GEORGE FOSTER PEABODY

George Foster Peabody

GEORGE FOSTER
PEABODY

Banker, Philanthropist, Publicist

by

LOUISE WARE

THE UNIVERSITY OF GEORGIA PRESS
ATHENS

Paperback edition, 2009
© 1951 by the University of Georgia Press
Athens, Georgia 30602
www.ugapress.org
All rights reserved
Printed digitally in the United States of America

The Library of Congress has cataloged the hardcover edition of this book as follows:
Library of Congress Cataloging-in-Publication Data

Ware, Louise.
George Foster Peabody, banker, philanthropist, publicist.
x, 279 p. port. 23 cm.
Bibliography: p. 257–272.
1. Peabody, George Foster, 1852–1938. I. Title.
HG2463.P4 W3
923.373   51-11005

Paperback ISBN-13: 978-0-8203-3456-1
ISBN-10: 0-8203-3456-1

Cover image reproduced from the *Dictionary of American Portraits*,
published by Dover Publications, Inc., in 1967.

Contents

	Foreword	vii
I	Early Life in Columbus, Georgia	1
II	Young Peabody in Brooklyn	10
III	Peabody As Banker	17
IV	Friendship With Shepard; Hampton Institute	30
V	In Search of a Home	37
VI	Business Affairs in the 1890's	47
VII	Party Politics	57
VIII	From Railroads to Sugar Beets	70
IX	Home Life and Local Politics	86
X	Peabody and Education	96
XI	University of Georgia Trustee	107
XII	Treasurer of Democratic Party	121
XIII	Retirement from Business	132
XIV	Jeanes Fund Trustee; Trask's Tragic Death	142
XV	Saratoga Springs Commissioner; Shepard's Last Days	155
XVI	Peabody and Wilson	161
XVII	The Busy War Years	174
XVIII	Post War Readjustments	186
XIX	The Wedding at Yaddo; The "Ladye" at Rest	196
XX	Warm Springs and Roosevelt	204
XXI	Yaddo, a Retreat for Artists	218
XXII	Peabody and the New Deal	230
XXIII	At Warm Springs	245
XXIV	In Conclusion	250
	Bibliography	257
	Index	273

Foreword

IN THIS BOOK, THE FIRST FULL-LENGTH ACCOUNT OF THE life of George Foster Peabody, the aim of the writer has been to present her subject as a person of many interests and activities. Special stress has been laid throughout upon his humanitarian ideas and philanthropic achievements. In the undertaking and carrying out of the project, the writer had the approval of Mr. Peabody's foster daughter, the late Mrs. Marjorie Peabody Waite. She and other members of the family, and many friends and associates, made available his voluminous correspondence and gave a free hand in the use of the materials. Additional material was obtained through research in various libraries.

George Foster Peabody was a native of Georgia. He lived from 1852 to 1938. As a young boy he was sent North to boarding school. Shortly thereafter his family, impoverished by the Civil War, left Georgia and settled in Brooklyn. Peabody was forced by poverty to leave school. He began his career as an errand boy in a Brooklyn mercantile house. Years later he became the partner of his friend, Spencer Trask, in the business of investment banking. The firm handled securities for great industrial enterprises in the last part of the nineteenth century and the first part of the twentieth. Its backing was an important factor in the building of railroads of the Rocky Mountain region and Mexico; it also helped to finance the electrical industry and the beet-sugar industry. Peabody built up a fortune in investment banking and in related activities.

He became a member of the board of directors of numerous companies which his firm financed. At fifty-four he retired from business to become his own executor in humanitarian work.

Like many other well-to-do men of his day, Peabody engaged in a wide range of activities. He took a prominent part in civic affairs, and was a supporter of many worthy causes; he was interested in the extension of the study of political science and in all that might help to bring about an enlightened electorate. He was a warm friend of several presidents, particularly of Woodrow Wilson. For many years he had a close contact with Franklin D. Roosevelt. He was deputy chairman of the Federal Reserve Bank of New York during its early, policy-forming days. He was a sponsor of the peace movement; he was a member of the Men's League for Woman Suffrage; he promoted music and the arts. He was one of the most prominent laymen of his day in Episcopal Church affairs.

One of his chief interests was education. His own formal schooling having been cut short when he was a young boy, he was always eager to help others to obtain what he had missed. He was a member of the board of trustees of many educational institutions, including Hampton, Tuskegee, Penn School, the University of Georgia, and Colorado College for Women. He gave large sums of money for the furtherance of educational work. He was a charter member of the Southern Education Board, and for many years was Treasurer of the General Education Board. In recognition of his services, he was awarded an honorary Master of Arts degree by Harvard University, and an honorary degree of Doctor of Laws by Washington and Lee University and by the University of Georgia.

Peabody is also known for the lavish hospitality which he accorded visitors at his Brooklyn mansion and at his

FOREWORD

Lake George estate. He was a loved and frequent guest at Yaddo, the beautiful Saratoga Springs home of Spencer and Katrina Trask. Eleven years after Spencer Trask's tragic death in a railroad accident, Peabody was married to Katrina Trask. At the time of the ceremony, Peabody was sixty-nine and she was sixty-eight. A few months later, Katrina died. Peabody continued to live at Yaddo, which now became a retreat for artists, under the terms of the will of Spencer and Katrina Trask. In his last years, he lived at his Warm Springs, Georgia, home part of the time; he died there in 1938. His ashes were buried at Yaddo.

It is the purpose of the book to review Mr. Peabody's life in its entirety. His major business operations are dealt with in some detail, but the files are incomplete and it is not possible to write a definitive account of this phase of his career at the present time. When all "the returns" are in, such an account will doubtless be written whereupon a just appraisal of his role in relation to the practices and codes of his day may properly be made.

In writing the biography of any person one must try to see the background of the time in which he lived. The more one does so, the more one finds that any one individual plays generally but an infinitesimal part in a great array of social forces. In a sense this is true of Peabody; yet, in his quiet, unspectacular way, he was a person of considerable weight—one who may well have turned the scales at many a crucial moment. He had in an unusual degree a feeling for the responsibilities of citizenship in a democracy, and, when he became wealthy, a feeling for the responsibilities which wealth entails. He was not, perhaps, one of the outstanding figures of his country and his time, but he was unmistakably a person of importance.

Acknowledgment is made to the family and friends of

Mr. Peabody who shared their memories with me. Their names are indicated in the interviews at the end of the book. Mrs. Marjorie Peabody Waite assisted me in many ways. Mrs. Waite and her sister, Mrs. Elizabeth Ames, Director of Yaddo, extended the hospitality of the estate to me while I was working on the letter files. I am indebted to Miss Allena Gilbert Pardee, long-time friend of the Trasks and Mr. Peabody, for her many courtesies and help—I thank her posthumously.

I am deeply grateful to Professor Allan Nevins of the History Department, Columbia University. He read the manuscript critically and made many valuable suggestions.

May I thank Miss Margaret Ladd Franklin for her generous assistance in literary criticism.

My sister, Ethel Kime Ware, read the manuscript and made many helpful suggestions. My brothers, Nicholas Benedict Ware and William Arthur Ware, gave me their encouragement.

A word of warm appreciation goes to my colleagues at Adelphi College and at the Association for the Aid of Crippled Children. They helped make the task pleasant.

Acknowledgment is made to Professor Thomas C. Cochran of New York University for courtesy extended me. I appreciate also the assistance of Dr. and Mrs. Ralph W. Hidy, versed in economic and business history, who read the manuscript and made suggestions.

Acknowledgment is also made to the members of the staff of the Columbia University Library, the New York Public Library, and the Library of Congress. I appreciate also the many kind acts of Miss M. A. Reilly and Miss Virginia Ackerley, secretaries in History Department at Columbia.

CHAPTER I

Early Life in Columbus, Georgia

ON JULY 27, 1852, IN THE BUSY LITTLE TOWN OF COLUMbus, Georgia, a son was born to Elvira Canfield and George Henry Peabody. He was their first-born child, and they named him George Foster.

The household in which George Foster Peabody grew up was of that period, much like other households of fairly well-to-do Southerners. As a small child he heard the murmur of slaves' voices in the family kitchen. He went to sleep to the tunes of Negro folk rhymes and spirituals. Everywhere about him were customs of the old South.

But back of this little boy were long lines of New England ancestors. His father was descended from one Francis Paybody, or Peabody, an early Massachusetts resident; his mother traced her descent in the male line—the Canfields—back to colonial Connecticut, and before that to England and possibly Normandy. Not much is known of the occupations of the Canfield forbears. The men of Peabody line were, in general, business men and bankers and professional men.

Young George's father, George Henry Peabody, was born near Woodbury, Connecticut, on January 29, 1807; of eleven children he was the third.[1] After a modest

---

1. George Henry Peabody's father was William Henry Peabody, born at Norwich, Connecticut, in 1760. He married Ruth Buckley on Feb. 19, 1795. Their eleven children were: Catherine Maria (b 1796); Henry

1

education, he migrated south with relatives in a search of business opportunities. Chance brought him to Columbus, Georgia, in the days when the town was young. Here he established himself in business as a merchant, running a general store. Trade was good and he prospered. He remained a bachelor until early middle age. We do not know whether all this time he had a sweetheart in Connecticut or whether, when he decided to get married, he felt that he would be more at home with the sort of girl he had grown up with. However that may be, he finally married Elvira Canfield, a comely Bridgeport girl seventeen years younger than himself.

The wedding took place in Bridgeport on November 1, 1851. Amid the well-wishings of their kin, the bride and groom packed their belongings and left for the South. Arriving in Columbus, they began housekeeping in a modest but comfortable home of ante-bellum style, a few blocks from George Henry's store.

George Henry, of course, already knew many of the people in the town. Elvira soon became acquainted. As a New England girl, she had many things to get used to— the sight of slaves on the way to the market, the drawling accent of her neighbors, the ever-present talk of cotton crops. Her husband had bought slaves[2] to do the work of the house, but she had to learn to direct them. She was adaptable and appears not to have had great difficulty; before long she had set her home in order and was also taking part in the affairs of the Presbyterian Church.

---

2. Peabody Papers, Yaddo files.

Buckley (b 1797); Charlotte (b 1799); Mary (b 1801); Lucy (b 1803); William (b 1805); George Henry (b 1807); Charles Alfred (b 1810); John Boadicea (b 1812); Augustus (b 1814); Frederic Gideon (b 1818). S. H. Peabody, *Peabody Genealogy* (Boston, 1909), p. 67. Elvira Canfield Peabody was born on November 11, 1824.

EARLY LIFE IN COLUMBUS 3

Children were born in due time; after George Foster came Royal Canfield, Charles Jones, and Eva Louise.[3]

2.

George Foster's boyhood home of Columbus was a busy manufacturing center, situated in midwest Georgia, on the bank of the muddy Chattahoochee River. The opposite bank was Alabama. The winding yellow waters of the river led to the Gulf and gave Columbus an outlook to farther ports. Stretching out beyond the town on the opposite side were cotton fields and yellowing corn-stalks and crooked red dirt roads.

Columbus had been laid out as a trading village in 1828. In the early days, twenty years and more before George's birth, Indians had come prowling on the outskirts. Upon occasion they had been hostile, but now in the 1850's they came only to buy in the stores. The presence of a large supply of cotton in the region had led to manufactures. By the early 1850's there were several large textile plants turning out yard goods and manufactured garments. The population had increased and now numbered several thousand.

In line with business needs, transportation had developed. Two stage coach lines terminated near the center of town, and weary travelers alighted to transact business with merchants and mill owners. Just a few months before George Foster's birth, a railroad line twenty miles long had been completed, connecting Columbus with other towns in Georgia.

Down the main street stretched a row of stores. From the open doorways came pungent smells—of bundled hay, of leather harness hanging upon racks in feed stores,

---

3. The children were George Foster, born July 27, 1852; Royal Canfield, Feb. 12, 1854; Charles Jones, April 25, 1856; and Eva Louise, born May 9, 1859, died June 18, 1861.

of various kinds of produce. Among these buildings was Mr. Peabody's general store, and one could see customers entering to buy things all the way from children's clothes to snuff.

A short distance from the center of town there was a slave market. Here dealers brought their slaves by day, carried on transactions, and—as required by law—retired at night with the remaining unsold slaves to an encampment outside the town.

Columbus in those days was a place of many interests. Horse racing was a favorite sport; there was a track at the edge of the town. Theatrical performances, using local talent, were popular, and lecturers addressed large audiences in the public hall. Lavish hospitality was extended by city officials to visiting dignitaries. Three newspapers received the latest news over the telegraph wires.

In the early 1850's, Columbus was quiet politically; but after the passage of the Kansas-Nebraska Act in 1854, the atmosphere became charged with feeling regarding states' rights and the slavery question. In the latter part of the decade there was talk of secession. George Henry Peabody's general store must have been a center of rumors, schemes and arguments, and even the children in his home must have felt the excitement in the air.

3.

In this active town with its cotton mills, its social affairs, its talk of secession, little George began to grow up. At home he learned his manners from his New England parents and also from the faithful household slaves. His mother was strict with him, desiring to rear her son in God-fearing ways. She taught him his prayers and read the Bible to him.

On Sunday the family went to church. Here they listened to Calvinist doctrines expounded by the preacher.

In later years George remembered well the kindly Presbyterian pastor.

Public schools had not yet been established in Columbus. There was at least one private school for boys in the town, but the Peabodys did not send their sons to this school. Elvira Peabody taught her eldest son at home until he was ten years old. We do not know how far she took him in his studies beyond the three R's, but she taught him to read the Bible. As a child he read all of the Old Testament once and started to read it again.

One day he was reciting his lessons at his mother's knee. Since he was only four or five, he could not remember some of the things his mother had told him. Elvira looked him firmly in the eye and said, "Think, George, think." This incident made a great impression upon him and he cited it many times in later years.

When he was ten, his parents decided to send him to school. They selected one which accepted boys but which was run mainly for girls. The sons of two of his mother's friends also attended the school; they were Nathan and Oscar Straus and Henry Goetchius. The Straus boys became well known figures in later years; Henry Goetchius became a lawyer prominent in civic affairs of Columbus.

As the oldest child George took the lead with his brothers. His relationships with them were marked by warm affection.

4.

In the early 1860's rumors of a possible break with the Union became more and more disquieting. Where would it all end? Where did one want it to end? On December 23, 1860, news reached Columbus of the secession of South Carolina. That night the whole town turned out in a wild celebration. Fireworks and bonfires flared in the streets. There was a torchlight procession. Perhaps the little

Peabody boys wheedled their mother into letting them go to the parade.

The secession of Georgia soon followed; and the small towns and hamlets all over the state began to prepare for war. Many of the able-bodied young men of Columbus left their peacetime pursuits and went off to battle.

Business men of the town contracted with the Confederate Government to make articles of war. The mills were turned into cap-making factories. Munitions works were erected. Several gun-boats were built in the yards on the banks of the Chattahoochee River. A plant for making matches was set into operation. Manufacturers kept their plants running night and day. If the Peabodys ventured out at night, they saw the eerie gas lights shining through the windows of the mills, and the steady hum of machinery filled the air.

Increased business caused inflation in Columbus during the war. Wages rose, and many persons had more to spend. Many homes were impoverished, however, and the town council had to help soldiers' wives and their families with grants of money.

We have no figures to show how much business merchant Peabody did at this time, but it is apparent that he made a comfortable living. He provided well for his family.

During the early part of the war, Columbus was untouched by the armies, but many feared this munitions center might be attacked. In 1864 Columbus mills were running full tilt. More of the town's sons had gone off to the colors. War had taken its terrible toll for three years; what would be the end? The answer came from the telegraph wires. Atlanta, only one hundred twenty-five miles away, was in flames, and the armies were on the march. A part of General Sherman's army was pressing forward toward Columbus.

Scarcely had the news of the burning of Atlanta been received when refugees from that stricken city began pouring into Columbus. Officials and other townsfolk were kept busy administering relief. Fear was mounting, for the guns of the approach troops were within ear-shot. Late in the afternoon of Sunday, April 17, 1865, soldiers entered the city. Throughout the night guns cracked and houses went up in flames. From the tops of buildings, frightened women and children watched the battle going on.

In the midst of this scene of panic and confusion, the Peabodys, out of force of habit, sat down to a hasty meal. Hardly had they lifted food to their lips when the door was pushed open and soldiers pressed into the dining room. The family was told to get up from the table and soldiers sat down to eat the food. George said later that his father was ordered to unlock a trunk in the attic and his mother was threatened with violence. Fortunately, however, none of the family suffered physical injury.

The fighting went on until Tuesday, April 19. Hospitals were crowded, and some of the wounded were brought into the Peabodys' home. When the shots had died down, the townspeople went out to reconnoitre. The sight that faced them burned itself into their memories. The town was in ruins; the ashes of buildings were smouldering. George Foster Peabody never forgot the day.[4]

5.

When the soldiers had withdrawn from the town, merchants went to the main streets to inspect the damage. Practically all of the buildings were a charred rubble. George Henry Peabody found only the remains of his

---

4. Copy of Mr. Peabody's letter to Henry Wise Wood, Oct. 13, 1916, Peabody Papers, Yaddo files. Statements by family and friends.

store. Boxes and bags were scattered; feedstuffs, implements, supplies were gone. There was little, if anything, to sell. Moreover, he knew that many of his former customers could not buy even if he had the stock, for their own resources had been wiped out. What could he do?

In the face of well-nigh insurmountable obstacles, Mr. Peabody decided that he would remain in business and would continue to make his home in Columbus. Having resolved thus, he made arrangements to go north in order to replenish his stock in markets now re-opened to the South. He left thirteen-year-old George, a manly boy, mature for his years, in charge of the store.

So earnest was the spirit of Columbus residents in their desire to start anew, that within a few weeks business had begun again. A short while later, the mills resumed operation on a peacetime basis. Though faced with all the difficulties of reconstruction, the leading men of the town were determined that Columbus should again become a manufacturing and residential center. A new day began, and the Peabodys were a part of it.

After the war a public school system was established in Columbus, but for some reason, possibly their old love of New England, Mr. and Mrs. Peabody decided to send their boys north to school. Resumption of business meant that the parents could afford the expense of a private school; they chose one in Danbury, Connecticut, Deer Hill Institute, an Episcopal boys' school of which two clergymen were headmasters.[5] Thus in the fall of 1865 young George entered a different world from the one that he had known. He took with him, however, many of the ways of the old South, especially hospitality and easy courtesy. He also retained sense impressions of the new Columbus—

---

5. The reason for choice of the school at Danbury is not known. Charles J. went North to school with George. (*New York Daily Tribune*, May 13, 1906.)

the sight of cotton mills whirring, the smell of turpentine as nails were driven into timber in the construction of homes and stores.

CHAPTER II

Young Peabody in Brooklyn

GEORGE HENRY PEABODY FOUND IT IMPOSSIBLE TO RECOUP his losses after the Civil War. A few months after the boys went north to school, he gave up his store. He and Mrs. Peabody then moved to Brooklyn, New York, where they settled down in a modest house which they planned to make their permanent home. Hard times in the family meant that the boys could no longer stay in school. At the end of that first year at Deer Hill, they said goodbye to their schoolmates and journeyed to Brooklyn, where parents and children had a happy reunion.

Brooklyn was a separate city then, with a history going back to Dutch days. The residents had shown intense loyalty and patriotic effort during the Civil War. Fine humanitarian service had been rendered by civic leaders. At Plymouth Church, the magnetic Henry Ward Beecher had inspired his congregation to volunteer their services in the war. The Academy of Music had been the scene of a great fair to raise money for war relief. It was a city of churches, of rows of brownstone fronts—a neighborly place where the policeman and the lamplighter knew the residents by name.

Like other cities, Brooklyn was recuperating from the war; its business and industrial life was rapidly expanding. Twenty-five years earlier, the population of the city had been about forty thousand; it was by the late 1860's three hundred thousand.

The business part of town had shifted to Fulton Street, not far from City Hall. On Fulton, Myrtle, and Atlantic avenues, many stores were erected.[1] It was before the days of the elevated railroad, and one could see bobbing horsecars, heated in winter by small stoves. Brooklyn Bridge was not built until the 1880's, but a ferry ran from Brooklyn to New York. Every day many business men walked down to the dock to take the boat for Manhattan.

The Peabodys, settled in their modest home in Brooklyn, felt the pinch of privation. Whereas in Columbus Elvira Peabody had set a bountiful table for her husband and the boys, she now had almost nothing to serve them. Eighteen months went by without the sight of any butter; staples were meager. Mr. Peabody sought work, but his health was poor after the rigors of war days and he was not able to cope with the situation. He could work at odd jobs only.

In keeping with her usual spirit, Elvira set her proud head to the task of helping to support the family. Perhaps she could take in boarders? In this way, the family would at least have enough to eat. Upon this course she decided, and they opened their home to "paying guests." Once more the dishes held enough food to satisfy the appetites of her growing boys.

Glance at the Peabodys as they begin their life in Brooklyn. Here is gentle George Henry, an infirm man of fifty-nine on whose face are written memories of war and failure. And here is Elvira, tired from hard work, yet staunch, reading her Bible for comfort. And here are their three boys growing tall like saplings.

1. The year 1867 saw forty-one brick buildings and twenty-four frame edifices erected for business purposes. A year later the Long Island Safe Deposit Company Building, the Mercantile Library Building, the Adelphi Academy, the Kings County Savings Bank, and other public buildings were constructed.

On June 20, 1866, George went to work for the firm of Farnham, Gilbert and Company, dry-goods commission merchants in Brooklyn. At first he was an errand boy at a wage of eight dollars a month; later he was employed as a clerk. The fourteen-year-old boy was self-reliant and alert, and he readily grasped the details taught him by Charles H. Welling, one of the partners. When, in 1868, this firm was dissolved, George went to work as a bookkeeper for Spaulding, Swift and Company. Two years later we find him working for White, Browne and Company—later renamed White, Payson and Company—of Boston, importers of dry-goods, alpacas, and silks.

It was an interesting period for a bright youth beginning work in the business world. Factories and stores throughout the country were readjusting after the Civil War. The mercantile business was one of the leading forms of enterprise. Wholesale merchants like Farnham, Gilbert and Company and White, Browne and Company bought up bolts of goods and supplied them to retail stores such as A. T. Stewart's, now Wanamaker's, in New York City. They shipped out boxes of finery, silks, satins, and cotton materials, to small town dealers in distant parts of the country.

George's job gave him an opportunity to follow the exciting and at times dangerous fluctuations of the market. He received first-hand impressions of the panic of 1873. He later said that he witnessed some of the early "rackets" and their operations.[2]

The excitement and interest of the business world did not wholly satisfy George's inquiring mind. Soon after he started work, he began to look around for some opportunity to read and study. There were, as yet, no free evening courses available in high school or college, but he

2. *New York Daily Tribune*, May 13, 1906.

learned that the Brooklyn Young Men's Christian Association had a library and arranged occasional lectures. He took out a membership card and began to visit the "Y" in the evenings. Night after night he read there under the flickering light. He always referred to the place as his "Alma Mater," and, years later, he made large contributions to it in recognition of what it had meant to him.

In the "Y" library Peabody read books on all kinds of subjects, and acquired an astonishing amount of information. He developed a taste for literature, especially poetry and the drama. He learned to express himself in a clear, though rather heavy, expository style. Letter-writing became one of his important activities. It was a matter of continuous regret to him that he could not attend college, but through his study, he went a long way towards giving himself the equivalent of a college education. Many considered him to be, on some subjects, one of the best informed men of his time.

Mrs. Peabody, and probably Mr. Peabody, attended the Reformed Church on Brooklyn Heights. George took an active part in Sunday school and at sixteen he became chairman of a committee to handle the Sunday school funds. One Sunday, General Samuel C. Armstrong, founder of Hampton Agricultural and Mechanical Institute, was the guest speaker. He explained the plans for Hampton and ended with an eloquent appeal for funds for the education of Negroes. George was deeply moved by the address. He suggested that the committee vote part of its funds to help the struggling project. It did so, and later the Sunday school contributed a scholarship to Hampton. This was the beginning of Peabody's long and intimate connection with General Armstrong and with Hampton Institute. He remained throughout his life a champion of the Negro.

2.

At Sunday school George met a young banker called Spencer Trask. Trask was a member of an old Brooklyn family and a graduate of Princeton. The two young men were drawn together by a common interest in church affairs, and they became good friends.

Young George also met Kate Nichols, daughter of George L. and Christina Nichols of Brooklyn. He was attracted to her from the beginning—he used to walk past the Nichols home in the hope of getting a glimpse of her, but he thought he was too poor to court her.

Kate Nichols had grown up in a family of means and position. Indulged by her parents, admired by her young brothers, she had an enviable security. She was pretty, with pink and white complexion, brown hair knotted softly at the back of her head, and blue eyes of a mystic beauty. Though short, she drew herself up to full height in statuesque fashion and appeared taller than she was. She had many admirers—among them not only George Foster Peabody, but also Spencer Trask.

Trask eventually won her promise to marry him. In due time, the invitations to the wedding were sent, including a white square to George Foster Peabody.[3] On November 12, 1874, the ceremony was performed—the girl Peabody loved married the man who was his friend.

For the first year after the marriage George seems to have seen little of the Trasks; then one day they invited him to have dinner with them. According to the family report, Trask told his wife, before the dinner came off, that young Peabody was rather reserved, and suggested that she "bring him out" in conversation. She did so, and found him interesting—a man of ideas. From that time on, Peabody and the Trasks often called on each other.

---

3. Interview with Miss Allena Gilbert Pardee.

3.

Spencer and Kate Trask established their home in Brooklyn. Their red brick house at 112 Willow Street, on the Heights, was large and hospitable. In the fashion of wealthy young matrons of her day, Kate directed a housekeeper and household staff. She arranged the flowers, wrote letters, read, and received her friends. Her husband, a busy Wall Street banker, perhaps stopped in at an art gallery or at his club on the way home. They entertained at dinner.

The Trasks' first child, Alanson, was born on December 19, 1875; their second, Christina Nichols, on May 25, 1877. After Christina's birth, Kate suffered a long illness; in 1879, she went to Europe to recuperate. She returned home much improved, but meanwhile the health of the little boy, Alanson, had become very poor. Anxiety deepened into grief for Kate and Spencer, for on April 23, 1880, their first-born child died.

4.

The Peabodys continued to live in Brooklyn. They were in better circumstances now. All three sons were in business. In 1879, Royal married Georgiana F. Sniffen; their son, Charles Samuel Peabody, born on April 8, 1880, became the idol of his bachelor Uncle George. George Henry Peabody had been in poor health for sometime; he died[4] a few months after Royal's wedding. The widow took the body to Connecticut for burial. Two years later, on December 7, 1882, Charles Jones Peabody was married to Helen A. Hoyt, formerly of Cleveland, Ohio.

George was now left alone with his mother in the home that had been so full of life. He had always been devoted to her, and he now became more solicitous than

---
4. He died on June 27, 1880.

ever for her comfort. They moved twice during the early 1880's each time to a home pleasanter than the one they had left. The "paying guests" were a thing of the past. Peabody's earnings in mercantile business, and later in banking, were ample for their needs.

Peabody had come to like the ritual of the Episcopal Church, and in 1880 he decided to change his affiliation and become an Episcopalian. He became a member of Holy Trinity Church on Montague Street, Brooklyn Heights. On Sundays he was a familiar sight as, tall and erect, he stepped down the aisle toward his pew. Upon leaving the church, he tipped his hat to acquaintances and was greeted as "Mr. Peabody." He had become a figure of importance in the community.

Toward the end of 1879, Peabody was offered, and accepted, a partnership in the firm of Trask and Stone, bankers. In January, 1880, he took up his new duties. A few months later, he became a partner in the reorganized firm of Spencer Trask and Company.

Members of the family tell us that George Foster was troubled when Spencer first spoke of a partnership. The business side of the proposal interested him, but he foresaw an awkward situation in the intimate association. He was still in love with Kate Trask; Spencer was his friend. He went to Trask to clear the situation. "Spencer," he said, "I am in love with your wife." Trask looked him in the eye with perfect candor. "I don't blame you, Foster; I am in love with her myself." In this matter-of-fact way, it is said, the subject was dismissed and the two men continued their discussions.[5]

---

5. Interviews with Miss Allena Gilbert Pardee, Mrs. Marjorie Peabody Waite, summer 1940.

CHAPTER III

Peabody as Banker

ON MONDAY MORNING, MAY 2, 1881, GEORGE FOSTER Peabody became the partner of Spencer Trask in the newly formed banking house of Spencer Trask and Company. He was soon busily at work at his roll-top desk.

Let us glance at this business which he had entered. Investment banking was not new, but in the industrial era after the Civil War it was being extended into new operations.[1] Both railroad expansion and industrial development and consolidation called for large-scale financing. The investment banker was a merchant of securities. He was a middleman between the promoter of the enterprise and the buyer of securities. He must establish contact with the organizer who needed capital, analyze and appraise the nature of the projected development, and gauge the chances for the success of the undertaking. He must contact the potential customer, acquaint him with the project, convince him of its soundness, and persuade him to help supply the needed capital. The capital thus received from the customer must be channeled into enterprises which should bring profits to the company, to the customer, and, in return for acting as go-between, to the bank itself.

1. F. A. Bradford, "Investment Banking," *Dictionary of American History,* J. T. Adams, editor (New York: Charles Scribner's Sons, 1940); Willis H. Parker and J. I. Bogen, *Investment Banking* (New York: Charles Scribner's Sons, 1936).

The usual investment banking firm of that period was composed of a small number of partners. These men were often well-known individuals whose names were synonymous with their businesses. The success of their work depended upon the confidence bestowed in them. In the mores of the time, the private banker must be a man of impeccable reputation. He must present a demeanor of dignity, and must deport himself in such a way as to inspire and keep the faith of his clientele. While he operated in a business where highly competitive enterprises were being financed, his business code did not sanction cutthroat competition with other banking houses. Where differences arose, these were settled by negotiation when possible. When the house advertised a flotation, the words such as "Our Mr. Peabody" were the thing to say to indicate the correctness of the transaction, and reassure the public on the strength of the partner's name.

In the ethical code of the investment banker, the customer's privacy was assured. Hence in writing the story of a particular investment banker, it is difficult to get, in any great detail, a picture of the operations he conducted.

Among the features of investment banking was the promotion of new enterprises and the reorganization of old ones. Investment bankers must be conservative, yet dynamic. In financing the new enterprise they must be shrewd analysts of existing conditions and wise prophets of conditions of the future. When sponsoring a new business they must study the market trends and endeavor to anticipate crises. In the reorganization of old enterprises, they would often take over some decrepit company, and improve the rolling stock by use of new machinery and equipment. In many cases they would negotiate a re-sale.

One of the features of investment banking was the assumption of some control in the enterprise under flotation.

One or more of the partners in the bank would be placed on the Board of Directors of the new or reorganized company. In this way the bankers kept a watchful eye on their own and their clients' investments.[2]

The firm of Spencer Trask and Company conformed to the general pattern of investment banking of their day. They financed new companies. They reorganized old companies, and helped to rehabilitate them and put them on their feet. In many of these enterprises they assumed some control by virtue of representation on the Board of Directors. It is astonishing to see the list of directorships held by Peabody within a few years.

2.

The partners brought to their work a broad experience from widely different backgrounds. Spencer Trask was thirty-eight, older than Peabody by nine years. He was a member of a well-known family on Brooklyn Heights. He attended Polytechnic Institute, and was graduated from Princeton University in the class of 1866. He then went to work in the firm of Henry Marquand, his mother's uncle. A few months afterward, he formed his own firm, which on February 1, 1868, became the partnership of Trask and Stone. In 1878, when Stone withdrew, Trask formed the firm of Trask and Francis, which lasted until 1881.

A man of means before starting out in his profession, by the time he took Peabody into partnership Trask had become a man of wealth. Even during the depression of 1873-1878, his firm had prospered. He had the wisdom that came through long experience in banking circles. His methods were on the whole conservative, though he

---

2. Charges were later hurled at these practices. Implications of the dangers of interlocking directorates and of possible money trusts were to be the subject of investigation.

liked to push the development of a new enterprise. He was shrewd, energetic, a man of vision, a promotor with his feet on the ground.

Peabody, now twenty-nine, was six feet tall, stalwart, compelling. He had the benefit of fifteen years experience in mercantile houses. He knew how to watch the shifting trends of business. He was expert at getting a clear picture of a situation and mapping out far-reaching plans on the basis of his findings. He knew how to see things in the large, without neglecting the importance of detail.

The partners worked well together. Though they did not always agree, they were congenial in matters of general policy. They were courteous in their dealings with clients, and the atmosphere in their offices was one of dignity.

The firm had a branch office at Albany and another in Philadelphia.[3] As business expanded, they opened branches in other cities and engaged representatives and correspondents in other areas. Peabody bought a seat on the New York Stock Exchange on May 27, 1886, for $24,000. Charles Jones Peabody, who had been serving in the Albany office, was made manager of that office. He was made a partner of Spencer Trask and Company the following year, and shortly afterwards moved to New York; he remained for many years in the firm's New York office. Other partners were added, among them Edwin M. Bulkley in 1887, and Acosta Nichols, brother-in-law of Mr. Trask, in 1897.

During the first few years, the firm handled mostly stocks; it is said that they had one of the largest stock brokerage businesses in the country. From the first, however, they had the reputation of being a substantial, conservative house. As time went on, they dealt more and more largely in bonds.

---

3. In each of these cities they had a resident partner.

Ramifications of the business reached over the entire United States, to Mexico, and to Europe. Through visits made by members and representatives of the firm, they made extensive connections with investors in England. Within a few years they were reported to have some twenty thousand clients.[4]

Trask's old firm had had many dealings in railroad and mining enterprises, and it required only an expansion of previous connections to bring Spencer Trask and Company into the forefront of the vast business of transportation that was opening up. After the Civil War the western part of the country developed rapidly; soon thousands of miles of tracks were laid. The first transcontinental railroad, the Union Pacific, was completed in 1869. Within the next two decades the names of the railroad magnates—E. H. Harriman, J. P. Morgan, the Goulds, James J. Hill, Collis P. Huntington and a few others—were carved into America's transportation legend. Spencer Trask and Company transacted business with all these men.

A large part of the work of handling railroad securities fell to Peabody. He called on pioneer promoters in their offices and discussed terms with them as they chewed the butts of their cigars. But he also saw things at first hand. His railroad passes, regularly used, covered the main lines of the United States. He went as far north as Ottawa, Canada, and as far southwest as Manzanillo on the Pacific coast. When he first visited the West, it was only a few years after Custer's last raid against the Indians. Leisurely bison, crossing the tracks, often held up the locomotives.[5]

Developments in railroad business in the early 1880's

---

4. E. J. Koop, *History of Spencer Trask and Company.*
5. From Mr. Peabody's statement quoted in the *New York Times,* July 26, 1931.

brought Peabody and his firm into contact with General William Jackson Palmer, one of the great pioneers in building up the Southwest. The two men began to discuss plans together. William J. Palmer had worked as private secretary to J. Edgar Thompson, president of the Pennsylvania Railroad. At twenty-five, he had left his job to head a troop in the Civil War. His energy and courage won quick recognition; after the war, he was promoted to the rank of brigadier general. He returned to railroading, however, and in 1869 went to Colorado. Within the next four years, he had succeeded in bringing to that state two railroads—the Kansas and Pacific, and the Denver and Rio Grande. He also organized a system of mountain railroads which, with their branch lines, criss-crossed the entire Southwest, and thus facilitated the transportation of settlers to that region. At the same time, he aided in the development of towns alongside the railroads; for example, he was prime mover in the building of Colorado Springs.

Turning to Mexico for his next major work, Palmer procured from President Porfirio Diaz and the Mexican Congress the William J. Palmer-James Sullivan concession, whereby he was permitted to build a railroad from Mexico City to Ciudad Juarez and another from Mexico City to Nuevo Laredo. Later, on the basis of this concession, Palmer and his associates organized the Mexican National Railway.[6] It was at this stage of affairs in the early 1880's that Peabody met Palmer and formed a close business acquaintance with him. The two men visited the West and Mexico. They studied and inspected natural resources. They saw untold wealth in the lead, silver, and coal mines which lay along their route. In Mexico, they

---

6. Its completion was financed by Matheson and Company of London.

traveled through rugged hills and along narrow trails on horseback and camped at night among the Indians.

Along their route bands of busy workmen were laying the ties for the first rails. Peabody was impressed by Palmer's injunctions to his men. "You are building a railroad," Palmer would say to them, "for the use of the Mexican people. They have their own ways which it is not for you to criticize. Try to adapt yourselves to these ways in a spirit of sympathy."[7] Peabody believed this to be a wise policy, and when the time came for putting it into practice himself, he did so.

Peabody and Palmer enjoyed working together. Gifted with a rich, powerful personality, Palmer was a man of bold action. A pioneer and adventurer, quick to meet the problems of laying rails over deserts and swamps, he was thrilled by the grandeur of mountain gorges. Peabody, with the background of patterned life in the South and in Brooklyn, partner in a conservative banking house, was less of the pioneer than Palmer, but he had imagination and perspective and shared Palmer's vision of the destined greatness of the West.

After making a detailed study, with Palmer, of the local terrain, Peabody returned to New York to discuss matters with Trask. The two men decided upon a policy of expanding their railroad interests in the Southwest, and Peabody was given free rein to go ahead. From 1885 to 1901, he was associated continuously with Palmer in planning and building railroads and in financing subsidiary enterprises.

The most important of these enterprises was the reorganization, development and final sale of the Rio Grande Western. This narrow-gauge railroad was turned into one of the most modern lines, and within a few years, it

---

7. Peabody Papers.

became a fifteen million dollar company. We shall trace its phenomenal career in a later chapter.

Concurrently with the extension of the Rio Grande Western, Palmer was building the Mexican National Railway. In this, too, Peabody was associated with him,[8] handling securities through Spencer Trask and Company. While engaged with Palmer in developing these railway enterprises, Peabody became interested in Mexican mining properties. Through Charles H. Towne, a promoter of mining operations, and later through D. C. Brown, he gained extensive holdings in these properties. In later years, much of his personal fortune was invested in Mexican enterprises.

In 1886 Peabody became a director of the St. Louis, Alton and Terre Haute Railroad; he was later made chairman of the board. In its report[9] of December 31, 1888, this railway was listed at $14,475,193. Peabody was very active in developing this road; he afterwards handled the negotiations which led to its sale to the Illinois Central.

4.

A second major activity of Spencer Trask and Company was the handling of public utility securities. While operating under the firm name of Trask and Francis in the late 1870's, Spencer Trask had given Thomas A. Edison some backing in his experiments.[10] After the inventor perfected his incandescent lamp, the Edison Electric Light Company was formed, but this firm was not permitted to do more than manufacture and operate the apparatus and have it licensed, and in order to engage in distributing

8. In the period from 1881 to 1888. They negotiated the sale to Spier and Company.
Report for the year ending December 31, 1888.
9. *Commercial and Financial Chronicle,* XLVIII (March 23, 1889), p. 397.
10. Drexel, Morgan and Company had also backed Edison, and Trask was in touch with them. (E. J. Koop, *History of Spencer Trask and Company.*)

electric current it was necessary to form a separate company. On December 17, 1880, the Edison Electric Illuminating Company of New York was formed. Two old four-story buildings at 255-257 Pearl Street were converted into a plant. At three o'clock on September 4, 1882, Edison turned on the switch and the distribution of electric current began.

From that day, the old flickering gas jets increasingly gave way to the steady bright flame of the pear-shaped electric light bulb. The number of customers in October, 1882, was fifty-nine; by 1893, it was over five thousand. At the turn of the century there were more than eleven thousand customers served by the company.[11]

Contributing to the success of the electrical industry were numerous factors. For instance, the first real skyscraper, an eight-story structure known as the Tower Building, was built at 50 Broadway in 1888. Then came other tall buildings. Tenants wished the convenience of using electric lights in their offices. Moreover, they grew tired of stair-climbing and demanded elevators—and these were now operated in the main by electric current instead of by steam. Another factor was the encouragement given the industry by many housewives. Weary of seeing their ceilings blackened by the gaslight's flicker, they sought the clean and easily turned on electric bulb. Before long, they were seeking appliances operated by electric current; the electric iron was inevitably to replace the old sad-iron in thousands of homes. Still another reason for the onward sweep of the electric industry was the fact that many people were growing tired of the old horse-drawn cars—they wished greater speed, and the electric trolley was the solution nearest to hand. After a

11. *Thirty Years of New York, 1882-1912*, pp. 229-230.

brief period of skepticism, it was apparent that the electric industry was here to stay.

Spencer Trask and Company, which had been interested in the new venture, was one of the first firms to use the current. Having been in on the ground floor, so to speak, they made the further promotion of the Illuminating Company one of their main concerns. Trask was elected president of the company on December 11, 1884. Peabody became a director, and was made a vice-president.[12] At J. P. Morgan's insistence, he was made president pro tem in 1889 for a few months while Trask was in Europe, and he retained his membership on the board throughout the 1890's.

Under Trask's presidency, and with the able assistance of Peabody and several others, the Edison Electric Illuminating Company of New York justified the faith which its backers had placed in it. In the course of two years, 1887 and 1888, distribution of current was extended to uptown districts. Installation of arc lamps on Fifth Avenue between Washington Square and Fifty-ninth Street was begun in 1892. The New York area was amply supplied with current and the value of the company's securities mounted. For the first half of 1897, the gross earnings[13] from the business, January 1 to June 30, reached $1,228,766, and the net earnings $571,715.

Spencer Trask and Company also promoted other electric illuminating developments. In 1889 the Edison General Electric Company was formed and the Trask firm

---

12. On April 21, 1885, the offices were moved from 65 Fifth Avenue to 16 Broad Street. This was done at Spencer Trask's request, as a matter of convenience to him as president. (E. J. Koop, *History of Spencer Trask and Company.*) *Thirty Years of New York 1882-1912*, p. 192.
13. *Commercial and Financial Chronicle*, Supplement, LXVII (July 30, 1898), p. 150. The Company listed 382,291 incandescent lamps as of December 31, 1897 (*ibid.*). In 1898 the Company decided to increase its capital stock to $10,000,000. *Commercial and Financial Chronicle*, LXVII (December 10, 1898), p. 1207.

took a leading part in its establishment and in the merger of this company with other interests into the General Electric Company in 1892. Trask and Peabody were both members of the board of directors of the General Electric Company; on that board's executive committee Trask served for a time; Peabody served for many years.

In 1894, the Trask firm undertook the financing of the Cleveland Electric Illuminating Company. Peabody himself took over the general supervision of this company. The firm also promoted the Detroit Electric Illuminating Company.

5.

We have seen how the firm of Spencer Trask and Company followed the practices of investment bankers of the day in the flotation of securities for new enterprises, and in the reorganization and re-sale of old companies. We have seen how they followed the practice of putting a member of the firm on the Board of Directors of the company to exercise some control in its affairs.

In later years, Peabody said he had felt, even in those early days, increasing concern regarding undesirable practices of big business.[14] He referred in particular to the situation in the railroad industry in the late 1880's. Cutthroat competition and railroad rate wars were coming to be matters of great concern in the financial world. To meet the problem, J. P. Morgan called a conference of railroad presidents and bankers in his drawing room at 219 Madison Avenue. The sessions began on December 21, 1888, continued several days, and were resumed in January, 1889. Meanwhile some stockholders, investors in railroad securities, put an advertisement in the papers

---

14. H. L. Satterlee, *J. Pierpont Morgan, An Intimate Portrait* (New York: The Macmillan Company, 1939), pp. 245-258.

urging stockholders of seven railroads not to re-elect the officials who had been engaging in rate wars.

As a result of the meetings, at Morgan's home, an "Interstate Commerce Railroad Association" was formed and an "Agreement of the Presidents of January 1889" was signed. This document was referred to as the "Gentlemen's Agreement." The chief obligations assumed by the parties were: to obey the Interstate Commerce law; to seek redress through the Association and not independently; to refrain from making private concessions to shippers; to build no parallel railroad lines. A trial period of sixty days was set, and the agreements were later renewed. In December, 1889, a new association, including the western lines, was formed, and a system of arbitration was provided. Railroad operators and security holders endorsed the new association. Government officials and the Interstate Commerce Commission approved it.

As a representative of some of the railroads, Peabody was present at Morgan's home when the agreements were drawn up.[15] He later said it disturbed him to see how often these "Gentlemen's Agreements" were violated. We do not have material available to show what part he played, if any, in the drawing up of the agreements, nor is it possible at this time to show what he did to uphold his standards of business ethics and influence the conduct of others in such matters.

In studying the role of any particular banker, one must take into consideration the business codes prevalent in the period in which he lived. Peabody's career in finance took place before the day of government regulation of securities trading. The old Roman formula, *caveat emptor*—let the buyer beware—was in effect. Watering

---

15. Mr. Peabody's statement to his foster daughter; correspondence in the files.

of stock was common. The customer took the risk; quick sale and re-sale of stock might make him rich today and leave him a pauper tomorrow.

The firm of Spencer Trask and Company took an attitude which was well-nigh universal among the brokers of that day. The partners were there to make money. It was Peabody's belief that the buyer of stocks should share the responsibility of the deal with the broker. The broker himself often bought shares in the same companies whose stock he recommended to his clients. He believed in informing the customer of the assets and liabilities as far as they could be ascertained. In announcements he took pains to describe the proposed improvements and the expenses attached. After that the customer must take the risk along with the promoter.

CHAPTER IV

Friendship with Shepard; Hampton Institute

WHILE STILL IN COLUMBUS PEABODY NO DOUBT HEARD discussion of Democratic Party politics at his father's general store. By the time he was sixteen the family had moved to Brooklyn; here he watched with interest the Presidential campaign of 1868—he would have voted for Horatio Seymour if he had had a chance. In 1876 he voted for Samuel Tilden. He became an active member of the American Free Trade League in 1880; later he became its treasurer. He was a lifelong advocate of tariff reform.

One of the men with whom Peabody's political interests brought him in contact was Edward Morse Shepard, a young lawyer living in Brooklyn, who became—next to Spencer and Kate Trask—his closest friend. Shepard's father, Lorenzo B. Shepard, an able young lawyer in mid-century New York, had died when Edward was six years old. The boy's mother, a calm and gracious woman, belonged to the Albany branch of the Morse family. Edward was born in New York City on July 23, 1850, the third of five children. A few years after the father's death, the family moved to a modest but attractive house in Brooklyn. Abram S. Hewitt, a close friend of Lorenzo B. Shepard, became guardian of the children. Hewitt was a well-known ironmaster and one of the leading civic figures of New York and Brooklyn, a man whose name was linked with reforms during the eighties and nineties. Under his guidance Shepard was reared.

Edward Shepard went to public school in Brooklyn, in New York, and—for one year—in Ohio. He then attended the College of the City of New York where, after a brilliant undergraduate career, he was graduated with highest honors in 1869. After serving a clerkship in a law office, he was admitted to the bar and began his practice. A few years later he was a successful corporation lawyer,[1] connected with the Mexican National Railway and other railroads, and with large mining and smelting interests in Mexico and in the West.

Influenced perhaps by the example of Abram S. Hewitt, Shepard soon took an active part in Brooklyn's civic movements. About 1880, a number of Brooklyn young men were devoting their energies to the cause of good government. From them originated such organizations as the Independent Republicans, the non-partisan Society for Political Education, the Young Republican Club, and the Young Men's Democratic Club.[2] Shepard and Peabody were among those who formed the Young Men's Democratic Club. Shepard was chairman of the executive committee from 1881 to 1883 and president from 1883 to 1885. Peabody helped draw up the club's constitution, which contained a clause prohibiting the members from holding political office. This restriction Peabody believed to be a leading factor in lending weight and influence to the organization.

1. He was counsel for the Rapid Transit Commission of New York City. He was also counsel for officials in planning the entrance of the Pennsylvania Railroad into New York City. (R. R. Bowker in "Edward Morse Shepard," *The City College Quarterly*, December, 1911.)
2. Among others important in organizing the club were Alfred C. Chapin, A. Augustus Healy, Fred W. Hinrichs, and David A. Doody.

Heated debates were held in the club rooms on issues of the day. In Peabody's opinion, these discussions were "perhaps a conclusive factor in 1884 in the nomination of Grover Cleveland rather than Thomas F. Bayard, who was a personal friend of both Mr. Shepard and myself, and greatly admired, but the politics of the situation seemed to us clearly to call for Mr. Cleveland's nomination."[3]

This Young Men's Democratic Club of Brooklyn was active from the early 1880's until 1891. It promoted the principles of the National Democratic party and supported Cleveland for President. Through the decade, the club worked for Civil Service reform. In the late 1880's, some of the charter members, including Shepard and Peabody, went over to an organization known as the Brooklyn Democratic Club where they continued to work for reform measures.

It is interesting to picture the two young friends, Peabody and Shepard, working together in political matters. Though sharing many interests and ambitions, they were different both in appearance and in personality.

Edward Shepard was a slight, frail man. His sensitive mouth was partly concealed by a small mustache. He had a well-shaped head, a thin nose, a high forehead, and keen brown eyes. His manner was reserved, even diffident. Shepard liked best to be in a small circle of close friends where he was at ease and where his powers of analysis and precise logical thought could be freely exercised. Amid these sympathetic companions, he would make dry jests and would express his views without hesitancy. His voice, when he spoke from the public platform, was thin and penetrating, but he had a good singing voice and often

---

3. Copy of Mr. Peabody's letter to Henry M. Morgenthau, Jr., June 26, 1934, is in Yaddo files.

sang for a group of friends. At his home in Brooklyn and later at his beautiful estate at Lake George, he gave delightful dinners at which he assembled kindred spirits from his old City College days and from his more recent political and professional contacts. He made two ventures as a writer: in 1884 he wrote a memorial to Richard Dugdale, author of *The Jukes*; in 1888 appeared his life of Martin Van Buren, published in the American Statesmen Series.

Shepard represented an interesting combination: he was an idealist and a reformer, but at the same time a party man. He was an ardent Jeffersonian Democrat and believed in adhering to party lines whenever possible. Compared with Peabody, he was a conservative. He did not, for example, share Peabody's enthusiasm for the Single Tax,[4] or even for Free Trade.

2.

On June 4, 1884, Peabody accepted his first trusteeship on an educational board; this was the beginning of his official connection with Hampton Institute. Let us glance for a moment at the school which for half a century was so close to Peabody's heart. At the end of the Civil War, General Samuel C. Armstrong had been asked to take charge of an encampment of Negroes near Norfolk, Virginia. While performing his duties, he became interested in the idea of establishing a school, and in 1867 he wrote to the American Missionary Association recommending purchase of the encampment property for that purpose. His suggestion was accepted; and in 1868 Hampton Agricultural and Mechanical Institute opened its doors. General Armstrong was made principal. With his

---

4. Peabody liked to think of himself as a radical. He read Henry George's *Progress and Poverty* soon after it was published, and became a wholehearted advocate of the Single Tax doctrine.

young bride, he settled down on the farm which was eventually turned into a campus.

Hampton offered the usual common school and collegiate courses, but its special purpose was the instruction of Negroes in agricultural, industrial, and mechanical arts. Under the leadership of the indomitable General Armstrong, the school grew rapidly. By 1878, the enrollment had reached 323; by 1886, 693. The staff, of course, had also been enlarged; in 1878 there were 24 members; by 1886, there were 70.

In accepting membership on the Board of Trustees, Peabody wrote:

> My Dear General Armstrong
> I am in receipt of your kind letter enclosing official notice of my election as Trustee of Hampton School, which I assure you I appreciate as a great honor. As I told you I am glad to be of service in its behalf and want to accept—I only feel rather guilty when I think that my time is so taken up. . . . I will accept the position however and do the best I can, trusting to you to let me know whenever you can find some one who will more effectively attend to the duties.
> I trust that you are feeling well after the term has ended and hope that I may see you this summer when you are on.
> Sincerely,
> Geo. F. Peabody

Shortly after becoming a trustee, Peabody was made a member of the Investment Committee, and was also appointed treasurer of the school. From the first he took an active part. On February 2, 1885, we find him writing:

> My Dear Gen. Armstrong
> My Grandmother died suddenly (after a long illness though) this morning and I shall not be able to accompany you this evening as expected. Mr. E. H. VanIngen, however, expects you to take tea at his house—122 Remsen St. between Henry and Clinton. . .
> I trust that you will not fail to be there, for I want him to know you and the work better. You know of him as a very square and common sense business man

and very generous but quietly so—he is one of Mr. Beecher's pillars of strength.

You will excuse the informality of this because of my hurried arrangements owing to my many engagements. I am very sorry to miss seeing you today.

Sincerely,
Geo. F. Peabody

Again on April 20, 1885, he wrote:

My Dear Gen. Armstrong

I think it is too bad that Hampton Endowment Funds should not be invested. Last summer was the time; now good Bonds are going up every day. I think the Govts should be sold and the proceeds invested in the new West Shore 4 per cent Bond as also the Cash.

Wishing yourself and fily and the School the Compliments of the Season

Yours,
Geo. F. Peabody

On April 24, 1886, he wrote:

My Dear General Armstrong—

I reached here this noon expecting to spend three or four days with you, and just after dinner I got a telegram stating that Mr. Trask has sprained his ankle and is laid up, so I start right off by Old Dom. Str. Very sorry indeed to have missed this visit—Hope to be on hand for several days at Anniversary Ex.

Sincerely,
Geo. F. Peabody

He visited Hampton as often as he could. When General Armstrong was in New York, the two men discussed school finances. On April 28, 1890, he wrote:

My dear Gen. Armstrong

I was sorry to be out of the City last week when you were to meet Mr. Monroe as I trust you did. I trust that your few days rest has greatly rested and strengthened you and that you are feeling better. I am sorry, however, to think that you are back again in Hampton for if I were in your place I should go off where I couldn't hear of negroes or Indians for several weeks to come at any rate. That is my theory of rest. I am writing to you now to say that my mother Mrs. Geo. H.

Peabody and her friend, Miss Jones have just started for a leisurely trip out through the West up through Colorado, then to Salt Lake City, then San Francisco and from there on up to Alaska! I thought it would please your mother and know very well it would very much please my mother if my mother were able to make a call upon your mother while in the City. . . . Pray be entirely frank and let me know if there be any possible reason why it might not be altogether convenient for your mother to meet strangers.

       Yours very truly,
       Geo. Foster Peabody

He discussed the problems of developing grounds and buildings with Gen. Armstrong from time to time. On October 20, 1892, he wrote:

> As to the matter of the entrance to the grounds the Architect presented an elaborate plan that was quite beyond anything that I had suggested to Mr. Trask and as a consequence rather staggered him and I am afraid rather weakened his interest in the matter—I am afraid the matter will have to drag on now for a while for Mr. Trask is too full of other things to take it up at present, and when I tackle him again I want to have had leisure enough to be fully informed myself as to what is proposed—I think it would be just as well to "look poor" next Spring when the visitors are there—they may help us on more—Please remember me to Mrs. Armstrong.

As business affairs crowded in upon him, Peabody found it difficult to visit Hampton as often as he wished,[5] but his interest in it never slackened. "My thoughts are often of Hampton and your noble self," he wrote to Armstrong;[6] and, again on December 8, 1892, he declared: "I think Hampton *the most* important educational institution in the U. S. . . ."[7]

---

5. Mr. Peabody was elected a member of the board of trustees of Hampton on May 21, 1884. He served as its treasurer from 1893-1898. He remained a trustee until April 24, 1930, when he resigned as active trustee and served as an honorary trustee until his death.
6. Hampton files.
7. *Ibid.*

CHAPTER V

In Search of a Home

Spencer and Kate Trask had felt the strain of sickness and grief. They wanted a summer home in a cheerful environment, far from the city, and decided to look for something in the neighborhood of Saratoga Springs.[1] This gracious community with its rambling old hotels, its large houses, its tree-lined streets, appealed to them.

They found that a large farm two miles from town was for sale—a beautiful place comprising seven hundred acres of rolling hillside and valley, threaded by running streams and little lakes. Dark forests, shrubs and vines added to the natural beauty of the spot. From the top of the hill, they could see the gentle outline of the Green Mountains forty miles to the east and to the west the Adirondacks. This seemed an ideal setting, and in 1881 they bought the place.[2]

They wanted a name for the new home, and little Christina had a happy thought. "Call it Yaddo, Mamma," the child exclaimed, "for it makes poetry; it sounds like

1. Saratoga was an old hunting ground of the Mohawks, sold by them to the citizens of Albany in 1684. Soon after 1789 the place became famous for its sawmills, owned by Gideon Putnam; in 1802 Putnam built a large hotel which marked the start of Saratoga's prestige as a fashionable resort. The race-track was established in 1864.
2. Upon the site in the days of Dutch settlement there stood the road-house of one Barhydt. The house remained an inn through a good part of the nineteenth century; among its guests were Daniel Webster and Edgar Allan Poe.

shadow, but it will not be shadow."³ And Yaddo it was called.

On March 23, 1884, another child, Spencer, was born. When he was a few weeks old, the family moved to Saratoga for the summer. Kate writes in her *Chronicles* of the joyful days free from the worries of the past few years. Each summer thereafter they spent at Yaddo. They had employed a French nurse to take care of the two children. When Christina grew older and Mrs. Trask sought a governess, she was fortunate in securing an admirable woman, Miss Allena Gilbert Pardee, for the position. Miss Pardee, member of an old Connecticut family, was visiting her artist aunt in New York. At first she came to the Trask home several days a week, but later she made her home with them as Christina's governess and Mrs. Trask's companion.

The summer of 1887 was one of the happiest of all at Yaddo. The two children, now ten and three, romped about the place, swung on the apple trees, played games in the big house. Kate and her young daughter were constant companions. In the fall, the family returned to Brooklyn for the winter months. Kate speaks of the "gay coach-load"⁴ bound for the city.

The winter season passed in a round of social activities, but on March 12, 1888, Kate Trask became ill with diphtheria. Before she recovered, little Spencer and Christina became gravely ill with the disease. On April 14th, four-year-old Spencer died at the home in Brooklyn, followed four days later by ten-year-old Christina. The parents' grief was almost unbearable. Their first son's death, the recent death of Kate's mother, and now the death of their two remaining children—it seemed as

---

3. Interviews with members of the family.
4. Katrina Trask, *Chronicles of Yaddo, 1888.*

though there were little left for them. Kate, anguished, went around like someone stunned. Spencer Trask, with rare understanding, encouraged her to express her sorrow in words. This she did by writing a familiar chronicle, and it seemed to give her relief. The result is an exquisitely touching story of Christina, which for many years only the family and a few close friends were permitted to read.

The months that followed were like a bad dream. Kate was fortunate in having Miss Pardee, Christina's governess, remain with her. On August 17, 1889, she gave birth to another child, Katrina, who lived only a few days.

Amid the many sorrows of his friends, the Trasks, Peabody was at hand to offer sympathy and encouragement. He visited them at Yaddo and was a frequent caller at their home in Brooklyn. Now more than ever he seemed a member of the family. After the loss of their children, Mr. and Mrs. Trask decided to visit Europe for a change of scene. They were away many months. Toward the end of their trip, Peabody joined them in France. He was relieved to find that the trip had helped them.

By the early 1890's the Trasks found life at Yaddo increasingly pleasant. They spent the winters at 112 Willow Street, Brooklyn, and a part of the year at Tuxedo Park; but summers were spent at Yaddo. As time passed, they extended the season, so that they were at Saratoga most of the year. They later made it their permanent home.

The original house on the place was destroyed by fire in 1891. The news reached Peabody at the office, and he brought it to Spencer Trask, who was ill with pneumonia at the time. It was sad news indeed, for memories of the children were bound up in the old house. But, without hesitation, Trask gave the order to rebuild.

The new mansion at Yaddo was a copy of Haddon Hall, the historic English castle—a great edifice of granite, with wings jutting off from the central part. It was set upon a high point on the hillside. Round about were tall pine trees; far away one could see the hazy line of mountains. A lovely stone terrace gave a view of half of Saratoga County. Below the house, at the foot of the slope, was a sunken rose-garden,[5] to the right of that was a greenhouse, and beyond were the vegetable gardens and dairy. In the valley were four small lakes, shaded by encircling forest; each of these was named for one of the Trask children.

Spencer Trask took constant delight in developing the place. Dressed in riding togs, seated in the saddle on a fine horse, the tall dark-bearded man was the picture of a country gentleman. He employed his former coachman, James Paul, as superintendent of grounds and farm and hired a corps of workmen. One of his first activities was to plant additional pine trees. He directed the laying out of the flower gardens, and, with an eye sensitive to natural beauty, landscaped the estate without spoiling its rugged appearance.

The visitor at Yaddo was ushered into a baronial hall. Near the entrance was a fountain with a marble statue as its centre. At the opposite end of the hall, some fifty feet away, glass doors opened out upon a broad portico. In the center of the hall, on the left, was a wide fireplace; over the fireplace was a mosaic representation of a falcon. The hall opened, on the left, into a grand salon, or library. This room was sixty feet long and thirty-five wide. Here was another big fireplace, with a glowing fire to welcome the caller. A life-sized painting of little Christina in riding clothes and another of her small brother Spencer were later given the place of honor on the walls. The room was lined with books—poetry, drama, history, and works

---

5. A pergola trellised with climbing roses was later added.

on art and music. Across the hall from the library was the large high-ceilinged dining-room, with French windows giving a view of the mountains. Beyond this room were several smaller rooms including the kitchen.

A wide staircase led up from the great hall. At the landing the stairway divided and circled in two curves to the second story. The broad hall on the second floor gave a vista of countryside and mountains at one end and at the other end opened to an upstairs porch shaded by the pine trees. There were several suites of rooms off this hall. Mrs. Trask's suite was up a brief staircase. From her sitting-room she could look down upon the rose garden at the foot of the terrace or far away to the hazy tops of mountains.

The Trasks enjoyed having house guests. Friends and acquaintances were constantly coming and going; some stayed for a weekend, some for a week, some for a much longer time. Interesting people of all sorts sat at the beautifully appointed table.

Mrs. Trask suffered from a chronic heart condition and she was often confined to her suite when guests arrived. On these occasions, Miss Pardee did the honors and made the guests comfortable. Whenever Kate was able, she would receive visitors in her suite. Dressed in a trailing satin gown and propped up on a divan in her luxurious living room, she held her intimate little salon.

Katrina Trask had been writing for a number of years. Before 1890 she had occupied herself intermittently with her "Chronicles" of Yaddo. After the death of her children, she turned to her writing more seriously. A volume of her poetry, *Under King Constantine*, was published in 1892. A second edition of this book appeared in 1893. Another book of poetry, *Sonnets and Lyrics*, was published in 1894. This was followed by two works of fiction, *White Satin and Homespun* (1896) and *John*

Leighton Jr. (1898). She followed these works by other books of poetry and drama. In all her works the romantic element is strong. She places her characters in an atmosphere of medieval pageantry and chivalry. In her plays there is always a conquering hero, mighty and good.

The grand manner, the sweep of color and of pomp, she carried over to the every-day life which surrounded her. With the capable assistance of her husband, who sought to gratify all her wishes, she wove a magic spell over the guests who came to Yaddo. Now and then a play would be presented. At the psychological moment Katrina would appear on the landing of the great staircase dressed in a trailing gown and wearing gleaming jewels about her neck.[6] Though short in stature, she appeared tall as she descended the stairs to join her faithful courtiers.

To the outsider looking back on such a scene the situation might seem artificial. In a period of American life when realism had set in, when novelists like Stephen Crane were writing of the sordid incidents in city slums, here, a few hours away, was Yaddo—a scene, as it were, in medieval drama. Yet to the persons who lived there and to those who visited and caught its spell, there was nothing artificial about it. They became a part of the scene and it took on reality. Later, a guest returning to the city could hardly describe the magic which had captured him.

In this atmosphere that carried an element of unreality and romanticism, George Foster Peabody spent many week-ends and holidays. His business transactions would require an evening conference with Spencer Trask, and he would come for a few hours of discussion—and then remain for a visit. He had his own suite of rooms. He was so much at home at Yaddo that he felt free to invite

---

6. A "feature story" on "Authors at Home," appearing in *New York Times* on November 12, 1898.

guests at will. The tall young man with courtly manners was a part of the place.

2.

Wealth gave Peabody the opportunity to move to his own more spacious home. In the 1880's he and his mother lived at 10 Lafayette Avenue; later they lived in a house on Remsen Street. From there they moved to 28 Monroe Place, Brooklyn, a house which Peabody bought from Spencer Trask's father, Alanson Trask.

The four-story brownstone mansion at 28 Monroe Place was one of the finest residences on Brooklyn Heights. Some of Peabody's friends lived near-by—the Trasks, Edward Morse Shepard and the Hewitts. Among his neighbors were the Lows, the Whites, the Pierreponts and the Beards—all prominent in Brooklyn's civic and social life.

In furnishing his large home, Peabody had the help of the best decorators and art dealers. He himself bought art treasures in this country and in Europe, and built up an interesting library of hundreds of volumes. The main room of the house was the library. On its walls, in spaces not occupied by books, were hung a dozen or more oil paintings; other works of art were several plaques and a bisque Diana. The room, though rather imposing, was one in which hosts and guests could take their ease; it contained a davenport and plenty of comfortable chairs and hassocks. Under foot were Persian and Angora rugs. A coal fire burned in the grate and shone on the polished brass of wood-box, fire screen, and andirons.

Peabody's personal suite was on the third floor. It consisted of a small front room and a large bedroom. These rooms were simply furnished; the bedroom contained a brass bed, four stands, four cane chairs (including a rocker), two chiffoniers, and two clothes presses.

On the walls were photographs of horses, of Western scenery, of tombs of the Medici, of a stained glass window, of the river Cam at Cambridge, England, of a frieze of children. On the mantel were family photographs. Later a photograph of Spencer Trask and an oil portrait of Mrs. Trask were added to the collection of pictures.

From the contents of this room one can capture something of the personality of the man. The simple, practical furniture; the likenesses of persons dear to him; the photographed frieze of children—all tell of an intimate side which was often unrevealed to the public.[7]

Mrs. Peabody had her own suite and spent much of her time there. Now that she had leisure, she turned to painting, a hobby for which she displayed considerable talent. Peabody employed a housekeeper and a staff of household help, so that his mother had no responsibility unless she wished it. He engaged a companion for her, a Miss Jones, who accompanied her on occasional trips.

On weekdays, Peabody would drive down to the docks and take the ferry for lower Manhattan. A short time later he would step into his office. A day of activity followed; conferences with his partner, meetings of the boards of directors of the railroads and utilities companies, wires to branch houses, letters to correspondents and representatives. Returning home in time for dinner, he would relax and enjoy himself. The setting was always somewhat ceremonious—heavy damask, massive silver; delicacies such as hothouse grapes graced the board. Yet the atmosphere was pleasant and friendly. Often there were guests, and the gentlemen would linger long around the table after the ladies had withdrawn.

Entertaining friends at home was Peabody's chief

---

7. Above detail is from inventory at time of dismantling of the rooms. Peabody Papers.

diversion. Occasionally he would arrange a musical evening; once he engaged an opera singer to come to the house in honor of his mother's birthday. In general his guests were persons engaged in business and professional life.

He liked to keep in close touch with his relatives in the South. His cousin, Miss Pocahontas Peabody of Columbus, Georgia, who later was married to Professor W. W. Daniels, of the University of Wisconsin, was one of his favorite guests. Other young kin came from the South for a visit. With evenings at the opera, at concerts, and at the theatre, with drives through the parks and to places of interest, he made their stay a delightful fairy-tale.

It was the custom of wealthy families of that day, as of this, to have summer homes in the country. The women folk and the household staff would open the estates in late spring and remain there until autumn; the men of the family would run up for week-ends and for longer periods of vacation. The beautiful scenery around Lake George, about twenty-five miles north of Saratoga Springs, attracted many. Peabody followed the mode of the day. He enjoyed Yaddo and decided to have his own home near there. In 1891, he purchased a large house with several hundred acres of land near Caldwell on Lake George. The place was named Abenia, which is Algonquin for "Home of Rest." The house overlooked the lake. It was a rather ungainly affair, with mansard roof; he decided to remodel it to suit his own taste and eventually did so. Under his direction it was made into something both more handsome and more comfortable. Around the edge of the roof, as a crowning touch, he planted geraniums. Atop the roof and on the piazza below he placed porch rockers so that his guests might fully enjoy the lake breezes.

Inside the house the appearance was similar to that of his Brooklyn home. Fur rugs covered the floors; the walls were lined with oil paintings of madonnas and cherubs. In the dining room bowls of beautiful flowers—in summer from the garden, in winter from the greenhouse—gave welcome and good cheer.

Each spring Peabody sent most of his household staff to Abenia, retaining only enough of it to keep the town house in order. His mother spent the summers at Abenia, and Peabody went up often. As the years passed, the stay of the family was extended into the fall, as was the case with the Trasks at Yaddo; and gradually the Lake George place became Peabody's home most of the year.

Peabody had been a generous host in Brooklyn, but at Abenia, he had an even better chance to practice his gifts in that line. He became famous for his house parties, each of them carefully planned so that a company of congenial spirits should be gathered together. He always liked to have his relatives come from the South for a visit. He played host to clergymen and educators who were attending near-by conferences.

One of his main interests was the development of the grounds. He preserved the natural beauty, as Spencer Trask did at Yaddo, planted trees and shrubs, and laid out beautiful walks over the estate. He continued to purchase property, and, in time, owned a thousand acres of wooded land.[8]

Tall and straight, he would walk with a visitor along the shady paths, naming every wild flower and plant. Or he and a friend would ride through the woodland as the sun glanced through the tops of spruces, and then return to the house for a chat on the porch with his mother and other guests. It was at Abenia and at Yaddo that Peabody felt most himself. At both these beautiful estates he could relax and enjoy the comforts of living and the pleasures of rich friendships.

8. He later donated some of his land to the state as a reservation.

CHAPTER VI

Business Affairs in the 1890's

WE HAVE SKETCHED THE ENTRANCE OF SPENCER TRASK and Company into the fields of railroad financing and public utilities. At first the partners handled chiefly large blocks of stock, but as time passed, they dealt more and more in bonds. Their operation in bonds became so extensive that in 1892 they opened a department for bond investments.

Peabody had become a director in many enterprises. These included not only the Rio Grande Western, the St. Louis, Alton and Terre Haute, and electrical companies of several cities, but also numerous Mexican railway and mining companies. He represented his company in various negotiations. He was a director in numerous railway, electrical industry, and mining enterprises, and in many of these enterprises he served as vice president or treasurer. Among his connections about 1891 were the following:[1]

Name	Office Held
Compania Metalurgica Mexicana	Vice Pres. and Dir.
Mexican Lead Co.	Treasurer and Dir.
Montezuma Lead Co.	Vice Pres. and Dir.
Potosi & Rio Verde Railway Co.	President and Dir.
Mexican Smelting & Refining Co.	President
Teziutlan Copper Co.	Vice Pres. and Dir.
Teziutlan Copper Mfg. & Smtg. Co.	Vice Pres. and Dir.

1. Letter from Mr. R. E. Safford, Secretary of the Mexican Northern Railway Company to author, April 18, 1940.

Towne Securities Corp.   Director
Mexican Northern Railway Co.   Vice Pres. and Dir.
The Fresnillo Co.   Vice Pres. and Dir.

Peabody's connection with the Denver and Rio Grande Western Railway continued as his most important single railway interest. In 1889 under the leadership of General Palmer and Peabody, this railroad was reorganized and the name was changed to Rio Grande Western. On June 1, 1889, the *Commerical and Financial Chronicle* recorded the reorganization as follows:[2]

> Denver & Rio Grande Western-Rio Grande Western. The latter title is the name of the reorganized Denver Rio Grande & Western. First trust mortgage 4 per cent 50-year bonds to an aggregate limit $16,000,000 have been authorized. The liabilities of the old company are under the plan of reorganization merged into the new 4 per cent bonds and preferred stock, so that the new mortgage is a first lien upon all the property, including rolling stock. The Reorganization Committee have authorized the sale of $5,500,000 of the new issue, the proceeds of which will be used for improving the line relaying it with heavier steel rails, broadening the gauge, new equipment and extensions. The Central Trust Company and Messrs. J. Kennedy Tod & Co. of this City are offering these bonds at 75.

The first annual meeting of the reorganized company was held at Salt Lake City in July, 1889. At that time a board of directors was elected and officers were chosen. Peabody was made a director. He also became first vice president. The other officers were William J. Palmer, president; D. C. Dodge, second vice president and general manager; C. W. Drake, secretary and treasurer.[3]

---

2. *Commercial and Financial Chronicle*, XLVIII, 729.
3. The Board of Directors included Charles J. Canda, James C. Parrish, Frederic P. Olcott, George Foster Peabody, J. Kennedy Tod, and William J. Palmer of New York; J. D. Potts of Philadelphia; Barthold Schlesinger of Boston; and D. C. Dodge of Denver. *Commercial and Financial Chronicle*, XLIX (July 27, 1889), 115.

The property covered is described as follows:

The main line, extending from Ogden, Utah, to Salt Lake City, and thence southerly and southeasterly, via Pleasant Valley Junction to Green River Station, Emery County, and thence easterly through Emery County to a point on the Colorado State line, a distance of over 310 miles; the branch from Pleasant Valley Junction southwesterly, via Pleasant Valley to coal mines in San Pete County, 19 miles; also, two branches commencing at Bingham Junction, one running easterly to Alta in the Little Cottonwood Mining District in Salt Lake County, a distance, including tramway, of about 18 miles and one running westerly to a point near Jordan Mine in the Bingham Mining district, a distance including tramway, of about 20 miles; also, two branches in Salt Lake County, one to lime quarries and the other to salt works, together about 2 miles; and a branch in Davis Co. to Salt Lake, about 2 miles; and also all other existing spurs or branches.[4]

One of the chief purposes of the reorganization was the improvement and extension of the line. When General Palmer built the road, he used a three-foot gauge. This had made it possible for trains to make their way along narrow mountain ledges and through deep canyons. The three-foot gauge had been economical. Developments in traffic since that time, however, had made it advisable to widen the gauge to the four feet eight and one half inches, which had by this time become the standard width.

The reorganization and improvement required a refunding of capital investment. In these operations Peabody, as a member of the firm of Spencer Trask and Company, played a major part.

To effect the new capitalization, bond-holders were urged to turn in their bonds with coupons attached. There was outstanding of the first mortgage bonds a total of $6,900,000, with coupons amounting to $1,345,500.

---

4. *Commercial and Financial Chronicle*, XLIX (August 24, 1889), 237-238.

In all, a total of $6,873,000 in bonds was turned in. One individual opposed the plan, however, and brought suit to compel the company to pay the coupons from its bonds.5 The Supreme Court of New York gave a decision favoring the company. In a report to the bond holders, the Reorganization Committee, of which Peabody was a member, wrote:

> Whatever the final result, it appears to be of slight consequence, as the new securities held by the Trust Co., and originally intended to be exchanged for these old Bonds, have now become so valuable that it is not unlikely that the recalcitrant bondholder may in a short time be placed at a disadvantage compared with those who joined in the plan of reorganization.6

After the new issue of bonds was placed, the company, under the leadership of Palmer and Peabody, made a careful study of the probable future business of the road. The general manager, Colonel David C. Dodge, assisted them. As a result, it was decided that further improvements in location should be made in order to shorten distance, procure easier curves and grades, and prevent washouts at dangerous points.7

Of the changes, the committee wrote:

> In addition to the decided advantages of this route in the respects above mentioned, your company has secured an additional section of grand canyon scenery which forms a noteworthy feature of the "Scenic line."
>
> An important decision arrived at in this same connection was that the increased tonnage of the modern freight car, the increased weight of the engines to properly handle the business of today, and the probability of a steadily increasing traffic made it desirable, as a

---

5. Report of the Reorganization Committee of the Denver and Rio Grande Western to bond and stockholders, May, 1891, pp. 3-6.
6. *Ibid.*
7. Among the improvements was a new line forty-four miles long across the Utah border; the building of sixteen miles of railroad in Colorado to Crevasse, a station on the Denver and Rio Grande about halfway between the border and Grand Junction. (*Ibid.*)

matter of true economy, to lay 65 lb. rails throughout on the main line, instead of a lighter weight.

Concerning other improvements, the committee continued:

> It was also decided that it would be true economy to have the most improved appliances placed upon all the new equipment, which accordingly, has been provided with the Westinghouse Air Brakes and Automatic Couplers of the Master Car Builders' type on all the freight cars and driver brakes on many of the engines, while the passenger equipment has the provision for heating by steam from the engine to take the place of the "car stove." The "Pintsch Gas" system for lighting the passenger trains was adopted, as affording the passenger sufficient light with which to read with entire ease; this required the erection of a plant for the manufacture and supply of gas to the cars at Ogden.[8]

These improvements caused a large outlay of funds, but they signified, according to the directors, a great advance over the equipment of any other railroad in the Western country. The road-bed, too, they stated, promised to be in the front rank.

In concluding their report, the Reorganization Committee of the Denver and Rio Grande Western wrote:[9]

> By the changes of location referred to, over 8000 degrees of curvature have been avoided, the maximum curve having been reduced from 20 degrees to 10 degrees, and the distance from Grand Junction to Ogden shortened by about 18 miles.
> The excess of expenditure for widening the gauge and purchasing the new equipment beyond the amount received from the first issue of Bonds, was provided by the sale of Bonds and Preferred Stock from time to time as there was need for the money.
> The entire amount expended by the Committee including the legal and corporate expenses in New York was . . . $4,949,314.30.

---

8. Report of the Reorganization Committee of the Denver and Rio Grande Western to bond and stockholders, May, 1891, pp. 3-6.
9. *Ibid.*

The report of the Rio Grande Western for years 1890 through June 30, 1893, shows:[10]

Year Ended June 30,	1890	1891	1892	1893
Mileage	387	407	512	514
Gross Earnings	$1,622,234	$2,346,130	$2,643,924	$2,496,462
Net Income	520,686	856,783	928,571	846,468
Dividends		255,369	312,398	312,416

In spite of the depression years which followed 1893 this railroad showed continuous development; on a later page we shall record details of its progress.

We have referred to Peabody's connection with the St. Louis, Alton and Terre Haute Railway. This railway was a successor to the old Terre Haute, Alton and St. Louis,[11] which was sold in foreclosure in 1861. In October, 1890, the main line of the road, consisting of 193 miles, was sold to the Cleveland, Cincinnati, Chicago and St. Louis for $10,000,000 in four per cent one-hundred-year gold bonds.

For the year ending December 31, 1892, Mr. Peabody, Chairman of the Board of Directors, reported that the officers considered the year's results very encouraging. Local traffic had shown a steady increase. Heavy expenses had been incurred, however, in laying heavier rails and in improving the property otherwise. And because of this outlay, Peabody wrote:

> In view of the necessity for more equipment, the board have incurred further loans to secure some additions at once. When the 7 per cent bonds shall have been retired in 1894 and the heavy payments on those of them in the sinking fund cease, they hope to be able to provide the ampler equipment which the President shows to be most desirable for the further enlargement of your business. The payment of your bonds will release all the

---

10. *Commercial and Financial Chronicle, Investors' Supplement*, LVII (November, 1893), 118.
11. *Commercial and Financial Chronicle*, LVI (April, 1893), 577.

bonds of the C.C.C. & St. L. Ry. Co., and put a large surplus of them in the treasury to provide for such equipment and other improvements necessary to enlarge the earning capacity of your company. It has not seemed wise to dispose of any of your holdings of these bonds in advance of the negotiation that will be necessary in connection with the payment of your first and second mortgage bonds; and consequently offers to purchase have been declined.

The larger portion of the bills payable have been incurred in connection with the retirement of the large amount of your preferred stock with accumulated arrears of dividend thereon that was canceled early in the year 1892. It being deemed desirable, as stated above, to keep together the balance of the C.C.C. & St. L. bonds, the retirement of this stock was accomplished by a cash transaction in connection with the Cleveland, Cincinnati, Chicago & St. Louis Railway Co., and a complete settlement of the main line sale; to this purchase the former lessor company contributed $60,745, and the balance was procured by your company on long time loans secured by ample collaterals. . . .[12]

Peabody's interest in the electrical industry increased in the early 1890's. We have seen that, with Spencer Trask, he was instrumental in helping to develop both the New York Edison Electric Illuminating Company and the Edison General Electric Company. He was also one of the leading figures in the development of the Edison Electric Illuminating Company of Brooklyn, of which his brother Royal was an officer.

On January 31, 1900, the General Electric Company, which was incorporated on April 15, 1892, as an amalgamation, showed on its consolidated balance sheet total assets of $29,532,697.09, while its liabilities of $29,532,697.09 included $20,827,200.00 in capital stock and $5,300,000.00 in 5 per cent gold coupon debentures. It was

---

12. *Commercial and Financial Chronicle*, LVI (April, 1893), 577. The St. Louis, Alton & Terre Haute was later sold to the Illinois Central on October 15, 1902.

generally prosperous except for a brief period after the 1893 panic. Peabody continued as a director of the company.[13] He also had a good deal to do with developments in the electrical industry in Cleveland and in Detroit.

2.

During the first few years of business Spencer Trask and Company had reflected the expansion going on in the country, particularly in the fields of transportation and public utility. Along with expansion had come difficult problems.[14] By the early 1890's business conditions were in a serious state. Several major factors were responsible,[15] among them the curtailed purchasing power of agriculture, slackened demand abroad for American products, and withdrawals of gold by foreign investors. Moreover, the new Silver Purchase policy, authorized by Congress in 1890, had created anxiety: it was a threat to the gold standard which was the basis of the currency. Another factor in the situation was that, during the vast expansion of railroad industry, much stock had been watered and some railroads had over-expanded. Early in 1893 many railroads and other businesses found themselves insolvent.

The first alarming event occurred on February 20,

13. *Commercial and Financial Chronicle*, LXX (April 21, 1900), p. 798; General Electric Company, *Eighth Annual Report*, January 31, 1900. C. A. Coffin was president. J. P. Morgan, Thomas A. Edison, Spencer Trask, and others also were interested in the company.
14. A. M. Schlesinger, *The Rise of The City, 1878-1898. A History of American Life*, X (New York, The Macmillan Company, 1933); Ida M. Tarbell, *The Nationalizing of Business, 1878-1898. A History of American Life*, IX (New York, The Macmillan Company, 1936); *Commercial and Financial Chronicle* issues.
15. F. P. Weberg, *The Background of the Panic of 1893* (Washington, D. C.: The Catholic University of America, 1929); A. Nevins, *Grover Cleveland, A Study in Courage* (New York: Dodd, Mead and Company, 1932); D. R. Dewey, *Financial History of the United States* (New York: Longmans, Green & Co., 1934).

1893, when the Philadelphia and Reading Railroad declared itself bankrupt. A second shock came in May, 1893, when the National Cordage Company, the rope trust, failed. In the next few months, over 17,000 business firms went into bankruptcy. Unemployment multiplied and breadlines of hungry men stretched along the sidewalks. Among the business corporations the hardest hit were the railroads. The Erie Railroad failed in July, the Northern Pacific in August, the Union Pacific in October.

The violent financial panic was a source of great anxiety to Spencer Trask and Company. The firm had heavy commitments, and many of its securities were stocks and bonds of Western Railroads. It was not possible to borrow money even on top grade securities, and the firm found it necessary to give notes. These notes were paid off in full within a reasonably short time and the firm resumed its normal activities.[16]

The General Electric Company, in which Trask and Peabody were interested, was in trouble for a time. The company had endorsed notes for several utility companies and as security had received stock and bonds of these companies. These securities, normally worth approximately $16,000,000 were now down to a fraction of their former price. In spite of these harassing problems, however, the company was able to show a profit because of the demand for its own securities. The same was true of the New York Edison Electric Illuminating Company; it felt the strain of conditions, but because of heavy consumer demand was able to weather the depression and show astonishing gains within the next few years.

In that panic year of 1893, Mr. Peabody, though concerned for Spencer Trask and Company holdings, was apparently not unduly alarmed. Indeed, he went on a

---

16. Interviews with members of the firm.

trip to Europe that summer and while there, made a sightseeing tour in company with his friend, Edward Morse Shepard, who joined him in London. Whether he combined business with pleasure and conferred with British firms is not known.

In 1895 Spencer Trask and Company organized the Broadway Realty Company, which constructed at 11 Broadway a building known as the Bowling Green offices. It was the largest office building in the city south of City Hall Park, and was designed to meet the needs of business men and shipping interests. At the same time, wishing to see improvements in that vicinity, Trask and Peabody used their influence to procure the removal of the Customs House from its old site to a commanding position south of the Broadway Realty Company building and facing Bowling Green Park. Trask was made president of the Broadway Realty Company. He was succeeded by Peabody, who remained its president for many years.

Another important activity of the partners occurred in connection with the reorganization and refinancing of the *New York Times*. In 1896, through an arrangement with Adolph S. Ochs, a Chattanooga publisher, Trask and several associates underwrote the re-organized paper, and Ochs became its publisher. While Peabody was less involved than Trask in making this transaction, he was interested in it. The contact thus made led to a friendly acquaintance with Mr. Ochs and the editorial staff. The newspaper respected his opinions and often printed letters from him on its editorial page.

CHAPTER VII

Party Politics

IN THE EARLY 1890's PEABODY WAS ALREADY A LEADING figure in Democratic Party politics in Kings County; he was also becoming more prominent in Party affairs in New York State. For many years now he had been a member of the Young Men's Democratic Club of Brooklyn; with Edward Morse Shepard and other well known civic figures he had worked hard for political reform.

The wave of industrialism and urbanization in the late nineteenth century had brought with it new social ills. Many remedies were being offered—some mild, some drastic. Socialists were painting utopias. Civil service reformers were busy. In the early 1890's New York City, which had been in the grip of corrupt politicians, had a housecleaning; through the famous Lexow Committee a sweeping investigation was conducted, and in 1894 a reform government was put in office. The organizations known as Good Government Clubs and the Citizens' Union were working for further municipal reform. Many men of wealth and prominence took their civic responsibilities seriously and became leaders in these movements.

Peabody, as we have seen, had long been interested in good government and social improvement. His interest was strengthened through association with his friends, Edward Morse Shepard and Katrina and Spencer Trask, who were all active in such causes; he had, too, much sympathy and encouragement from his mother. He was

57

also influenced by Henry George's writings, and by the man himself, whom he came to know personally.

In politics, Peabody was a "Cleveland Democrat"; he believed in a sound currency and in a downward revision of the tariff. He had viewed with regret Cleveland's defeat in 1888. Despite that defeat, he and other Democrats of like views believed in 1890 that Cleveland could again win the Democratic nomination, but several events in 1891 shook their confidence.

On January 21, 1892, the National Democratic Committee issued a call for the national convention; it was to be held in Chicago in June. Thereupon, the New York State Democratic Committee promptly issued a call for a state convention to be held in Albany on February 22. Upon hearing this, certain Brooklyn Democrats favoring Cleveland's nomination objected, characterizing the proposed state convention as a "Snap Convention," the real object of which was to promote the nomination of David B. Hill, Governor of New York. Some of the objectors swung into action to defeat such a plan; prominent among them were Peabody and Edward M. Shepard.

Shortly before the Albany convention, about twenty prominent Brooklyn Democrats gathered at the Clarendon Hotel. Peabody was among those who had called the meeting. He was appointed to serve on a committee of twenty-five, later increased to one hundred, which should arrange a mass meeting of protest at the Criterion Theater. As a result of these meetings, delegates were sent to Albany, and later plans were completed for a State Democratic Convention to be held at Syracuse on May 31.

Between February and May, the Brooklyn Democrats organized themselves as the Brooklyn Provisional Committee. They were referred to by other members of the Democratic Party variously as "The Provisional Committee," "The Irregulars", or "The Anti-Snaps." Ward organizations of voters in Brooklyn were formed. Literature was distributed, and the remonstrance now became known as the "Syracuse Movement." Peabody served as chairman of the executive committee, and thus was a prime mover in making arrangements.

On Decoration Day, May 30, 1892, the delegates went to Syracuse by special train. The cars were decorated with banners. Among the delegates were Peabody and Shepard; the latter was appointed chairman of the convention. The Syracuse meeting, held at the Athenaeum, condemned the February 22 convention as a violation of party practice, and chose delegates to send to the National Convention of the Democratic Party at Chicago. Among those chosen were Peabody and Shepard.

On June 21, the Kings County delegates were on hand at Chicago, having reached there several days in advance. They made an exciting, skillful canvass of sentiment. When they found that it was likely Cleveland would be nominated without the aid of votes from New York State, the delegates withdrew their claims for seats. However, they were assigned seats upon the floor of the convention behind the seats reserved for the regular delegates from New York.

Having witnessed Cleveland's nomination about four o'clock on the morning of June 23, the Brooklyn Provisional delegates wrote finis to the first part of their battle. They then returned home and quickly called the Brooklyn Committee together to map out an intensive campaign. Peabody was appointed chairman of the campaign committee. During the next several months, the committee arranged a large number of meetings throughout the city; at one of these, on October 19th, Peabody and Shepard were the speakers. As November drew near, a Committee on Election Day was named, with Shepard as chairman and Peabody as one of the leading members.

On Election Day, the Brooklyn Provisional Committee was represented by about nine hundred citizens, many of them men prominent in business and professional life. They wore badges of the committee and escorted people to the polls.

When the returns were in, the plurality for Cleveland in Brooklyn was found to be nearly thirty thousand. It was pointed out by the Committee that this increase was proportionately larger than the increase in any important city except Chicago.[1] The Brooklyn Committee had labored hard, and it was well satisfied with the election results. Cleveland would be the next President.

Having completed its work, the Brooklyn Provisional Committee disbanded, but members of the organization continued to work for other measures. Since 1890, some of these Reform Democrats had been working toward changes in the city and county offices and had nominated[2] several candidates.

As the Brooklyn city campaign of 1893 approached, the Reform Democrats decided they could no longer align themselves with the "Regulars" — with "Willoughby Street" as the organization was commonly called. The reformers called the Cleveland Clubs together and made a campaign which resulted in the defeat of "Willoughby Street"[3] at the polls in 1893.

In 1894 the Brooklyn Democratic Club, of which Peabody was now president,[4] was reorganized. The meeting at

1. Syracuse Movement, Kings County, *Proceedings on Dissolution of Central Committees*, Nov. 11, 1892, p. 44.
2. Their nominees included J. Warren Greene, Henry C. Wright, Henry Hentz, and John C. Kelley.
3. In a public address made at a later date, Shepard pointed out that Willoughby Street had made such a bad name for itself that in the mayoralty election of 1894, one third of the Democrats of Brooklyn voted for a Republican (some for the regular Republican candidate, some for the "Partisan Republican").
4. Shepard was president for several years beginning with 1888.

which the reorganization was effected took place on April 4 at the Brooklyn Academy of Music. More than two thousand persons entered to the strains of stirring music by Conterno's Band. Six hundred were seated on the stage, and the boxes were occupied by well known citizens.

In 1895 Edward M. Shepard was the independent Democratic candidate for Mayor of Brooklyn. Peabody, who was a firm believer in Shepard's abilities, gave him staunch support. He was, however, defeated.

2.

Peabody approved of Cleveland's stand for currency stabilization. In a letter to the Brooklyn Eagle on December 2, 1892, he had warned of the grave danger which threatened the country and had maintained that the chief duty of the hour was to demand repeal of the Silver Purchase Act.

After Cleveland took office in March, 1893, the problem of the currency reached a critical state. The economic collapse in that year focused public attention on the subject to an increasing degree. The "debtor class" and its spokesmen put the blame for the collapse upon a shortage of circulating medium; business and financial leaders traced the trouble to silver inflation. With the eyes of the country upon him, President Cleveland announced that he and his cabinet would act to maintain parity between gold and silver. In August, 1893, he summoned a special session of Congress which, after a battle of more than two months, repealed the Silver Purchase Act.[5]

During the two long depression years that followed,

---

5. By the terms of the Sherman Silver Purchase Act of 1890, the government was required to buy silver at the rate of 4,500,000 ounces a month. The bullion was coined into silver dollars and silver certificates were printed. The result was an accumulation of silver money which decreased in value, and caused the withdrawal of gold.

the currency question continued to be in the forefront. It was obvious that bi-metallism would be a paramount issue in the campaign of 1896.

3.

At the Republican party convention of 1896, William McKinley, sponsored by his wealthy friend, Marcus Alonzo Hanna, was nominated for president. The party platform called for a strict adherence to the gold standard, and McKinley could be counted on to pursue that end. At the national convention of the Democratic party at Chicago in July, 1896, William Jennings Bryan was nominated on a platform which demanded free and unlimited coinage of both gold and silver at the legal ratio of sixteen to one. Thus the two parties were lined up against each other on this, the main issue of the day.

Many Democrats, however, were opposed to "free silver," and were alarmed by the nomination of Bryan, its leading advocate. A movement was set on foot to nominate another candidate. The group of insurgents became known as the Gold Democrats. Peabody was one of its leaders.

The Gold Democrats met in a convention at Indianapolis on September 3 and 4, 1896. Organized as the "National Democratic Party," they denounced the "costly patch-work system" of paper currency as a danger to the country, and endorsed a policy of sound money. They condemned protection, advocating tariff for revenue only. They praised the Cleveland administration for its wisdom and energy, and for its dignified handling of foreign affairs. For president, they nominated eighty-year-old General John M. Palmer of Illinois, a Civil War veteran; for vice president, General Simon B. Buckner of Kentucky.

The Gold Democrats, or Sound Money Democrats, mapped out a brisk and intensive campaign. They set up national headquarters at 39 East Twenty-third Street,

PARTY POLITICS 63

New York City. Peabody, in charge of the Eastern States campaign for the Palmer-Buckner ticket, worked night and day.

The next few weeks saw one of the most spirited campaigns in American history. Mark Hanna spent a hundred thousand dollars of his own money and raised between three and a half and four million dollars in campaign funds. Bulletins and pamphlets were broadcast. McKinley was described on a large poster as the "Advance Agent of Prosperity." This appealed to many who were still impoverished from the depression. The scene looked bright to the Republicans.

Bryan, on the other hand—then thirty-four, but referred to as the "boy democrat"—was swaying crowds along his fifteen-thousand-mile tour of the country. His famous "Cross of Gold" speech, delivered at the convention, was followed by other dramatic speeches. Though opponents denounced him as a demagogue who would stir up class and sectional strife, his oratory won great numbers to his side.

The Gold Democrats strained every nerve to bring about the election of General Palmer and his running mate General Buckner. A number of prominent democrats, including Hoke Smith, Secretary of the Interior, joined the new wing of the party. Peabody continued to work indefatigably at New York Headquarters.

On Election Day, almost fourteen million persons went to the polls. Of that number, McKinley received 7,111,607 votes, Bryan 6,509,052, and Palmer 134,645. Writing to Dr. Frissell at Hampton on November 5, Peabody said that he was pleased at the size of the sound money vote in the South, where little work was done during the campaign.

After the election, the Gold Democrats ceased to exist as a party. Many of them had voted the Republican ticket at the last and of these many remained Republicans.

Others returned to the Democratic fold. Peabody, having made the powerful effort in favor of a sound currency Democratic candidate, took the defeat with good grace and renewed his old party allegiance. He continued, however, to exert himself in favor of a stabilized currency.

4.

The campaign had shown the need of a thorough study of the money situation with a view to determining what reforms were called for. At a special meeting of the Board of Governors of the Indianapolis Board of Trade on November 18, 1896, Hugh H. Hanna read an urgent message addressed by President Cleveland to the Chamber of Commerce. Hanna requested that action be taken at once, proposing that a letter be sent to the more important boards of trade in the central western states inviting them to send representatives to a convention. His proposal was adopted. The date chosen for the convention was January 12, 1897.

Delegates from twenty-eight states and the District of Columbia attended this convention. More than one hundred cities sent representatives. An executive committee was appointed with Hugh H. Hanna as chairman; George Foster Peabody was one of the members. The committee was instructed to select a commission which should draw up suggestions to be presented at the next meeting of the convention. Peabody afterwards wrote to an acquaintance:

> I have always taken pride for my part in arranging for the meetings which resulted in these appointments at the house of my partner, Spencer Trask, in Saratoga Springs.[6]

Among those selected to serve on the commission were George F. Edmunds of Vermont, Chairman; Charles S. Fairchild of New York; and J. Laurence Laughlin, econo-

---

6. Copy of Mr. Peabody's letter to John J. Mitchell, President of Illinois Merchants Trust Company, Nov. 9, 1927, Yaddo files.

mist, of Illinois. One of the staff members appointed by the commission was Professor H. Parker Willis, economist.

The commission spent a year in making its report.[7] On January 25, 1898, the Indianapolis Monetary Convention reconvened, and considered the findings. The recommendations based on these findings were, in brief: that a gold standard be maintained, with the paper currency convertible to gold; that the volume of the currency be adequate for general needs and elastic enough to permit expansion in business transactions; and that, in order to furnish credit facilities to the entire country, a banking system embodying these principles should be set up.

The Indianapolis convention advised against too rapid contraction of the currency. Steps should be taken to ensure the eventual retirement of all classes of United States notes by a gradual and steady process. Interest-bearing bonds should not be issued except in case of unforeseen emergency. Silver dollars should be used as subsidiary coins, side by side with gold.

Peabody can be given a large amount of credit for the work of the Indianapolis Monetary Convention. As a member of the executive committee, he not only helped to select the members of the commission which drew up the report, but he was also active before the convention met in starting public discussion of currency problems. He helped meet the expenses of the staff.

After the convention he was asked to collaborate with Hugh H. Hanna in unifying the efforts of the New York Reform Club, the National Sound Money League, and the Indianapolis Monetary Association. This work brought

---

7. *Commercial and Financial Chronicle,* LXIV (Jan. 16, 1897), 100-101, commenting upon the report of the convention, said it was a great gain, "to have had the practical business man's idea" put into such a vital shape; it met the needs of the country.

him into close association with Hanna, who became one of his personal friends.

The triumph of the Gold Platform in the campaign of 1896, and the recommendations made by the Indianapolis Monetary Convention, assured the acceptance of the gold standard; this was achieved by an act passed in 1900. The evils of the old system of inelastic currency, resulting from the National Banking Act of 1862, were not, however, corrected.

Peabody believed that progress had been made in stabilizing the currency, but he was convinced that more reform was needed. During the next few years he kept calling attention to the recommendations of the Indianapolis Convention, and prodding public officials to carry these recommendations into practice. It was the ground work which he and Hanna and others laid in the Indianapolis Convention that formed the basis of the Aldrich monetary plan of 1908 and of the Federal Reserve Act of 1913 providing for the Federal Reserve Bank system. He may accurately be called one of the pioneers of the Federal Reserve movement.

One is naturally curious to know the extent of Peabody's penetration into economic problems such as that of the currency. Though not a college man, he had read widely in political economy. His knowledge of actual conditions in the business and financial world was, of course, very thorough; he had seen what would and would not work in a world of free private enterprise. His study of economic theory was therefore illumined by his practical experience. As a banker, he saw the stability of the country resting upon a more adequate regulation of the currency.

While he remained, in general, an adherent of the classical school of economic theory, Peabody respected the work of the rising body of economists, among them

Professors J. Laurence Laughlin and H. Parker Willis, who were engaged in reformulating the science of economics to meet the needs of the new industrial life. After the Indianapolis Monetary Convention, he was in touch with Laughlin and Willis for many years; later he was in touch with Professor Irving Fisher of Yale. On the whole, it may be said that he was a conservative with an open mind, a practical man with an appreciation of the value of theory.

5.

After 1896, Peabody not only continued his active efforts in behalf of an improved currency system, but also devoted much time to several other causes which he had long regarded as important. An advocate of free trade, he aligned himself with organizations working toward this objective. Likewise, having been converted to single tax by Henry George's book *Progress and Poverty* years before he gave his support to Louis Post, editor of *The Public*, an organ devoted to the subject. For many years he kept up an extensive correspondence with Post.

One of his most significant activities from this time was his increasing effort in behalf of government ownership of railroads. At first thought, this seems a strange paradox. Here was a man who had made his fortune in the handling of railroad and public utilities stocks and bonds. The foundation of Spencer Trask and Company business was the system of private enterprise. How could he reconcile his philosophy of government ownership of railroads with his practice?

His files throw some light upon this question. Although he had been, and still was, an active figure in railroad manipulations, his reasoning told him that it was important for this form of transportation to be operated as a public service rather than for the advantage of private interests. Perhaps the ideas regarding the nationalizing of land which he had derived from Henry George may have carried over in his mind to the nationalizing of railroads. It is possible also that the disposal of his largest railroad interests, namely the Rio Grande Western in 1901, and the St. Louis, Alton and Terre Haute in 1902, may have had some bearing on his attitude, for after this time he was less heavily involved in large scale competitive enterprises, and consequently may have felt that he had less at stake in the fortunes of private railroads. It must be remembered, however, that he still held important securities in Mexican railway companies and was to continue holding them throughout his life. Peabody the capitalist, the railroad financier, and Peabody the advocate of government control of railroads—it is an interesting dualism which is not easily explained.

6.

During the late 1890's Peabody was in touch with Tom L. Johnson, Mayor of Cleveland, whom he had met earlier in connection with electric illuminating developments. He also met Newton D. Baker, a young lawyer who came to Cleveland in 1899 and was Tom Johnson's assistant. A close personal friendship with Baker began in this way. The two men exchanged their views on various issues. Baker, who was beginning his political career, respected Peabody's opinions. How much he consulted Peabody in those earlier years is not known, for the letter files of that period are scanty. From 1914 through the early 1930's, the letters are numerous and show a relationship of mutual confidence.

7.

At the turn of the century we find Peabody a busy man indeed. He was known as a leading banker and as a promoter. He was a figure in politics. He was active in the world of education: he was still a trustee of Hampton; he was a member (appointed in 1898) of the Board of Trustees of Colorado College; and he was greatly interested in a new educational undertaking which we shall describe in detail later on—the Southern Education Conference.

CHAPTER VIII

From Railroads to Sugar Beets

INDUSTRIAL DEVELOPMENTS OF THE 1890's CONTINUED TO give Spencer Trask and Company additional opportunities. The company's historian states that a list of the firms in whose financing the Trask bankers played an important part would read much like a list of all the great industries of the country.[1]

The phenomenal expansion of big business at the end of the century led to the forming of huge consolidations, the greatest of these being the United States Steel Corporation, which was created in 1901 when Andrew Carnegie sold his gigantic holdings to J. P. Morgan. Railroads were in process of being merged into mammoth enterprises, controlled by six great interests.

In the course of these consolidations, Spencer Trask and Company effected several of their biggest deals. Two of these were the sale of the Rio Grande Western to Kuhn, Loeb and Company, and the sale of the Brooklyn Edison Illuminating Company to the Anthony N. Brady interests. At this same time Spencer Trask and Company—chiefly as a result of Peabody's negotiations—were extending their holdings into the beet sugar industry, and Peabody was widening the scope of his activities in connection with the Mexican railways and with railroad and mining enterprises in the western states.

1. E. J. Koop, *op. cit.*

FROM RAILROADS TO SUGAR BEETS 71

Under the able leadership of Palmer and Peabody, the Rio Grande Western had continued to prosper. Interesting reports were issued by the railroad each year which were a barometer of mining conditions at that time. The *Commercial and Financial Chronicle*, in referring to the railroad's report of 1896, said:

> Gen. Palmer shows that as far as the Rio Grande Western is concerned the recovery in silver mining following the great depression in 1893 has been so marked that the traffic derived by the road, both direct and indirect, from that industry was actually greater in the late year than it had been in 1893. . . .[2]

The report showed that many new silver discoveries had been made in Utah. Gold mining was developing throughout Utah and Colorado. Reference was made to some of the other industries, such as the growing of beet sugar along the railroad route. Nineteen thousand tons of beet sugar had been carried by the railroad during the preceding year.

The report showed an interesting shift in the kinds of business carried between 1892 and 1896:[3]

	Year ending June 30, 1896			
	1895-96	1894-95	1893-94	1892-93
Passengers carried	261,814	219,813	213,450	293,489
Total tons carried	736,621	678,539	635,561	667,451
Of Which				
Bituminous coal	217,912	259,151	223,927	----------
Ores	153,482	84,065	106,435	----------
Charcoal & Coke	33,388	30,669	27,833	----------
Lumber & Wood	30,616	19,373	13,115	----------

Two years later the Rio Grande Western Annual Report showed net earnings of $1,293,111 from operations. The directors announced additions which had been made to property and equipment. The expenditures, they said,

---

2. *Commercial and Financial Chronicle*, LXIII (Oct. 17, 1896), 681-682.
3. *Ibid.*, p. 697.

had been made "almost exclusively for new tracks, including the double tracking of the Mountain Division, new buildings and lands, and a new additional telegraph wire from Salt Lake City to Grand Junction."

The report[4] showed that the receipts were over 27 per cent larger and the net earnings $32\frac{1}{2}$ per cent larger than those of the largest previous fiscal year.[5] Except in sugar, sugar beets and asphaltum, every class of commodity carried showed an increase. There semed to be no reason to feel further anxiety regarding business in relation to mining in Utah, for other ores besides silver were showing a gain.[6]

The report of the Rio Grande Western for the year ending June 30, 1899, showed receipts from operation to be $3,352,988, and net earnings $1,268,463.[7] Haulage of coal had contributed 42 per cent of the total tonnage;[8] the carrying of coal and coke was twice what it had been in 1896. Furthermore, during the preceding year three additional beet sugar works had been completed, or partially completed, at or near stations on the Rio Grande Western line in Utah and Colorado.

Because of improvements undertaken at this time, a new consolidated mortgage was arranged by the company. The purpose of the mortgage was described in a circular as follows:[9]

> Issues have been made of the fifty year 4 per cent Gold Bonds under this Mortgage as follows:

4. The report stated that for safety on the eve of the outbreak of the Spanish-American War, it had been deemed wise to borrow $180,000 the previous April for equipment. Settlement was being made for chair cars and coaches, with the Pullman Company. *Commercial and Financial Chronicle*, LXVII (Oct. 15, 1898), 794-795.
5. The record year before this had been 1891-1892. *Ibid.*
6. *Commercial and Financial Chronicle*, LXVII (Oct. 15, 1898), 794-795.
7. *Ibid.*, LXIX (Oct. 28, 1899), 910-911.
8. *Ibid.*
9. *Ibid.*

1st: To acquire the $2,850,000 First Mortgage Bonds (being the entire issue) and all other securities of the Tintic Range and Sevier Railway branches covering 110 miles at $20,000 per mile (formerly in the Company's Treasury Reserve) ___$2,200,000
2nd: To retire the same amount of old First Mortgage Main Line Bonds held in the Company's Treasury as a Capital Reserve _____$800,000
3rd: To provide additional equipment and to discharge car trusts and other indebtedness for equipment and to pay for certain additions to the property _____$1,000,000

	Total	$4,000,000
Which with an additional		500,000

not yet issued (but now issuable for 25 miles of the new line completed since June 30, 1899) make up a total of $4,500,000
Of these Consolidated Bonds there were sold in March last and delivered in June   1,500,000

Leaving in the Treasury Reserve, of Consolidated Bonds $3,000,000

On March 31, 1900, the Rio Grande Western directors announced an increase in stock. It was stated that the shareholders would vote on April 30 at Salt Lake City on the question of amending the articles of incorporation by increasing the common capital stock by five million dollars. This would make a total authorized common capital stock of fifteen million dollars.[10]

The Railroad later announced a sale of stock. On May 19, 1900, the *Commercial and Financial Chronicle* reported:

The directors have accepted an offer from Spencer Trask & Co. to purchase the remaining $700,000 of preferred stock at the price of 90 per cent less a bankers' commission of 2½ per cent. The bankers, as agreed, offer all of the stock to the present stockholders for subscription up to and including May 25 at 90 per cent. This

---

10. *Ibid.*, LXX (March 31, 1900), 633, 895.

issue disposes of the full amount of preferred stock ($7,500,000) authorized. The proceeds "will be used in part payment for expenditures made to change the gauge and reduce the grade of the Utah Central R.R. . . . for further betterments on various lines."11

On November 24, 1900, the *Commercial and Financial Chronicle* carried an editorial captioned "Rio Grande Western's Progress" and commented:

> The lines of the Rio Grande Western, as is known, are located in Utah, a silver-mining State, but the depression in that industry has not served to check the company's prosperity. The outcome shows what intelligent management can do for a road in the United States running through a good territory and not exclusively dependent upon one class of traffic, either locally or in movement of through traffic . . . the road forms an important link in a trans-continental line across the country . . . The Company holds an ample capital reserve, there being on hand June 30, 1900, $2,484,800 of the 1st Mortgage 4 per cent consolidated gold bonds, besides $500,000 issuable but not yet issued at that date; also $260,000 Utah Central R. R. bonds and $1,000,000 Western Express Company stock. But additional provision has been deemed wise, and accordingly last April the stockholders were asked to give authority to issue $5,000,000 more common stock from time to time. As yet there has been no occasion to make any issue under this authorization, but it is a resource which remains available when needed. . . .
> The management are desirous of keeping the road's fixed charges low, and therein they are evincing the conservatism for which they have long been distinguished.12

Under the able direction of General Palmer and Peabody and the Board, the road had become an admirable example of modern equipment. By now the Rio Grande Western had extended its operations westerly through Utah. It was, moreover, a desirable link in a projected transcontinental rail line over the Southwestern Pacific route.

11. *Ibid.*, LXX (May 19, 1900), 997.
12. *Ibid.*, LXXI (Nov. 24, 1900), 1040.

At this time Palmer and Peabody believed that the time was ripe for the sale of the railroad. Other great mergers were taking place and consolidation was in the air. They began negotiations with Kuhn, Loeb and Company, and on May 29, 1901, Kuhn, Loeb wrote a check for $15,246,666.66 in favor of the firm. This represented the passing of control of the Rio Grande Western to the Denver and Rio Grande. The check is said to have been the second largest which had passed through the New York Clearing House up to that date.[13] The profitable sale of the railroad was a source of great satisfaction to Peabody and to Spencer Trask and Company. The partners declared a bonus of a year's salary to all the employees.

A large transaction effected shortly after this was the sale of the St. Louis, Alton and Terre Haute Railroad to the Illinois Central Railroad on October 15, 1902. Peabody had been a director since 1886; he had served as chairman of the board and had spent many hours helping to build the railroad up.[14] He was one of the chief negotiators of the sale.

2.

In the field of public utilities as well as in that of railroads, Spencer Trask and Company made large sales and mergers during this period. We have noted the earlier interests of Peabody and Spencer Trask in the New York Edison and in the Brooklyn Edison illuminating companies. We have also seen that Peabody and Trask were members of the board of directors of the General Electric Company. All of these companies had prospered except

---

13. E. J. Koop, *op. cit.* (In May, 1901, after the sale was effected, George J. Gould was made chairman of the Board and E. H. Harriman was made a director.)
14. The details of the many problems which Peabody had to solve in connection with this railroad are so far not available.

for a recession for a brief time after the panic of 1893. In the late 1890's Anthony N. Brady, who had extensive interests in Albany utilities, began a process of buying up electrical interests in and near New York. The first of the illuminating companies to be sold by Spencer Trask and Company was the Edison Electric Illuminating Company of Brooklyn; it was sold to the Kings County Electric Light and Power Company, one of the Brady interests. The announcement was made in 1898:

> Mr. George Foster Peabody, of the board of directors of the Edison Electric Illuminating Co. of Brooklyn, acting in consultation with the officers, has today closed, in behalf of stockholding interests represented by his firm (Spencer Trask & Co., Pine St., N. Y.) and equally for all others, a proposed sale of the stock of this company to the Kings County Electric Light & Power Co. upon terms which the members of the board of directors unite in thinking for the permanent advantage of the stockholders. Counsel are preparing the papers in detail to carry out the agreement provided it shall be accepted by two thirds of the stockholders.
> As soon as these details are in proper shape the matter will be fully submitted to each stockholder of record. The result to the stockholders will be in substance that the right to subscribe to 25 per cent additional stock at par, will be secured to them and that for the whole amount of stock they will then be offered par in ninety-nine year 6 per cent purchase money mortgage bonds, to be secured by the deposit of the Edison Stock so sold, and additionally by a junior mortgage of the Kings County Company upon its property, and further by the deposit of a guaranty fund of $1,000.000.[15]

The official circular which gave the terms for the sale of stock stated that the Stockholders' Committee, consisting of George Foster Peabody, Ethan Allen Doty and Edwin M. Bulkley, would continue until investment was made of the $6,125,000 of Edison first consolidated

---

15. *Commercial and Financial Chronicle*, LXVII (July to December, 1898), 177, 482.

bonds which had been reserved for extension and improvements.[16]

This sale is interesting because it brought under one control—that of Brady and his associates—practically all the electric light business in the borough of Brooklyn.

Having consummated the sale of the Brooklyn Edison Company, Peabody next turned to the sale of the New York Edison Electric Illuminating Company. His shrewdness as a banker was never more clearly shown than in this deal. In the late 1890's the New York Edison Electric Illuminating Company had continued to develop rapidly. In 1892 the Company had paid five per cent dividends. From 1894 to 1898 it was paying six per cent. In 1897 gross earnings of the Company were $1,228,766, net earnings were $571,715; in 1898 gross earnings were $1,541,723, net earnings $685,208.[17] By the turn of the century the capital stock was $10,000,000 paying nine per cent dividends and earning a surplus in addition. The stock, unwatered, was selling at approximately 170 in the market.

Meanwhile Anthony N. Brady, who had purchased the Brooklyn Electric Illuminating Company and other interests in a merger, had organized the New York Gas & Electric Light, Heat & Power Company and had purchased the Westinghouse high tension plants in Harlem. To pay for these and other plants, his company issued $15,000,000 in bonds. In compliance with the New York law, he then proceeded to sell an equal amount of stock to validate the bonds. Immediately Wall Street rumors spread to the effect that Mr. Brady had an affiliation with Tammany, and that he might use his connections to interfere with the Edison Company's open-

---

16. *Ibid.*, 482. September 3, 1898.
17. *Commercial and Financial Chronicle, Supplement*, LXVII (July 30, 1898), 150. Spencer Trask was still president of the company.

ing the street pavement in upper New York to extend the Edison wires.[18]

As a result of the rumors, Edison stock fell to 120. Stockholders were anxious, and wanted to sell. Peabody thought the rumors being circulated were insufficient basis for selling. He went to the largest stockholder, reasoned with him, and won him over. He realized, however, that only a few would "have the courage" to hold on to their stock.

The situation required drastic action. He went to the other large stockholders. If they were unwilling to show faith in their stock and insisted on selling, he would dispose of the stock for them at 200, if they would place it in his hands, as a representative of Spencer Trask and Company. Would they do this? The answer was yes. The large interests, including Morgan, turned over practically all of their stock to Spencer Trask and Company for sale.

Peabody wished next to contact Brady, but he waited for Brady to make the first move. In due time Brady asked for an appointment. He came to Peabody's private office and they discussed the matter. What figure? asked Brady. Peabody said the price was 200. Terms could be arranged if the payment were made in bonds. Brady left without committing himself.

A second conference followed. Brady said his company

---

18. Memorandum dictated by Mr. Peabody, November 12, 1934. Interview with Dr. Lewis Franklin, formerly a member of Spencer Trask and Company staff, July, 1944. *Commercial and Financial Chronicle*, LXXII (May 25, 1901), 1038 records the New York Edison Electric Company merger: "This new company was formed on May 23 by consolidation of the New York Gas and Electric Light, Heat and Power Co. and the Edison Electric Illuminating Co. of New York. The Consolidated Gas Co. owned the entire $36,000,000 capital stock of the Power Company and the latter owned $8,926,500 of the $9,200,000 stock of the Edison Company. The authorized share capital of the new company is $45,200,000. . . ."; *Ibid.*, LXVIII, 41, 129, 380, 429.

would give 180, no more, or the deal was off. Peabody replied that the deal was off, and said good-day.

A short time later, Brady sent word to Peabody that the latter was a "pretty tough sort of negotiator,"[19] but that Brady's company would pay the price set. Whereupon Peabody crisply replied that the price was now 220. At this point, the price was agreed upon and paid.

The stock which was thus sold to the New York Gas & Electric Light Heat & Power Company had originally been issued at 100 a share; but, as Peabody later pointed out, the business of the company had increased to such an extent that he considered the 220 a share warranted. The sale of this original Edison Company stock amounted in round numbers to twenty-one million dollars, in bonds.

3.

While Peabody was engaged in negotiating the sale of the Rio Grande Western and of the Brooklyn and New York Edison Electric Illuminating Companies, he and his firm were also playing a large part in the development of the beet sugar industry. In the early days sugar had been produced chiefly from cane, but by the 1890's much of it was produced from the sugar beet. Bradstreet's, in an editorial appearing on Dec. 23, 1899, stated that at that time two-thirds of the world's sugar was produced from beets.

Until the time of the Louisiana Purchase, almost all the sugar made in the United States was made from maple sap. What cane sugar there was was imported from the West Indies and refined by "sugar bakers," who remelted the raw sugar and made it into moulds. After 1803, the year of the Louisiana Purchase, the sugar refining industry soon made great headway; as time went on,

---

19. The incident is recounted by Mr. Peabody in dictated notes, Yaddo files.

improvements were made in sugar mills, and new mills were built in several parts of the United States. Through one deal after another huge consolidations were formed. Among the powerful figures of the sugar refining business were Claus Spreckels and Henry O. Havemeyer.

Meanwhile, the sugar beet industry had come to the fore. In the first quarter of the nineteenth century, sugar beets had come to be extensively cultivated in Europe. In this country factories for the manufacture of sugar from beets were slow to develop, partly because of the expense of constructing them and partly because of the intrenchment of the cane sugar refining business. At the end of the century, however, the American beet sugar industry made rapid progress. In 1890, three factories existed in the United States for the manufacture of sugar from beets, two in California and one in Nebraska. In 1895 a large part of the sugar supply in this country was still imported, but beet sugar manufacture was gaining ground; it was to develop into one of the great industries of the country within a few years.[20]

Peabody's interest in sugar was probably an off-shoot of his connection with western railroads. When the Rio Grande Western began to carry thousands of tons of beets, he saw that the beet sugar industry would require much hauling of coal, limestone, and other supplies.

In 1899 Spencer Trask and Company in association with Kuhn, Loeb and Company formed a syndicate.[21] The business, known as the American Beet Sugar Company, had a capital of $20,000,000 of which $5,000,000

---

20. V. S. Clark, "Sugar Industry," *Dictionary of American History*; P. O. Ray, "Sugar Trust," *Dictionary of American History*; T. G. Palmer, *Beet Sugar—A Brief History of Its Origin and Development*, March 2, 1903, Fifty-Seventh Congress, Second Session, Senate Document Number 204; H. W. Wiley, *The Sugar Beet: Culture, Seed Development, Manufacture, and Statistics*. U. S. Department of Agriculture, Farmers' Bulletin Number 52, (Washington, 1897).
21. *Commercial and Financial Chronicle*, LXVIII (Feb. 11, 1899), 280, 616.

was six per cent preferred stock. Of the preferred stock $1,000,000 was a treasury reserve. The company took over the beet sugar properties of Henry T. Oxnard[22] and W. Bayard Cutting—that is, a factory at Grand Island, Nebraska, with a capacity of 350 tons of beets a day; another at Norfolk, Nebraska, handling 350 tons of beets a day; another at Chino Ranch, Southern California, with a capacity of 750 tons of beets a day, and another located in Southern California, capable of handling 2,000 tons of beets a day. The Company also acquired 7,500 acres of the best farming land surrounding its California factories. A report dated December 2, 1899,[23] stated that the company had acquired a large tract of irrigated land in Colorado and would build a sugar factory with a capacity of 750 tons daily. The new property would cost nearly a million dollars and would be paid for partly from the accumulated earnings and partly from the earnings of the next three years.

Peabody served on the board of directors of the new company and was a member of the board's executive committee. W. Bayard Cutting, chairman of the board, and his brother R. Fulton Cutting, a director, were warm personal friends of his. It was these three—Peabody and the two Cuttings—who handled most of the financial affairs of the company.

Although the American Beet Sugar Company faced strong opposition from cane sugar interests,[24] it made

---

22. The American Beet Sugar Company was incorporated under the laws of New Jersey, March 24, 1899. It consolidated the Oxnard Beet Sugar Company, organized April 15, 1890, and several other companies. *Moody's Manual of Industrial and Miscellaneous Securities* (New York, 1900), 779, 780.
23. *Commercial and Financial Chronicle*, LXIX (Dec. 2, 1899), 1149; LXIX (December 16, 1899), 1250.
24. In August, 1901, Henry B. Oxnard, the president, reported that the company had twenty-eight factories under way. This development had aroused the Spreckels syndicate, he said. *Commercial and Financial Chronicle*, LXXIII (August 3, 1901), 238.

rapid progress; in time it became one of the most important companies in the field. For over thirty years, a partner in the firm of Spencer Trask and Company served on the board of directors.

4.

All this time Peabody and Palmer had continued their association with each other. Through General Palmer's official connection with the national railways of Mexico, the Trask firm had interested itself in the building of railroads in that country, and in the opening up of lead, silver, and coal mines along the routes of the railroads. As we have noted, Peabody held numerous directorships in Mexican companies.

It was a period when many foreign investors were competing in Mexico. The country was being both exploited and developed by these financiers. Spencer Trask and Company enlarged their interests in the early 1900's. On July 20, 1901, they issued a statement to the bondholders of the Compania Metalurgica Mexicana, one of the most profitable of the mining companies: the steadily growing business of the Compania necessitated a larger capital provision; hence a mortgage was being drawn to finance the operations. The circular continued:[25]

> Our Mr. George Foster Peabody is the First Vice-President of the Company, and expects hereafter to take even a more active interest in the conduct of its business than he has during the past ten years of his association with it.

25. Spencer Trask and Company to Bondholders of Compania Metalurgica Mexicana, July 20, 1901. This company was incorporated under the laws of New Jersey in 1890. In 1900 it owned extensive smelting works in the city of San Luis Potosi, Mexico, and had a capacity for smelting 20,000 tons of ore per month. It also owned extensive lead and silver mining properties at Sierra Mojada, State of Coahuila, Mexico, and it controlled the Mexican Lead Company, the Montezuma Lead Company, and various other companies mining and transporting ore. Its capital stock was $4,000,000 in 1900. (*Moody's Manual*, 1900, p. 1101.)

Peabody was also engaged at this time in organizing and developing the Mexican Coal and Coke Company. He and his associates acquired some cactus-covered prairie land in Mexico which was reported to be a coal field. The report was well founded. With Peabody as a director of the company, production was quickly got under way, and within six years the land was yielding approximately $600,000 worth of coal a year.[26]

5.

Mr. Peabody was also a director of the Morton Trust Company, with which the State Trust Company had been consolidated in 1900. Among the other directors were John Jacob Astor, George F. Baker, James B. Duke, Abram S. Hewitt, Levi P. Morton, Elihu Root, and Thomas Fortune Ryan. The resources of this great company as listed in *Moody's Manual* (pp. 221-222) were $34,217,-014. Its profits, January 1 to June 30, 1900, were listed as $566,023.

6.

It may be of interest to observe the methods of work of a man who engaged in these large enterprises and yet found time for other things. Peabody's day began about seven o'clock in the morning. He would start by dictating letters, usually on education, church work or philan-

---

26. *New York Times*, May 13, 1906. The Mexican Coal and Coke Company was incorporated under the laws of New Jersey on June 29, 1899. Its purpose was to develop coal mines located in the Baroteran coal district, Mexico. In 1900 the stock of the company was listed at $5,000,000, par value $100. The officers included J. T. Gardiner, president; G. F. Peabody, vice president. Charles J. Peabody was also an officer. Acosta Nichols, Kate Trask's brother, was on the board of directors (*Moody's Manual*, 1900, p. 759). The Montezuma Lead Co. listed a capital stock of $500,000 seven per cent cumulative preferred and $2,500,000 common stock, par value $100 in 1900. (*Ibid.*, pp. 759-760.) The Mexican Lead Co. was incorporated under the laws of New Jersey, July 31, 1899. Its purpose was to operate mines near Monterey, Mexico. Its capital stock was $1,250,000 seven per cent. The Compania Metalurgica owned a majority of the common stock.

thropy.[27] At eight-thirty a secretary would report on his way to the office to receive directions and make up the schedule for the day. After that would come breakfast, and then the trip to the office. Peabody spent the day in absorbing activity. Being a director in many corporations, he had frequent meetings to attend. About three o'clock he would go to his private office on an upper floor and work until six or six-thirty.

He worked quickly and required speedy service from his subordinates. One of his former secretaries says that Peabody would ring for a messenger who would be sitting on a bench at the far end of the office. The youth would spring to his feet and start running, for Mr. Peabody would begin to issue his orders while the young man was on the way.

He was particular about meeting his obligations and insisted that his secretary draw cheques as soon as bills were rendered. Although generous with hospitality and with donations, he would brook no waste on the part of his staff. On one occasion a secretary who had put too many words into a telegram received the following pencilled note:[28]

> "This is very extravagant—you should have given more thought to it. G F P 14 words instead of 33."

When he went to Lake George or to Saratoga Springs, he would often take his secretary as far as Poughkeepsie. For this post he usually picked promising young men who were interested in learning business methods.

He had his secretaries keep files of receipted bills, business letters, and letters relating to philanthropies. Some, not all, of his personal letters were also placed in the files. Most of his correspondence prior to 1900

---

27. He employed several young men for his secretarial work, including one Negro.
28. Yaddo files.

was destroyed by a secretary on one occasion when Peabody moved, but for the years from 1900 on, the letters filled rows of boxes. The filing was in the main chronological, but a few boxes were listed in topical form.

CHAPTER IX

Home Life and Local Politics

BY THE TURN OF THE CENTURY PEABODY WAS A MULTI-millionaire. It was possible for him to enjoy every luxury that money could buy. With his town house at 28 Monroe Place, Brooklyn, and his large summer home on Lake George, he had all the comforts of a rich man of his day.

His family had remained a closely knit unit. His brothers had their own places at Lake George. Royal was associated with Peabody in several business enterprises, although he was never a partner of Spencer Trask and Company. He was himself an able business man, perhaps overshadowed by his prominent older brother. Royal's son, Charles S., affectionately nick-named Carlos, now a Harvard student, was a favorite with his indulgent Uncle George.

The younger brother, Charles J. Peabody, had been associated with Spencer Trask and Company as a partner for many years. He was an able, intelligent man, active in civic and church affairs. His two children, Eva and Dudley, were a source of pleasure to their devoted uncle.

During the summers the families visited back and forth at Lake George. In the winters, Royal and Charles and their families were frequently at 28 Monroe Place.

Both at Monroe Place and at Abenia, Peabody's mother presided over the household. Born of sturdy New England stock, religious, conscientious, Elvira Canfield Peabody had schooled herself to meet any situation with equanimity. Through the trying time of reconstruction in the South, and later in the family's impoverished circumstances in Brooklyn, she had held up her head. She had faced the broken health of her husband with courage, and had taken most of the family responsibilities upon herself. She was always deeply mindful of her obligations to her three sons. She had artistic talent, and though by the time she had leisure to cultivate it, her sight was failing, she was able to complete several paintings which were a delight to her son George.

In many ways, Peabody was like his mother, though with opportunities for creative endeavor that were beyond her reach. From her he received both stimulus and commendation for his educational and philanthropic work.

The winter of 1901 saw Elvira Peabody presiding as usual over her son's home at 28 Monroe Place. Though she had put on some weight since her young days, she was still a small woman. She was seventy-five, and she did not look younger, but her blue-veined hand grasped the arm of her rocker firmly, and she kept her clear mental faculties to the end.

The weeks slipped by in a round of activities. Peabody was busy with plans to take guests to an educational conference in the South. He was discussing the approaching mayoralty campaign with his friend Shepard. He was working on the big deal of the sale of the Rio Grande Western.

In the spring Mrs. Peabody became ill with an ailment that at first seemed only minor. Pneumonia set in, however, and she grew steadily worse. On May 3, 1901, with her three sons by her side, Elvira Canfield Peabody passed away. Funeral services were held at the Reformed Church and burial took place in Greenwood Cemetery, Brooklyn. At the same time, plans were made to transfer the remains of her husband, George Henry Peabody, from Connecticut to a grave beside hers. Peabody handled the situation with his customary poise and, though sorrowing, was able to be a comfort to his two brothers. He was himself helped by the sympathy of his many friends, especially the Trasks[1] and Shepard.

The mansion at 28 Monroe Place now housed only Peabody and his household staff. When he was in town, he dined frequently at one or another of his clubs; moreover, he spent as much time as possible at Abenia and Yaddo. After his mother's death, the Brooklyn residence became more of a town convenience and less of a home.

2.

As the months passed, the lonely man took pleasure in social life with his friends. He continued to purchase objects for his home. He kept his stable horses and harnessed them with fine leather and brass. For instance, from Mark W. Cross in June, 1901, he purchased:

> June 25 - 24 white cord pillar reins with brass snap @ $1.25 - $30.00; 6 white buff leather fronts @ $1.00 - $ 6.00;
> June 27 - 1 set 1 in. super quality ... horse buggy harness with box loops, enamel leather folds, half-cheek snaffle bits, overdraw cheeks, Swiss style breast collar with Stoll's rubber bars $200.00.

An interesting item is his storage list at Balch Price and Company on July 1, 1901, with evaluations:

> Mink cape (32 tails and 16 heads), Nat Beaver Robe $200.; Tiger Rug $20.; Wolf Rug $10.; Polar Bear Rug $60.; White Bear Skin $40.; 2 white Fox Skins $10.; totaling $340.00.

It was his pleasure to order rare gems, cutglass and silver for his friends. On one occasion he ordered: "Scent

---

1. Mrs. Trask wrote a poem, "In Memoriam—Elvira Canfield Peabody," to express her sympathy.

bottle ... $55.00"; "Four Leaf Clover Brooch ... $6.00"; "Gold and Sapphire Brooch ... $15.00"; "Baroque Pearl Brooch ... $17.00"; "Pearl and Diamond Scarf Pin ... $30." He ordered several portraits painted by the artist Ferraris, including one of his mother and one of Mrs. Trask.

On December 23, 1901, he purchased a house and two lots on Willow Street, Brooklyn. This property he turned over for a nominal sum to his brother Charles.

On January 17, 1902, his brother Charles wrote him about the new electric brougham:[2]

> We made a great run last night in the electric brougham, taking sixteen minutes to the ferry, and Helen was quite delighted with her novel experience, although some of the sharp turns seemed to disturb her head a little.
> Sincerely yours,
> Chas.

It was not long afterward that Peabody sent in his own order for one Knoxmobile, Model B, at a cost of $1,014.95. The dealer acknowledged the order, and added:[3] "We note that your vehicle is to be equipped with Dunlop tires, wheels to be enameled black, Dietz lamps, and the complete set of tools that are sent with each wagon. . . ."

3.

Peabody's files are filled with acknowledgments for his acts of philanthropy at this time. The gifts were both large and small. An example of one of the larger gifts was a donation to the Young Men's Christian Association in Columbus, Georgia. Wishing to do something for his boyhood home, he wrote in behalf of himself and his brothers on September 20, 1901:[4]

2. This letter and above lists of items are in the Yaddo files.
3. *Ibid.*
4. *History of the Central Y.M.C.A. of Columbus, Georgia,* (Columbus, 1941).

My dear Sir:

    I beg now, upon behalf of my brothers, Royal Canfield Peabody and Chas. Jones Peabody, and myself, to formally confirm our offer to erect a building to cost not less than $35,000, suitable for occupancy of the Y.M.C.A., and to be placed upon a plot of ground to be provided and deeded to the Association by other friends free of lien. This offer is conditioned upon the purchase and payment for this lot of land, and upon the raising of as much as $10,000 in cash to be invested and held by the trustees of the Association for an endowment fund.

    I am
        Very truly yours,
        George Foster Peabody.

At a meeting of Columbus citizens, a rising vote of appreciation was given for the generous offer. The following resolutions were adopted and sent to the Peabodys:

RESOLVED, That, this Association, realizing its work can be properly done and with the greatest success only in a home of its own, it is with peculiar pleasure that we have received from our friends and former fellow citizens, Mr. George Foster Peabody and his brothers, Mr. Royal Canfield Peabody and Mr. Charles Jones Peabody, their generous proposition to erect in our midst a suitable home for this Association.

RESOLVED, further, that immediate steps be taken to comply with all these conditions.

RESOLVED, further, that Mr. George Foster Peabody and his brothers be notified immediately of our acceptance, and that we manifest gratitude to them by a greater and more earnest work for the young men in our midst and thereby become better and more worthy laborers in the Master's cause.

Mr. Peabody was present at the formal opening and dedication of the beautiful new building.[5] At that time, the City Council joined the committee of the Y.M.C.A. in entertaining him. The exercises covered a period of three

---

5. The dedication took place on December 2, 1903. The building cost $53,575 which was paid by Mr. Peabody and his brothers. They also gave an additional $3,000 toward the cost of the lot.

days; they included a reception to the Peabody brothers, attended by thousands of persons. Among the prominent men taking part in the ceremonies were Dr. Cuthbert Hall of Union Theological Seminary, New York; Dr. Edwin A. Alderman, President of Tulane University; and Chancellor Walter B. Hill of the University of Georgia.

Mr. Peabody kept in contact with the Y.M.C.A. at Columbus, often calling in person to discuss matters with the Association secretary. He followed up the gift with a check for the construction of another building[6]—one for the use of Negro residents of Columbus. He took a special interest in the work of this branch Y.M.C.A.

4.

Peabody's interest in politics drew him into the New York City election of 1901. He had long been an advocate of municipal reform. One of his activities as a member of the Young Men's Democratic Club of Brooklyn had been to help rout machine politics.[7]

The cities of the country had gone through a period of great expansion since the Civil War. Thousands of persons seeking industrial jobs were moving in from rural districts. Each year brought many ship loads of immigrants from southern and eastern Europe as well as from the northern countries which had been the main source of earlier influxes. Most of the immigrants settled in the big cities. Problems of bad housing, poverty, and vice grew more and more vexing; evils in municipal government reached the proportions of great scandals. New York City had been in the grip of corrupt politicians under "Boss" Tweed for several years when his career ended

---

6. This second building was authorized on July 17, 1905, and was completed during 1907.
7. Above information from Mr. I. C. Moyer, General Secretary, Y.M.C.A., Columbus, Georgia; *History of the Central Y.M.C.A. of Columbus, Georgia.*

with a prison sentence. The Tweed ring was duplicated on a smaller scale in Brooklyn, which until 1897 was separate from Manhattan.

The famous Lexow investigation of the New York City Police System in the early 1890's, to which we have referred, showed a scandalous state of corruption and malpractice. To correct this situation, a reform administration under Mayor Strong was inaugurated in 1894. Strong made a valiant attempt to clean up the city. He was encouraged by the Reform Club, Good Government Clubs, and other forces pushing municipal reform. In the late 1890's there was a second, though less sweeping, investigation, known as the Mazet inquiry. After this there was again some improvement, but it was obvious to reformers that Greater New York needed a further overhauling. Reform was to be the chief issue in the campaign of 1901.

As their candidate for mayor, the Republicans chose Seth Low. Low was a resident of Brooklyn, a man well known for his civic interests and his devotion to educational and philanthropic causes. He was active in several reform organizations, among them the Citizens' Union. He had the respect of the community, and it was obvious that his name on the ballot would bring a large vote. Peabody had known Seth Low for years and respected him highly.

The Democrats in seeking their candidate cast about for a man who would satisfy the demand for reform and at the same time be acceptable to Tammany Hall. He must be widely enough known to have a good chance of winning. With these qualifications in view, officials of the party went over the list of possibilities. Peabody's name was placed at the top at first. He was not as widely known as some of the others, but he was respected. He refused to consider running for office, however. Among the others singled out for consideration was Edward M. Shepard.

Shepard was a regular party man. He was not a popular type—he was too quiet, too reserved, to catch the imagination of the man in the street—but, having reviewed the possible choices, the Democrats settled upon him. Thus the small, scholarly man, long a friend of Peabody, was selected to run for the most prominent post in New York City.

At this point, Peabody was in a dilemma. For years he had been boosting the work of the Citizens' Union. The organization now gave its support to the reform candidate, Seth Low. Had Peabody been selected as Democratic candidate, it is likely that the Union, or at least many of its members, might have supported him. It was expected by some of his fellow members that he would support Seth Low.

On the other hand, Shepard was a close friend of many years' standing; it was as if a member of his family were running. Moreover, Peabody had profound respect for Shepard, believing him to be a man of the utmost integrity, who would use the office of mayor to institute reforms. It was a difficult choice to make, but Peabody decided to support Shepard. He even resigned from the Citizens' Union, thus making his decision the more conspicuous.

Some of the newspapers found it hard to reconcile Peabody's promotion of Shepard with his previous career as a reformer. It was charged that he had sacrificed principle to party manipulations. The *Tribune* took him to task for consorting with Tammany. In a story captioned "Peabody With the Boss" on October 16, 1901, the paper reported Peabody's interview with Richard Croker, Tammany head. The two men met at Shepard's headquarters, said the *Tribune*. They talked earnestly and went into a private conference in an alcove. When they emerged from their conference, Mr. Peabody was asked the subject of their conversation. He replied that the visit was only a social one, that it was the first time he had met Mr. Croker. On being further queried as to his opinion of Croker, Peabody replied that Croker was a forceful man. He said he had talked campaign issues, chiefly, the general cleaning up of the city government. He said he had informed Croker of the work of the Committee of Fifteen and of their proposed program.

The *Tribune* stated that when Mr. Croker was asked afterwards what he thought about Mr. Peabody, he said Peabody was all right. When asked what they talked about, he said Peabody did all the talking.[8]

Peabody, as Shepard's representative[9] in the campaign, was tireless in his activities. On October 24, he took part in a debate on campaign issues held under the auspices of the Young Men's Union for the Society of Ethical Culture. From the platform he deplored the vice which had persisted and increased in New York in spite of all of the efforts of the Citizens' Union, the Committee of Fifteen, the Republican Club and the City Club; he excoriated politicians who had used their power to sway the public to their own ends; he urged a leadership which would work for the welfare of the people; and he declared that Shepard was the type of leader that was needed. Shepard, he said, had never been willing to further his personal career by "bending the knee to Baal." He explained the candidate's political activities by saying that Shepard had learned from his father a love of his party and a conviction that it was through conscientious work within the party ranks that he could most effectively use his intellect for the public good.

At this meeting, Peabody was referred to as a

8. *New York Daily Tribune,* Oct. 16, 1901.
9. *Ibid.,* Oct. 10, 1901.

man of political independence, one whose name bore considerable weight in anything he might support.[10]

What success Shepard might have had in reform is a matter for conjecture. Seth Low was elected Mayor.

10. *Ibid.*, Oct. 25, 1901.

CHAPTER X

Peabody and Education

EVER SINCE HIS ACCEPTANCE OF A TRUSTEESHIP AT Hampton, Peabody's name had been identified with the education of Negroes in the South. In the late 1890's his interest in education broadened into a new connection which established him as one of the leaders in promotion of education in the South.

The South, emerging from the painful problems of reconstruction, was reaching out to a new social order based upon a dual economy of agriculture and industry. Like the rest of the nation, this section was faced with the task of improving its educational system to meet the new day. Toward the close of the century there was a distinct educational revival manifest in the South as well as in other parts of the country. But State legislators found it difficult to vote appropriations for new schools and for teachers' salaries when the tax funds of the still impoverished states were at such a low ebb.

To help meet the situation, particularly in the rural districts, Northern philanthropists contributed large sums —George Peabody[1] in 1867 and 1869, three and a half million dollars; John F. Slater, in 1882, one million dollars; Daniel Hand in 1888, a million and a half dollars, and so on.[2] As a result, more schools were established

1. A distant cousin of George Foster Peabody.
2. Special contributions had also been made to Hampton Institute and Tuskegee Institute.

and provision was made for a systematic training of teachers.

What with aid from the North and intensive efforts in the South itself, the cause of free education was progressing.[3] But as yet appropriations were far from adequate. There was a great deal of illiteracy; log cabin school-houses, often windowless and without equipment, were common.

It was at this time that a new movement known as the Southern Education Conference was founded. The idea for the conference originated with Dr. Edward Abbott, an Episcopal clergyman of Cambridge, Massachusetts, who had been impressed by educational needs while on a tour of schools in the South. He arranged a first meeting at Capon Springs, West Virginia, in June, 1898. The guests included thirty-six persons: ministers, college presidents, and others. The following summer another meeting was held. Among the guests was Robert C. Ogden, head of Wanamaker's store in New York. Following his custom of taking guests to Hampton commencement, Ogden brought about twenty-five men and women whom he hoped to interest in Southern education. Peabody also attended, and like Ogden, he brought a number of persons[4] with him in his private railway car.

The highlight of this second conference in 1899 was an address by J. L. M. Curry, agent of the Peabody and Slater Funds, who spoke on "Education in the Southern States." His address afforded subject matter for discussion for the next ten years. A third conference was held in the

---

3. C. W. Dabney, *Universal Education in the South* (Chapel Hill: University of North Carolina Press, 1936), Vol. II, p. 6.
4. His guests included the Rev. S. D. McConnell of Brooklyn; Dr. Edwin Knox Mitchell of Hartford; Dr. Albert Shaw of the *Review of Reviews*; St. Clair McKelway of the *Brooklyn Eagle*; Clark B. Firestone of the *New York Evening Mail*; Stanhope Sams of the *New York Times*.

summer of 1900 and a fourth in 1901. At the 1901 conference, held at Winston-Salem, North Carolina, the Southern Education Board came into being.

On a summer's day in 1901 the town of Winston-Salem was abuzz with visitors. Robert C. Ogden had invited a party of guests, among whom was John D. Rockefeller, Jr.,[5] a young man beginning his career of philanthropy. Peabody also was present. The hospitable community opened its homes to the guests. Tables groaned with platters of fried chicken and hot biscuits. The quiet Moravian chapel, where the meetings were held, was packed with a notable audience from North and South. Governor Aycock, known as "The Educational Governor," addressed the assembly. President Dabney of the University of the South made an exhaustive statistical report on conditions in the common schools.

The Southern Education Board, which had its inception at this meeting, took upon itself the task of encouraging existing systems of schools in the South and developing additional facilities. Robert C. Ogden, as chairman, was asked to select an executive committee of seven members which would organize the work of the board.

Back in New York, Ogden invited a small group of men to come to his private offices at Wanamaker's store in June, 1901. These men were Peabody, Walter H. Page, Albert Shaw, and Charles W. Dabney. On August 2, Ogden appointed the executive board, and Peabody was one of the members.

The first meeting of the Southern Education Board was held in Ogden's office at two o'clock on November 4, 1901. Every day thereafter until November 9, there was a meeting at 10:30 in the morning. Ogden was elected president and Peabody, treasurer. The organization was a

---

5. Interview with Mr. John D. Rockefeller, Jr., June 10, 1940.

simple one, without constitution. There were no by-laws. The program adopted was based upon the considerations brought forward at the four Southern Education Conferences and upon the deliberations at Ogden's office.

Now that the organization was formed, how was it to be financed? A Finance Committee was appointed, with Peabody as its chairman. He offered to underwrite anonymously the expenses of the board to the extent of $40,000 for the first year. The sum of $10,000 was raised from other sources, and he paid the remaining $30,000.

In the process of forming the board which was composed of five Southern born men and three Northern born, Peabody, the treasurer, was as prominent a figure as Ogden, the president. Peabody aided Ogden in organizing the work and gave every item his careful attention. His years of service in behalf of Hampton were invaluable in preparing him for this important new educational service.

A word about the men who, together with Peabody, made up the board. Robert Ogden was the descendant of early Connecticut and New Jersey settlers. He had worked his way up from office boy in a dry-goods store. The only formal education he had was gained before he was fourteen. As a young man he traveled in the South as agent for his clothing store. He served in the Union army in Pennsylvania. After the War, he forged ahead in his business career. He had long been a member of the board of trustees at Hampton. Kindly, good-humored, he was a well-known figure in the South, respected by school officials. His indefatigable labors for Southern education and his tours were known as the "Ogden Movement." He and Peabody, both men of action, were congenial spirits.

The supervising director, J. L. M. Curry, was a Georgian by birth. He was a graduate of the University of Georgia and of Harvard Law School, a former Southern legislator, and also a professor. In 1881 he became agent of the George Peabody Fund, and, later, was also agent of the Slater Fund. When the Southern Education Board was formed, he was already acknowledged as a leader in Southern education. A big man full of vitality, he was an eloquent and forceful speaker. Acquainted with principles of education and possessing a broad knowledge of Southern school conditions, he supplemented the work of the philanthropist-builders, Ogden and Peabody. Unfortunately his death in 1903 cut short the contribution that he was making.

The other members of the board were men of established reputation. The secretary was Dr. Charles D. McIver, educator, of Greensboro, North Carolina. The executive secretary was the Rev. Edgar Gardner Murphy, of Montgomery, Alabama. Edward M. Shepard was employed as counsel.

Having made some far-reaching plans, the board began operations. Under the leadership of Ogden and Peabody, a campaign committee was appointed to awaken the South to its own educational needs. This committee worked with state superintendents and served as an agency of communication between the states. Its advantage lay in the fact that it did not attempt to dominate, but instead encouraged local endeavor. Visits, tours, and conferences were arranged. Members of the board carried on an extensive correspondence with leaders in the South and through their zeal inspired many a struggling local group. Their work has been referred to as educational statesmanship of a high order.

It is difficult to assess the contributions made by the Southern Education Board because of numerous other forces operating at the same time to improve education in the South. The renaissance in education which had begun to be evident at the end of the century was in full swing now. From 1900 to 1914 the amount of illiteracy was greatly reduced. Annual expenditures for public schools increased by many millions during this period. Hundreds of new high schools were built, and many extended their terms from two to four years. Emphasis was increasingly placed upon teacher training. The quality of personnel was generally improved. It is not possible to state what specific parts of this advance were made as a result of the Board's activities. Although it made definite suggestions, perhaps its greatest contributions were the confidence and enthusiasm, the tireless energy, of men like Ogden and Peabody who believed in the future of the South.

Meetings of the board were held regularly. These occasions were a time of good fellowship. Sometimes they met in the South, again at Ogden's office or home. A favorite meeting place for the summer conference was at Peabody's Lake George home. In this restful and invigorating atmosphere, leaders from North and South gathered to spend a few days in delightful association.

On the broad piazza at Abenia, they discussed matters of vital import. In the summer of 1904, they discussed the bond issue in Louisiana; the status of school library progress in North Carolina; Dr. E. A. Alderman's election to the presidency of the University of Virginia; women's work in improving schoolhouses. Walter Hines Page wrote Peabody of the inspiration he had received under the ideal conditions of this conference. In the summer of 1906, Albert Shaw referred to meetings at Abenia as occasions of both hospitality and widely radiating influence. At the conference held in 1909, Dr. Charles W. Stiles gave an illustrated address on the life history of the hookworm parasite and its relation to educational work— an address which moved the Reverend F. T. Gates, Mr. Rockefeller's benefactions adviser, who was present at the conference, to recommend to Mr. Rockefeller the establishment of a Sanitary Commission for the eradication of hookworm disease in the South.[6]

Peabody's activities on the Southern Education Board resulted in a new connection—his treasurership of the General Education Board. For some years John D. Rockefeller had been giving large sums of money for education and research. His gifts to the Baptist Education Society, to the University of Chicago, and to the Rockefeller Institute for Medical Research are examples of his philanthropy. He was largely influenced by the advice of Mr. Gates, and recently also by that of his son, who had been taking over many of the responsibilities of administering the large fortune.

John D. Rockefeller, Jr., was a serious young man, earnest in his desire to meet his responsibilities. He had schooled himself for a career of philanthropy. After graduating from Brown University, he had entered his father's offices where he learned the business and, with Gates's advice, handled the appeals which came to his desk. He liked to see things at first hand, and for that reason had accepted Robert C. Ogden's invitation to go as a guest to the Southern Education Conference at Winston-Salem, in 1901. On that occasion he was deeply impressed by the reports of education needs in the South.

While the Southern Education Board's work was highly important, its function was only that of giving stimulation and advice; it did not supply funds. Moreover, its field extended only through the Southern states. A more general program, of similar vision but with wider scope, was sorely needed. To such a program the Rockefellers now turned.

On the evening of January 15, 1902, two months

---

6. Correspondence in the files at Yaddo.

after the forming of the Southern Education Board, a small group of men gathered at the home of the banker Morris K. Jesup. They were John D. Rockefeller, Jr., Robert C. Ogden, George Foster Peabody, J. L. M. Curry, William H. Baldwin, Jr., and Wallace Buttrick. They discussed next steps in the movement for widening educational opportunities and raising educational standards.

On February 27, 1902, a second meeting was held, this time at John D. Rockefeller, Jr.'s home. Around the dinner table, in addition to the original six, were Daniel Coit Gilman, Albert Shaw, Walter Hines Page and Edward M. Shepard. The climax of the evening was reached when it was announced that John D. Rockefeller, Sr., would give $1,000,000 for the inauguration of an educational program.[7] Thus the General Education Board began.

The first president of the Board was William H. Baldwin, Jr. He held the office until 1905, when Robert C. Ogden succeeded him. Peabody was elected treasurer and held this office until 1909. From the beginning until 1917—when he became president—Wallace Buttrick was executive secretary. Buttrick, a native of New York State, was a Baptist minister, preaching at Albany. In 1902, he gave up his pastorate to become secretary of the General Education Board. Upon taking up his duties, he studied needs at the source. He was so pleasant and persuasive, and had such a fund of quaint humor, that his enthusiasm was generally contagious. He was a man

---

7. In June, 1905, he gave the first permanent endowment of $10,000,000. This supplemented his earlier gift of $1,000,000. In February, 1907, he added a further gift of $32,000,000 (*The General Education Board, An Account of Its Activities*, 1915). The General Education Board was established by Act of Congress in 1903. Incorporators were George Foster Peabody, Robert C. Ogden, J. L. M. Curry, Daniel C. Gilman, Morris K. Jesup, Albert Shaw, F. T. Gates, William H. Baldwin, Jr., and Walter H. Page. (*Ibid.*, p. 212.)

of wisdom, modest, courageous and far seeing, to whom is accorded a high place as an educational administrator.

On December 11, 1902, Peabody wrote to John D. Rockefeller, Jr.[8]:

> Dear Sir:-
> I beg to acknowledge the receipt of your cheque for $100 representing a contribution from Mr. Rockefeller to the expense incurred in publishing the report of the Fifth Conference for Education in the South.
> Thanking you very heartily on behalf of the Committee for this generous aid, I am,
> Yours very truly,
> *George Foster Peabody*
>
> P.S. May I take this occasion to send to you and to your father congratulations upon the remarkably successful founding of the General Education Board which I believe has a future of usefulness not exceeded by any other human enterprise I know.
> I must too refer to the extraordinary character and capacity and fitness of Doctor Buttrick whose selection indicates again the remarkable judgment of men which has been a feature of the preeminence of Mr. John D. Rockefeller, only his remarkable and persistent simplicity being more eminent.
> Very truly yours,
> *George Foster Peabody*

The General Education Board now set itself to pursue the objects set forth in its charter, namely, "the promotion of education within the United States of America, without distinction of race, sex or creed." Through its secretary, it made an educational survey of the South, state by state. Likewise, it studied the educational needs of the entire United States. Its policy was to give aid through existing organizations for the improvement of educational facilities. It did not plan to undertake independent work.

Limited space does not permit a detailed treatment

---

8. Letter by courtesy of Mr. John D. Rockefeller, Jr.

PEABODY AND EDUCATION 105

of the distinguished work of this board. Since our subject is Mr. Peabody, let us glance at his relation to it. Entrusted with the treasurership[9] of funds amounting to one million dollars at the start and increasing to a total of forty-three million after Rockefeller's third big gift in 1907, he had a grave responsibility on his hands. Though all matters were discussed, and all decisions made, at the Board meetings, Peabody had the individual responsibility of studying the investment market and of making recommendations regarding securities. His work entailed frequent conferences with F. T. Gates. With the same ability which characterized his business enterprises, he made appraisals of opportunities for investing the General Education Board's funds.[10]

As a member, as well as treasurer, he took a prominent part in the councils of the Board. The tall, courteous man was held in affectionate regard by his fellow members seated around the conference table. He generally had something important to say, and his opinions were deferred to.[11]

Because of his wide acquaintance in Southern educational circles, it would often happen that some particular institution in the South appealed to him to plead its cause before the Board. On at least one such occasion, he wrote to an educator explaining that the Board was proceeding slowly according to a general plan of development and that he doubted whether a donation would be made to this particular cause at the time. He did place specific needs before the Board from time to time, however. He also wrote to the younger Rockefeller individually, calling his attention to some of the conditions in need of improvement.

9. He was treasurer from 1902 until 1909.
10. Yaddo files.
11. Interview with Mr. John D. Rockefeller, Jr., June 10, 1940.

In the early years of the General Education Board a pleasant personal acquaintance was established between Peabody and Mr. Rockefeller, Jr.; it continued until Peabody's death. In July, 1904, Mr. and Mrs. Rockefeller, Jr., then a young couple, visited the Trasks and Mr. Peabody at Yaddo and Abenia. In anticipation of their visit, Peabody sent them two books of Mrs. Trask's poetry, referring to her as a "remarkable genius with exceptional attraction."[12]

News of the appointment of Peabody as Treasurer of the General Education Board was received with approval by those who knew him. The *Brooklyn Daily Eagle* in an editorial ("George Foster Peabody," May 2, 1906) said the country was to be congratulated upon having the services of a man of his character and administrative ability as treasurer of the fund.

Like the other members of the Board, Peabody referred to the administration of the Fund as the "stewardship of God's money." Though he was out of sympathy with many of Mr. Rockefeller's ideas and disapproved of some of his practices, he roundly condemned those critics of Mr. Rockefeller who impugned the latter's motives in the setting up of philanthropic funds.[13]

---

12. Yaddo files.
13. Yaddo files.

CHAPTER XI

University of Georgia Trustee

PEABODY'S ATTENDANCE AT THE SOUTHERN EDUCATION Conference led to an important new interest in the field of education. At the conference he had met Dr. Andrew H. Patterson, professor of physics at the University of Georgia. Dr. Patterson invited him to attend the centennial celebration to be held in June, 1901, and he accepted the invitation.

The University is the nation's oldest chartered state institution of higher learning. It was founded by Abraham Baldwin, and chartered by the state legislature, in 1785. In 1801, its doors were opened to the young men of Georgia. It was the center of the state's educational system. Situated at Athens, in the red hills of North Georgia, seventy-odd miles from Atlanta, the University had the look of age. The older buildings, darkened by time, were sheltered by lofty trees.

During the centennial celebration, Peabody was the guest of Mr. and Mrs. Edward R. Hodgson. Mr. Hodgson, class of 1868, lived in one of the fine old Southern houses on Milledge Avenue. He was an ardent supporter of the University. His son, Harry Hodgson, class of 1893, was one of the leading younger alumni. The Hodgsons were so closely identified with the University that it was hard to think of its life without thinking of them. At the elder Hodgson's beautiful home, Peabody enjoyed the hospitality of his host. They sat long around the dinner table swapping stories, talking of many things, and especially discussing the University and its future.

The centennial banquet was the crowning affair of the week. Mr. E. R. Hodgson was chairman of the committee on arrangements and won congratulations from the Chancellor, who dubbed him a "Prince." Nearly seven hundred loyal alumni came together to honor their Alma Mater. Distinguished guests paid tributes.

Peabody, self-educated since his fifteenth year, listened intently to the speeches of men who had spent their lives in educational endeavor. His interest in the University was deeply aroused. At the end of the week, he said good-bye to his hosts, knowing that he would return to Athens. Back in New York, he ordered a silver loving cup for Mr. Hodgson and had engraved upon it the inscription,[1] "Rightly esteemed the Prince among men."

The next summer, 1902, he was responsible for bringing the Ogden party to Athens for the Southern Education Conference. The party this time included Charles W. Eliot, president of Harvard University, and many other guests. The town turned out to welcome the distinguished group of publicists, educators, editors of magazines and newspapers. Guests and their hosts lingered long over the dinner table, North and South getting better acquainted. Within the old halls of the University they discussed the year's progress and planned next steps.

On this visit to the University, Peabody asked to see the library. It was housed on the second floor of the Academic Building. When shown some of the rare books, he was troubled for their safety, for the building was not fireproof. How much would it cost, he asked Dr. Hill, the Chancellor, to build a new library to safeguard the collection? Hill figured a rough estimate: it would take

---

1. Statement by Mr. Harry Hodgson.

fifty thousand dollars. Peabody directed him to build it and send him the bill. This was his first gift to the University. In all he gave about $250,000 to the institution.

Although concerned with the development of the whole University, his chief interest was the library. He remarked on one occasion that he was glad that he preceded Mr. Carnegie in making this gift. He gave the collection his personal attention and later, as chairman of the Library Committee of the board of trustees, had an active part in the acquisition of additional books, including many rare volumes.

At the time of the Centennial celebration he also studied the needs of the State Normal School, a part of the University system, located in Athens. A few months later, on April 4, 1902, the *New York Times* announced his gift, made through Chancellor Hill, of $10,000 to erect a new practice school building and $3,000 for equipment, his only stipulation being that the house be named for the Georgia county in which he was born—Muskogee. In this way young teachers were enabled to gain experience at the model school on the Normal School campus.

In the ensuing connections with the University of Georgia, Peabody's friendship with Chancellor Hill deepened into a rich experience for both men. Hill, about Peabody's age, was a man of vision. With Peabody's encouragement, he looked ahead to a great future for the University. Together the two were a "human dynamo." There was also about their acquaintance a warmly personal note. Peabody's sympathies and affection reached out to the devoted Hill, who put his whole soul into the work. He also became the friend of Mrs. Hill and of their young son.

The University was fortunate in having a large group of loyal alumni. Many were leaders in business, professional life, government, education. They were ready to give their Alma Mater endorsement and support. Among these men none was more devoted than Harry Hodgson. A successful business man, head of the Empire State Chemical Company at Athens, Hodgson had lived in the University atmosphere from childhood. He was reaching out to be of further service to the institution. Now in his early thirties, he derived satisfaction from his contacts with Peabody, whose broad experience and vision he respected. He found that he could write Peabody frankly about University matters and receive a frank letter in return.

Friendships grew up, too, between Peabody and a number of other officials and alumni. Mention is made in his correspondence of Professor David C. Barrow, the beloved "Uncle Dave" of the students, and of a number of alumni, among them Thomas J. Shackelford and Judge Callaway. As time went on, he became each year better acquainted with the members of the board of trustees, and with faculty, alumni, and students. Within the span of a year or two, the University of Georgia became his deepest single educational interest, next to Hampton.

2.

Plans for the University went forward. In 1904 some of the alumni formed an auxiliary to work on the proposed developments. Harry Hodgson was the chairman and seven others were on the committee.[2]

One of the chief activities of the auxiliary was to promote the development of the reorganized Georgia State College of Agriculture, a part of the University system. Peabody was one of the prime workers in the plans of the group. He aided them in buying fifty-five

---

2. The advisory board included J. L. M. Curry (1843), Walter B. Hill (1870), Joseph M. Terrell, W. B. Merritt, Clark Howell, Robert Emory Park, and George Foster Peabody.

UNIVERSITY OF GEORGIA TRUSTEE 111

parcels of land to enlarge the campus of the College of Agriculture to 1,000 acres, and made from his pocket the first payments on the purchases. After the land was bought, he engaged the services of the engineering firm of Charles W. Leavitt of New York to survey the property and lay out a landscape plan. A booklet with the plans was later mailed to alumni. The purchase of the additional property was accompanied by efforts to get an appropriation for the reorganized College of Agriculture. A bill was placed before the legislature to authorize an expenditure of $100,000.

At this crucial moment when the bill was pending, Mr. Peabody conceived a plan to take the members of the board of trustees and prominent legislators, newspaper men, and their wives on a week's trip to the University of Wisconsin. They could in this way see the work that was being done in agriculture in one of the foremost educational experiments in the country.

Having decided upon such a plan, he communicated with Samuel Spencer, president of the Southern railway, explaining the object of the proposed trip. Mr. Spencer supplied a special train. Mr. Peabody paid all expenses for food and service, but insisted that Chancellor Hill be the official host on the trip.

On a day in late November, 1904, the party[3] set forth for Wisconsin. Arriving at Madison, the visitors were met by University officials who cordially welcomed them. At the assembly the first day, Governor LaFollette of Wisconsin introduced Governor Terrell of Georgia, who was followed by Chancellor Hill and other speakers. The next two days were spent in a thorough study of the structure and life of the University. Before many hours had passed, friendship between the two institutions was cemented.

3. About forty persons (Peabody Papers).

Peabody was enthusiastic over the agricultural program of the University of Wisconsin. It gave him ideas for developments along this line which could be sponsored at the University of Georgia.

When the conference ended, the party returned to the special train which was to bear them back to Athens. In their ears were the rousing cheers of the students of the University of Wisconsin. A newspaper, describing the incident, said these representatives had forged a new and strong link in the chain binding North and South together.[4]

The trip was an object lesson of great value. It served to convince the state authorities of the need to support the plans for extension of the University's program. Peabody was so well pleased with the results that he paid the expenses of the new board of trustees of the Agricultural College for a trip to Cornell University at Ithaca, New York, to study the agricultural program in operation.

On the newly acquired property adjoining the campus, the University set up an agricultural experiment station. Also on the property the officials established a school of forestry. This school owes its origin to Mr. Peabody, who had developed his own thousand acre estate as a park, and wished to see a program of forest conservation in Georgia. He endowed it for a period of three years.

His offer of $2,500 a year for three years to apply on the salary of the first professor of the chair of forestry, was gladly accepted by the University. He then helped to find a professor for the position. Upon his recommendation, Alfred Akerman, a native Georgian and an alumnus of the University, at the time State Forester in Massachusetts, was selected to head the new department.

---

4. Yaddo files.

In naming the new school of forestry, the officials of the University wished to honor Mr. Peabody.[5] They proposed to give it his name. He was reluctant, preferring to remain in the background, but consented when his friends urged him to permit his name to be used because they believed it would draw support for the new school.

Peabody's friendship with Chancellor Hill had deepened during the five years after they first went over the grounds and buildings that Centennial week. They had spent many hours in going over plans for new developments. Hill was devoted to his work. On one occasion, after the Wisconsin trip, he was so tired from overexertion that Peabody insisted upon buying tickets for the Chancellor and his wife and son, and sending them to England for a rest and a visit to Oxford and Cambridge.[6] A few months after his return, Chancellor Hill contracted pneumonia and died.

The death of Chancellor Hill was a calamity to the University. They had looked to him for his vision and leadership. It would be hard to find a successor to carry on his work. He was a loved figure on the campus.

Peabody was shocked and deeply grieved over the loss of his friend. He could hardly picture the University without its buoyant leader. He immediately communicated with Mrs. Hill and offered his assistance, and kept in touch with her and Roger Hill in the years that followed.

During the time when the question of who should succeed Chancellor Hill was being considered, Peabody

---

5. The school of forestry thus designated as the George Foster Peabody School of Forestry was later enlarged to include a director, two full professors, one associate professor, and two assistant professors. About 1,000 acres of campus were assigned to the school. A large building and several smaller buildings were erected to house the classes. Students came to the school from many states and from some foreign countries.
6. Statement by Mr. Harry Hodgson; correspondence in Yaddo files.

exchanged correspondence with officials and alumni. He discussed the matter in detail with Harry Hodgson.

Professor David C. Barrow, beloved by the college community, was selected. He had a hard task in following Hill but approached the job in a spirit of devotion. Peabody, who had had some hand in the choice, thought Barrow had the ability needed. As time went on, he and Barrow worked together with intense enthusiasm.

The officials of the University wished to bestow further honors upon Mr. Peabody, besides naming the new school of forestry for him. At commencement in 1906, they conferred upon him the honorary degree of Doctor of Laws, and the tall man with greying hair made a striking figure in his silk doctoral robe as he stood on the platform to receive the hood. On August 28, 1906, the Governor of the State of Georgia by special act of the Legislature confirmed his appointment as a non-resident trustee of the University, the only person recognized in this way.

The act of the legislature and of the University officials in naming him a trustee at first troubled him, for he feared that being a non-resident, he might be unable to discharge his duties adequately, but he was overruled by friends. He considered the appointment a great honor and made it a point to attend board meetings regularly, often travelling long distances to be present. He served on the committees and kept up a continuous correspondence with Chancellor Barrow, Harry Hodgson, and others.

3.

Besides being connected with the University of Georgia, with Hampton, with the Southern Education Board, and with the General Education Board, Peabody had several other educational interests which were long continued. He was a trustee of Colorado College, as we have noted, and took an active part in its affairs. He visited the college several times and was a large contributor to its support.[7]

His long connection with Penn Normal Industrial and Agricultural School began in 1901. This school had been founded in the 1860's at St. Helena Island, South Carolina, by Laura M. Towne, for the education of Negroes. At the turn of the century, when Miss Towne was no longer able to continue her work, the school was reorganized. Dr. Hollis B. Frissell, successor of General Armstrong at Hampton, helped in the reorganization. He appointed two of the board members of Hampton to become members of the Penn School board—namely Mr. Peabody and Mr. Arthur Curtiss James. Dr. Frissell was made chairman of the board and Mr. Peabody, treasurer.[8]

Mr. Peabody took a personal interest in the school. He invited Miss Rossa B. Cooley, a member of the faculty at Hampton, to be one of his guests at Abenia. While she was there, he asked her to accept a position as head of Penn School and she consented. He helped to raise funds and enlisted the interest of many persons of wealth in the training offered the Negro residents of the island. He gave constant encouragement to Miss Cooley and her associate, Miss Grace House, in their task of developing the program and improving the buildings and equipment. He visited the school often.

Another of his interests was the connection with Fort

---

7. He was elected to the Board of Trustees in 1898 and served until February, 1932, when he resigned. In June, 1931, the Board elected him Trustee Emeritus (letter from Mr. W. W. Postlethwaite, Museum Director, to Acting President C. B. Hershey, May 15, 1944).
8. The school was incorporated in 1901 (Penn School records, July 27, 1944). After Dr. Frissell's death Mr. Peabody became chairman of the board, and retained the office until 1927, when he became honorary chairman. He remained a trustee until his death. (Letter from Miss Rossa B. Cooley, June 26, 1944.)

Valley Normal and Industrial Institute at Fort Valley, Georgia. Arriving at his Lake George home in the summer of 1902, he learned through his sister-in-law, Mrs. Royal C. Peabody, that a quartette from the school had pleased the summer cottagers with their spirituals. A few days later the principal called on him. As a result of their talk, Peabody became a member of the board of trustees. From that time on, he took an active part in the affairs of the school.[9]

One of his main interests was the work of Tuskegee Institute. It is not known when or how his interest in Tuskegee started; perhaps it was an outgrowth of his connection with Hampton and of his contacts with Booker T. Washington, President of Tuskegee, whose work stemmed from Hampton training. There are several brief letters from Peabody among the Booker T. Washington papers in the 1890's.

He is listed as a member of the board of trustees of Tuskegee for the year 1900-1901, and for each year thereafter through 1911. He made several gifts to the school, among them a donation of $950 in 1900.[10] He had a warm appreciation of the work that Booker T. Washington was doing.

Tuskegee was founded in the early 1880's with the idea of establishing in Alabama a school patterned along the lines of Hampton. The tale of Booker T. Washington's zealous efforts to secure vocational and academic training for Negro youth—efforts which were indispensable to the

---

9. He was also actively interested in the Voorhees School for Negroes in South Carolina.
10. Owing to pressure of many other duties in the period between 1911 and 1917 he appears to have had less intimate contact with the school. Thereafter, through the head, Dr. Robert R. Moton, he increased his efforts. In the 1920's he was one of the chief promoters of a campaign to endow Tuskegee and Hampton. The information regarding his Tuskegee connection comes from Charles G. Gomillion, Director of Records and Research, at Tuskegee.

success of the Tuskegee experiment—is a classic in the annals of American education and humanitarianism. Traveling up and down the country, under exhausting conditions, to win support for his struggling school, this former slave boy, who had worked his way through Hampton, won the sympathy and admiration of all who heard him. In his book, *Up From Slavery*, published in 1901, and in other books, he expounds his thesis that manual training, including training in agriculture and in the industrial arts, is indispensable in helping the Negro worker to find his place in society. He said this training should have a prominent place in the curriculum.

In looking over the correspondence in Mr. Peabody's files, one glimpses less of the personal note in his connections with Tuskegee than with Hampton. He visited Tuskegee, but not as often. He was, nevertheless, one of the most positive voices in enlisting support for Tuskegee. Booker T. Washington and his successor, Robert R. Moton, elicited his respect. Dr. George Washington Carver, Tuskegee's eminent professor and one of America's leading scientists, said of Peabody:

> He was a wonderful character. Mr. Peabody was a great friend of the Negro, and a great friend of Tuskegee. He had the real Christ Spirit.[11]

When Booker T. Washington's book *Up From Slavery* was published in 1901, Mr. Peabody ordered copies for a large number of his friends and relatives.

4.

Peabody's notable efforts in behalf of education were recognized by special honors. In 1903, he was awarded two honorary degrees—that of Master of Arts by Harvard University,[12] and that of LL.D. by the University

---

11. Interview with Dr. George Washington Carver, by author.
12. President Charles W. Eliot, in his address, referred to Peabody as "wise counsellor."

of Washington and Lee. In 1906, as we have seen, he was awarded the honorary degree of Doctor of Laws by the University of Georgia.

To the man whose poverty had prevented him from going to college, whose "alma mater" was the Y.M.C.A., this recognition meant a great deal. In the earlier years of his connections with schools he had been a counsellor and financial consultant, a magical god-father, in the institutions which he had served. He now enjoyed the role of honorary graduate, and as an honorary Doctor of Laws, was often referred to as Dr. Peabody.

5.

Peabody had attended church services since he was a small boy in Columbus. As a youth of sixteen he had been active in Sunday School affairs. At twenty-eight he had changed his affiliation and became a member of the Episcopal Church. He liked the organization and unity of both Roman Catholic and Episcopal Churches, but preferred the latter because he believed it to be more democratic. He soon became prominent in Episcopal church circles. He was head of the vestry of Holy Trinity Church.

In 1903 Holy Trinity was seeking a new rector. The church was an important one in Brooklyn, with potentialities for even wider influence, and the vestry wished to select the rector with care. At this time Peabody went to New Orleans on a business trip. On the way back he stopped over at Cincinnati and while there heard a young clergyman preach—the Reverend J. Howard Melish. He was impressed, and invited Melish to preach a sermon at Holy Trinity. On his return to Brooklyn, he met the vestrymen in a session and told them about Melish. He extolled the young preacher and indicated that here was his choice.

On a day in February, 1904, the young Reverend

Melish arrived at the Pennsylvania Railroad Ferry at the foot of Fulton Street.[13] Here Peabody met him in a new automobile. High in the seat sat the chauffeur.

The next Sunday Melish preached his sermon at Holy Trinity. His message, firm, clear, forceful, appealed to the church officials.[14] It did not take them long to make their decision. The young rector from Cincinnati was invited to take the pulpit.

A warm friendship grew up between Peabody and Melish. They found themselves akin on social issues, and spent many hours discussing problems of the day. At Peabody's dinner parties, the Reverend Melish was a welcome guest. He also became a friend of the Trasks.

Mr. Melish tells of an incident[15] of those days which made an impression upon him. A dozen young men, ranging in age from sixteen to twenty-one, in whom he had been interested in Cincinnati, visited him in Brooklyn. Before their arrival Mr. Melish told Mr. Peabody he was expecting some young guests, whereupon Peabody invited them to dinner. The young men had never seen a millionaire before. To their astonishment, the distinguished dark-bearded gentleman who entertained them did not seem very different from anyone else. They were impressed by his kindness and his solicitude for their pleasure. Afterward they said, "Why, he is religious!" although he had said little, if anything, about religion.

Peabody's duties as senior warden at Holy Trinity and his other church activities brought him into prominence in affairs outside the parish. He was a delegate to conventions of the Episcopal Church.

After 1904 he spent more time each year at Lake George, and found it impossible to attend services regular-

---
13. Interview with the Reverend J. Howard Melish, March 26, 1940.
14. Peabody Papers, Yaddo files.
15. The Reverend J. Howard Melish to author.

ly in Brooklyn. He attended the Lake George Church and became identified with its activities. He helped to find the new rector, the Reverend Edward M. Parrott, who began his services in February, 1906.

At church conventions he widened his circle of clergymen friends. Often he invited them to Abenia for conferences. Among his best friends were Bishop Doane of the Albany Diocese, and the Reverend J. Sylvester Nash of Boston. The Reverend Henry Van Dyke was an old friend who was also close to the Trasks. His acquaintance with other clergymen reached to the west coast. It may be safely said that by 1906, Peabody was one of the most widely known laymen in Episcopal Church circles, and one of the most influential.

CHAPTER XII

Treasurer of Democratic Party

POLITICS CONTINUED TO BE ONE OF PEABODY'S CHIEF concerns. We have noted how, in his early thirties, he helped to organize the Young Democrats in Brooklyn. We saw him, in 1896, becoming a national figure as a Gold Democrat. We also watched his efforts in support of Edward M. Shepard in the New York Mayoralty Campaign of 1901. From his study at Abenia, or at Yaddo, he sometimes appears like an Olympian reaching out to suggest or persuade through letter or telegram. He was especially good at arranging conferences at his home so that there might be an exchange of views. At these conferences he was dominant, but not dominating.

As the presidential campaign of 1904 drew near, Peabody did what he could to boost Edward M. Shepard as a possible Democratic candidate. The failure of Shepard at the New York City polls in 1901 had in no way dimmed his friend's confidence in his abilities. On February 10, 1903, Peabody wrote an acquaintance that he had been trying to put Shepard before the country and had arranged to have him deliver the baccalaureate address at the University of Georgia, an address at the Jefferson Club in St. Louis, and one at Tulane University.

It was soon apparent, however, that Shepard had slight chance of being nominated for President. Nomination for the governorship of New York might be more feasible. With the latter office in mind, Peabody wrote H. F. Hollis from Abenia:[1]

> I am confirmed in my thought that it would be a very great service if just now men from without the state of New York who believe it [that Shepard should be nominated] should write to C. F. Murphy, at Tammany Hall, W. F. Sheehan, David B. Hill and to August Belmont, and to Judge Parker respecting the advantage that it would prove to the National ticket in other states.

But his hopes were soon dimmed, and he wrote to a friend:[2]

> The conditions were made almost impossible when Senator McCarren, the leader of Mr. Shepard's own county, announced his unalterable opposition and stated that he could not carry the county.

Thus once again it became clear that Shepard lacked sufficient support to win high office. Though disappointed, Peabody refrained from pushing the matter further at this time.

Meanwhile, preparations for the national conventions moved forward. The Republicans met in June at Chicago. By acclamation, they nominated Theodore Roosevelt for President. For Vice President, they selected Charles W. Fairbanks of Indiana.

The Democratic Party met in July at St. Louis. Many of the members of the party had favored Cleveland, but he had refused to permit his name to be used. Some of the delegates favored William Jennings Bryan, being attracted by his "free silver" policies and his glamorous personality. Others leaned toward the newspaper publisher, William Randolph Hearst. The delegates finally nominated a "dark horse"—Alton B. Parker, presiding justice of the New York Court of Appeals. Henry G. Davis, a wealthy West Virginian, was nominated for Vice President.

1. Peabody Papers, Yaddo files. Letter dated August 4, 1904.
2. Copy of Mr. Peabody's letter dated September 23, 1904, in Yaddo files.

The Democratic platform, calling for such matters as revision in tariff schedules and added powers for the Interstate Commerce Commission, was silent on the currency question. Hence it was a surprise when Judge Parker, just after the nomination, wired W. F. Sheehan, chairman of the executive committee, that he stood for the gold standard. He offered to withdraw if his stand were unacceptable to the Democrats. After considerable debate, the party declared that since currency was not likely to be an issue in the campaign, there was no objection to Parker's holding the views which he had expressed. The "gold democrat" was retained as the Democratic nominee, and the party proceeded to map out the campaign.

Peabody was not enthusiastic over the nomination of Parker, but preferred him to Bryan because of the latter's views on the currency. He thought that Parker should be supported in order that there should be no cleavage in the party ranks. His main desire, he said, was to keep "plutocratic tendencies" from increasing in the government. The chairman of the National Democratic Campaign Committee was Thomas Taggart. In August Edward M. Shepard prevailed upon Peabody to accept the post of treasurer of the National Democratic Party. He was reluctant to do so because of other commitments, but was assured that he would be relieved of the details of handling the funds. An assistant treasurer was appointed to do the bookkeeping.

Soliciting of contributions in political campaigns was a long accepted practice. It often happened that a corporation or an individual would actually make donations to the campaign funds of both parties; and the public tolerated secrecy in the use of funds. But the practice of accepting gifts from corporations was seriously questioned during the 1904 campaign. The Republican Party bore the brunt of the attack. An editorial in the *New York World* on October 1 challenged Roosevelt for placing George B. Cortelyou, Secretary of Commerce and Labor, in the post of National Chairman of the Republican Party. The Bureau of Corporations was located in the Department of Commerce and Labor, and it was maintained that corporations might assume they were buying protection in contributing to the Republican Party under Cortelyou's chairmanship.[3] Roosevelt denied that there was anything in the nature of extortion. He did not, however, deny that big gifts were being made by corporations to the Republican Party campaign fund. Evidence later showed that a large per cent of the amount contributed came from corporations.[4]

The Democratic Party, too, was busy soliciting funds. Its 1904 records were never made public, but testimony later revealed that August Belmont gave between $100,000 and $250,000, and that Thomas Fortune Ryan gave a substantial sum. William F. Sheehan testified that a total of approximately $1,000,000 was contributed during the campaign.[5]

Years later, members of both parties were called upon to testify before a congressional committee investigating campaign contributions. Peabody, as former treasurer of his party, was asked to appear. In his testimony he said he did not remember anything about the individual contributions made in 1904. An excerpt from his statement follows:[6]

3. H. F. Pringle, *Theodore Roosevelt* (New York: Harcourt, Brace & Co., 1931), pp. 435-455.
4. "Campaign Contributions." Testimony before a Sub-Committee of the Committee on Privileges and Elections, United States Senate, 62nd Congress, Third Session; Pursuant to Senate Resolution 79, S. Res. 386 and S. Res. 418 (Washington, 1913), Vol. I, pp. 1-80.
5. *Ibid.*
6. *Ibid.*

Senator Jones: As I understand, you have no distinct recollection of any particular contributor to the campaign fund?

Mr. Peabody: No sir; there were no large contributors as far as I have personal knowledge.

Senator Jones: What is the largest contribution of which you have personal knowledge that was made at the campaign?

Mr. Peabody: I can not speak accurately, but my impression is that $5,000 is as large as I have any recollection of. I have no record of anything. I have no question but there were larger ones, but I have nothing that I could give real testimony on. The $5,000 was my own, I think, although I am not entirely certain whether that was the amount or not.

The Chairman: I understand that you had nothing to do with and knew nothing of the efforts to secure the funds for the campaign?

Mr. Peabody: No sir. I declined to take any part, except that I may have been present at the meetings when discussions were going on as to trying to get other people to do the work.

Senator Jones: Do you know who had special[7] charge of that work?

Mr. Peabody: As I say the executive committee, Mr. Sheehan and Mr. Belmont of that committee, I should think, would be the men who were probably more active. You know the custom, I suppose, Senator, that in these committees you call together 50 or 100 merchants and bankers and all sorts of fellows and have a sort of honorary finance committee and they go around and try to get $100 or $50 from the trade, and there was a large number of men of that kind, but I do not know, because of my not feeling responsible for that part of it. . . .[8]

Mr. Taggart, in testifying before the Congressional sub-committee, said:[9]

I will state this, that Mr. Peabody, as I said, was the

---

7. *Ibid.*
8. *Ibid.*
9. *Ibid.*

treasurer; he had charge of the finance committee.

The hearing continued:[10]

> *Senator Oliver*: Mr. Peabody was here last week and he did not know as much about it as you do.
> *Mr. Taggart*: I was going to explain a little further, that Mr. Peabody resigned after the election. I do not know whether it was because he was overworked or because he was disgusted. Mr. August Belmont was appointed treasurer in his stead.

The experience as treasurer was extremely distasteful to Mr. Peabody. He told friends that he believed some of the members of the party were disloyal. He afterwards said that he was in favor of having contributions to campaign funds made public before rather than after a campaign.[11]

2.

Judge Parker proved to be a poor match for his Republican opponent. Though a man of intelligence and many fine personal traits, he was little known outside his own state. Roosevelt won an overwhelming victory at the polls.

After the election, Peabody was anxious that the new administration consider the perennial currency question. On December 30, 1905, he wrote to Mr. Hanna:[12]

> Do you not think in view of Secretary Shaw's reference in his annual report to asset currency that strong effort should be made through Mr. Root or Mr. Taft to have the President informed respecting the recommendations of the Monetary Commission as to asset currency....

He followed up the matter with a letter[13] to Thomas Fortune Ryan on January 24, 1906:

---

10. *Ibid.*
11. The matter of campaign contributions was kept alive after 1904. Further investigations resulted in the enactment of federal legislation forbidding corporations to contribute to political campaigns and calling for publicity regarding campaign accounts.
12. Copy of letter in files at Yaddo.
13. *Ibid.* Mr. Hanna was in New York for meetings of the Southern Education Board and the General Education Board.

My dear Ryan:
My friend, Mr. H. H. Hanna of Indianapolis is here and I have asked him to be sure and not leave the city before having a talk with you, if possible, respecting the currency situation and the advisability of legislation. You probably will recall that Mr. Hanna was chairman of the Executive Committee of the Indianapolis Monetary Conference, which Committee was able to secure the enactment of the present law assuring, to a large extent, the stability of our single gold standard. Of course Mr. Schiff has recently brought up the question here, and Mr. Hanna has had some talk with him, but I am very anxious that Mr. Hanna should be in touch [with you]. Of course he has learned of your very large influence naturally, but I want as a *personal* matter, if you are strong enough that you should have a conference with him. He is, of course, not seeking money or anything else excepting counsel and instructions as to the best thing to do now.
I want also that you shall if possible, write Secretary Root, asking that he have some talk with Mr. Hanna when he may go to Washington, respecting this question. . . .[14]

At the same time Peabody was in close touch with the Single Tax advocates, including his old friend Henry George, and John Moody. On November 18, 1905, he wrote to an acquaintance:[15] " I am and have been for years a really cheerful subscriber to the New York Tax Reform Association. . . ."[16]

A few days later, he wrote to R. R. Bowker, a former business associate:[17]

Henry George, Louis Post, Lawson Purdy, John Moody and I hope T. M. Osborne of Auburn come at my request to talk over some method of making conservative presentation and real advance in the expression of Single Tax sentiment in this country, with the immediate emphasis on the best means of securing regular and accurate reports in the press of this country

---

14. *Ibid.*
15. Copy of letter to Allen R. Foote, Chicago, Illinois.
16. An organization devoted to the spread of the Single Tax doctrine.
17. Copy of letter to Mr. R. R. Bowker, November 26, 1905.

of the coming English campaign in which the Liberal
party are likely to emphasize the ground rent issue. . . .
Perhaps Shepard can be with us for a day although
he is not a Single Taxer. . . .

He gave money on a number of occasions to further
the Single Tax movement. For instance, on March 10,
1906, he sent $500 to be used for propaganda for this
purpose. The idea was that through intensive effort, a
score or more of men sympathetic to the movement might
be elected to the sixteenth Congress.

Other aspects of taxation engaged his attention also.
On February 26, 1906, he wrote to an acquaintance:[18]

> I have thought for some time that this country ought
> to go much further with *Inheritance tax* laws than even
> England has done. I have thought that . . . *estates*
> beyond a certain amount to be fixed, might well be
> taxed to the extent of 90 per cent. . . . It [would be]
> to my mind the one addition to the *land tax* and *franchise
> increment*. . . .

3.

Meanwhile his personal life had both joys and sorrows in the years 1904 and 1905. News from Carlos in Paris was pleasant. The art course was going well. Moreover, Carlos's fiancee had arrived in Paris and the two were going to be married in a happy, simple ceremony.[19] Mr. and Mrs. Royal Peabody, Carlos's parents, were to be on hand for the occasion.

But Peabody was troubled about Katrina Trask's condition. Early in February, 1905, in a letter to Dr. H. B. Frissell, he spoke of a hemorrhage which she had suffered in one eye as the result of a long-standing heart ailment, adding, "she lies in a darkened room at Yaddo."[20] Later in the year, he wrote to a clergyman friend, "Mrs. Trask

---

18. Professor John L. March of Schenectady, New York.
19. Letter from Charles S. Peabody, Yaddo files.
20. Copy of Mr. Peabody's letter to Dr. Frissell, Feb. 8, 1905.

is very ill to our deep sorrow. . . ."[21] And on the same day, he wrote to Dr. McIver that he was returning to Yaddo.[22] To Miss Rossa Cooley, on November 2, 1905, he wrote of his "fear that she is losing."

He himself was not well. He was suffering from extreme exhaustion and was in a rather depressed state. He wrote Dr. Frissell that he would call this a year of rest. Taking his condition in hand, he retired to Abenia to recuperate.

His rest was broken into, however, by correspondence, business appointments, and the entertaining of guests at Abenia. Responsibilities in behalf of schools were constant.

4.

Early in 1906, Peabody became actively engaged in an interesting church controversy. By this time there was hardly a layman in the country who was better known in Episcopal church circles than he was. His attendance at general conventions of the church had brought him in touch with clergymen throughout the United States. Bishops and rectors were frequent house guests at his home in Brooklyn and at Abenia. Any question of importance that came up in the church, especially in a New York State diocese, was sure to be brought to his attention.

One of the most hotly debated issues to arise in the Episcopal Church in New York State in the early years of the century was that of the Reverend Algernon Crapsey's unorthodox views. In a series of sermons preached in 1904-1905 at St. Andrew's Church, Rochester, New York, the Reverend Crapsey had questioned some of the church doctrines, particularly that of the Virgin Birth.

---

21. Copy of Mr. Peabody's letter to a New Orleans clergyman, Sept. 4, 1905.
22. Copy in Yaddo files.

His statements reached the ears of church authorities, who summoned him to be tried in the Diocesan Court of Western New York on April 17, 1906. The decision went against Crapsey. His counsel, Edward Morse Shepard, appealed the case to the Higher Church Court. This court confirmed the action of the Diocesan authorities, and Crapsey was dismissed from the church.

Peabody, on hearing of the controversy, took up the cause of the Reverend Crapsey. It was his view that some of the authorities were too narrow in their interpretation. His own religious views were simple. He believed in the Virgin Birth as well as in the ethical teachings of the New Testament. He was not disturbed, however, when the literal truth of the Bible stories was called into question. One could question the details of the stories, he asserted, without questioning any of the basic truths of the Bible.

Believing that the church should take a more liberal attitude, he wrote to clergymen and prominent laymen setting forth the issues involved. He sent hundreds of letters, some of them to persons as far away as the west coast. One is impressed with his tremendous zeal in this cause which he considered just.

Soon after the trial, the Reverend Crapsey left the church and took up other work. Peabody sent him letters of encouragement, and continued to keep in touch with the family for many years. Although the church authorities held to their view regarding the case, Peabody thought that the discussion of the issues involved had resulted in a more liberal outlook on the part of church members generally.

5.

Matters of the church had been making more and more inroads upon his time. He had taken some responsibility in connection with church schools, such as St. Paul's school for Negro youth. He was a prominent figure in the American Bible Society.[23]

Early in 1906, after preliminary correspondence with church officials, he invited a number of prominent Episcopal churchmen to dine with him. When they came, he spoke to them of the need for improving and expanding the church's program in behalf of education of Negroes. As a result of the meeting, plans for an organization to carry out such a program were drawn up.

The new organization was given the name of American Church Institute for Negroes. Under the general direction of the church, the institute was to foster and co-ordinate the work of a number of schools for Negroes. Mr. Peabody was one of the incorporators and became a member of the board of trustees. He considered the work so important that he later stated that if he had a million dollars to give for education of Negroes, he would donate at least two-thirds of it to the American Church Institute.[24]

---

23. He had served on the finance committee of the Society (*New York Daily Tribune*, March 23, 1902).
24. He was a trustee and treasurer of the American Church Institute in 1906-1907, in 1909-1910, and again from 1912 on.

CHAPTER XIII

Retirement from Business

PEABODY HAD REACHED HIS FIFTY-FOURTH YEAR. Although giving the appearance of robust energy, he had been overworking for years. His doctor had long advised him to take a rest. This he had sometimes consented to do, but it was always a rest with many interruptions—especially interruptions for conferences, for committee meetings, and for commencements and special occasions of the schools with which he was connected.

The days that he spent at Abenia and at Yaddo were a delightful respite. On February 10, 1906, he wrote to a clergyman friend of the "gorgeous day here with 22 inches of dry snow from yesterday, with beautiful sunshine, a little too warm possibly, but likely to be colder tonight." He wrote on February 26 of having the new rector and his wife and children visiting him at Abenia, and added that he was expecting guests for a house party over the following week-end.

On March 7, 1906, he suffered an accident. He had boarded a train for New York at Saratoga Springs. He stepped to the end of the car to get a drink of water, and as he did so, the train jerked with a sharp lunge that threw him off his feet. His head was bruised and his muscles strained. Trainmen and passengers hurried to assist him, and he was taken to Yaddo and put to bed.

News of his injury spread quickly. His concerned friends sent messages from all over the country. Two hundred neighbors met at the local schoolhouse and passed resolutions of thanks for his escape from more serious injury. A week's rest set him on his feet, but he felt the after effects of his accident, and physicians sent him to Abenia with firm warnings against any activity.

It was at this time that Peabody decided to retire from business, and his physical condition may have been partly responsible for the decision. There were other reasons, however, which undoubtedly weighed more with him—above all, his desire to devote himself to educational progress and philanthropy. Having announced his retirement, Peabody wound up his affairs as a partner in Spencer Trask and Company. This did not mean that he severed his connections with the firm, for he retained investments made through the company. In fact, his personal association with Spencer Trask was so close that it would have been difficult to break away even had he wanted to do so. He had extensive holdings in Mexican railroads and mining developments. He also had money invested in the Broadway Realty Company. From these holdings he derived the bulk of his income in his later years. Although officially retired from Wall Street, he went there frequently on his personal business and in order to invest funds entrusted to him as treasurer of the General Education Board, Tuskegee, Hampton, and other organizations.

It appears likely that, had he continued in business, Peabody would have amassed a larger fortune. At the time of his retirement he was already an outstanding figure in the financial world. The extent of his wealth at any particular time is not known, one reason being that he gave away such large sums while he was still building up his fortune. The fortune, at any rate, was not so great as to be classed with those of Carnegie or of Morgan or of Rockefeller. His former business acquaintances have made estimates which range from three million to forty million dollars. At the peak of his business career, early in the century, he must have had at least three or four million dollars.

His retirement was announced in the papers on May 6, 1906. The *Tribune,* on May 13, carried the caption "Abandoning Business for Life of Humanitarian Effort." Reporters interviewed him: He said he had never wanted to be rich, but that he had always believed he would some day be rich. And he added that wealth is a trust given by God to be used for the benefit of mankind.[1]

It is interesting to look back at the business careers of the able organizers of industry who made their fortunes at the end of the nineteenth century and the beginning of the twentieth. Their adroit manipulations have been the subject of controversy or the object of criticism these many years. Volumes have been written about them. Besides the classic works of Ida M. Tarbell and Henry D. Lloyd, there are F. L. Allen's *The Lords of Creation,* Matthew Josephson's *The Robber Barons,* Gustavus Myers' *The History of Great American Fortunes,* and Allan Nevins' *John D. Rockefeller—The Heroic Age of American Enterprise.* Others, too, have told the remarkable story of these giants of industry.

As for Peabody, in building up his fortune he had followed the usual practices of business men of his day. He had bargained shrewdly, as we have seen, in selling the Rio Grande Western to Kuhn, Loeb and Company for a cool $15,000,000. He had skilfully manipulated the sale of Edison Company stock to Anthony N. Brady for $21,000,000. It was his view that the broker should make a careful analysis of the securities, and that he could then expect the buyer to share the responsibility.

1. *New York Daily Tribune,* May 13, 1906.

It is possible that the indictments hurled against the giants of capital as "malefactors of great wealth,"[2] were a factor in bringing about Peabody's decision to retire, but it seems certain that the chief element in the case was his longing to spend the rest of his life in aiding humanitarian movements. He had been saying for years that his chief interest lay in matters other than business. His activities as publicist, as vestryman, as trustee in educational institutions, bore him out.

In commenting upon Peabody's retirement, the newspapers praised him. They remarked upon his broad culture and his many interests. In point of fact, he "retired" into a life that was as active as his business career. Energetic and forceful as ever, he simply applied his energies, from that time on, to non-wealth-producing tasks.

2.

It would be difficult to estimate the total of Mr. Peabody's contributions to humanitarian causes. His files covering the period before 1900 were destroyed; hence one can gain only a sketchy account of his earlier donations. Moreover, he said little about his gifts and one must trace them through acknowledgments made by others. That he was always a generous giver is clear. There was a constant stream of contributions; they ranged all the way from a donation of several thousand dollars to a one-dollar token of encouragement.[3]

His greatest gifts were made to the University of Georgia, to Y.M.C.A.'s, and to churches for the purchase of organs. He also gave a large sum for the erection of an amphitheatre at Long Island College Hospital.

---

2. In 1905 the Reverend Washington Gladden, an Ohio clergyman, scathingly condemned the "malefactors of great wealth" with special reference to John D. Rockefeller, Sr.
3. Mr. L. W. Noland, one of his former secretaries, estimates that in the period of World War I, the smaller gifts amounted to about $100 a day.

His gifts to the University of Georgia amounted to approximately $250,000;[4] among them were a gift to the library of $50,000 for a new building and a contribution of $60,000 to the University's War Memorial Fund. In addition to his cash donations he made numerous gifts of rare editions of books to the University Library and gifts of books to various faculty members.

He was a contributor to Colorado College which was founded by his friend General Palmer and which he himself later served as a member of the board of trustees.[5] From 1897 until 1932 he gave a total of about $42,000 to this college alone.

He gave substantial sums of money to Skidmore College, of which he became a trustee. It is not possible to know the exact amount, because many of his gifts to the institution were given anonymously. Miss Kathryn Starbuck,[6] Secretary of the College, states that a conservative estimate would be $20,000 to $25,000.

To other colleges, too, he made generous contributions. Often his donation would be in the form of a special gift. To Hampton he gave a stained-glass window reproducing Sir Joshua Reynold's painting "Hope," and also the Malone collection of books and documents. He gave a large plot of land at Greensboro, North Carolina, as a park for the young women students of the State Normal and Industrial College.[7]

His gifts to the schools for Negroes with which he was

4. Statement by Mr. Harry Hodgson; Peabody Papers at Yaddo.
5. Letter from Mr. W. W. Postlethwaite, Museum Director, to President C. B. Hershey, Colorado College.
6. Miss Starbuck's letter to the writer, Sept. 8, 1944. She states that in "addition to his personal contributions, Mr. Peabody was instrumental in securing gifts from others."
7. He gave money to Harvard University; for instance, the sum of $920 in securities on Dec. 23, 1919 (Peabody Papers, Yaddo files).

connected flowed in a steady stream.[8] He supplemented his gifts to the institutions themselves with contributions for specific purposes to the individuals serving these schools. For instance, he gave a house at Lake George to Miss Rossa B. Cooley and Miss Grace House of Penn School, so that they might have an opportunity to experience wider contacts after their confining years on St. Helena Island. With the assistance of Mr. Arthur Curtiss James, he also bought a home for them on a remote part of St. Helena Island, where they could rest and entertain their friends and eventually retire.

He was one of the chief backers of the work of Booker T. Washington. He subsidized the work of several individuals who made a study and compilation of Negro spirituals.

His active interest in the Young Men's Christian Association had continued through the years. He was a member of the advisory board of the Brooklyn Y.M.C.A., and between 1900 and 1905 he gave a total of $22,000 to the building fund of this organization.[9] In November, 1901, he bought for $22,000 a house in Montgomery, Alabama, which he turned over to the Y.M.C.A. at a nominal rental.

We have noted the contributions which he and his brothers made to the Young Men's Christian Association in their boyhood home of Columbus, Georgia,—$3,000 for a lot and $53,575 for a building. He also gave more than $10,000 for a Y.M.C.A. building for the Negro residents of the town. He gave $5,000 toward a new "Y" building at Schenectady, and made substantial contribu-

8. He also administered the fund left to Hampton by his friend, W. J. Palmer.
9. He also gave a substantial sum for the library of the Central building and a sizable amount for one of the branch Y.M.C.A.'s (*New York Daily Tribune*, May 13, 1906).

tions to the Y.M.C.A. at Colorado Springs. Likewise, he gave a large sum for the construction of a Y.M.C.A. building at Salt Lake City, Utah. He also contributed to the Portland, Oregon, Y.M.C.A., and to several Y.W.C.A.'s.

His interest in music led him to donate a number of organs to churches. In selecting an organ for Holy Trinity he had become acquainted with E. M. Skinner, who was then New York representative of an organ company. Years later, when Mr. Skinner was forming his own company for the manufacture of organs, Peabody was so impressed with the fine tone produced by Skinner's craftsmanship that he took a large block of stock in the new company and became a member of its board of directors. He made it clear that his interest was rather in assuring the manufacture of organs of fine quality than in the making of profit. He and his brother, Charles J. Peabody, gave an organ to St. Paul's Chapel at Columbia University. With the members of his family, he also later gave a Skinner organ costing more than $50,000 to Holy Trinity Church in Brooklyn[10] in memory of his brother Charles. He likewise gave several other smaller organs, and paid extensive amounts for repairs for several organs.

An amusing anecdote is told regarding his gift of one of the smaller organs. One Sunday, the minister of the church concerned was addressing the congregation from the pulpit. In one of the pews he noted the presence of a distinguished tall figure, a stranger. At the conclusion of the service, he shook hands with the visitor, who began to question him about the organ and the music. Pleased with the stranger's friendly interest, the clergyman spoke his mind on the theme of how much the church needed a better organ.[11] At this point, the visitor, without further

---

10. In 1926. He also gave a large sum for an organ for an Episcopal church in Albany, New York.
11. Files at Yaddo.

ado, told the clergyman to order an organ and send him the bill. It took the astonished preacher some time to convince himself that the visitor was George Foster Peabody!

He made at least one large contribution in the field of medical service. On May 13, 1905, he, with his brothers, gave $47,000 to provide the Skene amphitheatre and adjoining room at the Long Island College Hospital. To this sum they added $3,000 for a stained glass window in memory of their friend, Henry W. Maxwell.

He made substantial donations to the Brooklyn Bureau of Charities, to settlement houses, to the Brooklyn Society for Prevention of Cruelty to Children, to the Volunteers' Prisoners League. He pledged $5,000 toward the building fund of the General Theological Seminary,[12] and made contributions of many thousands of dollars to Holy Trinity and to the other churches with which he was connected.

Week in and week out his mail brought him appeals for aid to a variety of humanitarian causes scattered over the country. Sometimes he would dictate a refusal and follow that by a gift upon reconsideration of his finances. Almost any cause which had a logical program drew from him a response.

He often made gifts of books and of subscriptions to magazines, and he distributed reprints of articles on various subjects. He subsidized the publication of several books, and paid for having copies sent to a substantial list of acquaintances. He paid for the reprinting and distribution of Mrs. Trask's works on the subject of peace. Of her poem *Christ of the Andes*,[13] one hundred thousand reprints were made at his expense; by November 10, 1905,

---

12. Letter of Robert C. Beadle to the Reverend J. Howard Melish.
13. Letter from Benjamin Trueblood of American Peace Society to Mr. Peabody, July 20, 1905, Yaddo files.

seventy-three thousand copies[14] had been sent out by the American Peace Society. Again, he ordered ten thousand reprints[15] of Mrs. Trask's poem *Rise, Mighty Anglo-Saxons*.

Among the most appealing of all his gifts were the checks which he sent to acquaintances to add to their comfort. We have noted his contribution of a home at Lake George to Miss Rossa Cooley and Miss Grace House and the gift of a trip abroad to Chancellor Hill of the University of Georgia. At various times he would surprise a young relative with a fat check for a trip to New York. On one occasion at least, he sent money to a clergyman who was preaching in the summer at Lake George, so that the trip he had to make each week might be made in comfort. On other occasions too numerous to mention here, he supplied the funds for struggling clergymen, educators, students, writers to realize some objective that would have been impossible otherwise. Nevertheless, he did not hesitate to turn down a request when it appeared that the person making it would profit little by the gift.

Most of his donations were made without reservations of any kind. He did sometimes make a few gifts contingent upon the raising of a similar amount, or at least a certain amount by the local recipients.

He said little about his benefactions. In fact, he often made a gift and then forgot all about it. He once visited a college to which, years before, he had given a large sum for the construction of a building. In the auditorium that day, he was referred to as the generous benefactor. He was embarrassed at having no recollection of the contribution![16]

14. Letter from Benjamin Trueblood to Mr. Peabody, November 10, 1905, Yaddo files.
15. Letter from Albert Brandt, publisher, to Mr. Peabody's secretary, April 4, 1906, Yaddo files.
16. Statement of Mrs. Marjorie Peabody Waite to writer, summer, 1940. Mrs. Waite was with Mr. Peabody on that occasion.

From the beginning of his career of philanthropy, he preferred to plan his own contributions rather than employ a secretary for this purpose. One of his secretaries at the office would take care of the details of the correspondence after receiving directions written in pencil by Mr. Peabody on the margin of an appeal. While he did not hesitate to make gifts through constituted philanthropic organizations, Peabody liked to feel the personal touch in giving.

It was this desire to have personal supervision over his philanthropies that led him to retire from business in order to become, as he put it, his own executor. He had a distaste for the "dead hand" in benefactions, believing that future generations should not be hampered by commitments made in legacies. He preferred to give away his whole accumulated fortune in his lifetime, thus serving as a "steward of wealth" in the Biblical sense.

Investments carefully made prior to his retirement in Mexican mining and railway stocks, and his Broadway Realty Company holdings, insured his ability to continue commitments already made to educational institutions, and permitted him to add some new responsibilities. As it turned out, however, he lived longer than he had anticipated, and he was unable towards the end of his life, to keep on widening the scope of his beneficence.

It was a period when many rich men were turning over large sums for humanitarian causes. In the case of some philanthropists, it has been said that they were actuated largely by a guilty conscience—the desire to atone for the sin of amassing great riches at the expense of the public, sometimes by questionable methods. Peabody, however, seems to have been moved more by the precepts of the church and by the intense interest in education engendered in him by his early struggles to educate himself.

CHAPTER XIV

Jeanes Fund Trustee; Trask's Tragic Death

Mr. Peabody now had more time for educational work. He was active in the affairs of Hampton, Tuskegee, Penn School, Colorado College, and the University of Georgia. He helped to plan the program of the American Church Institute for Negroes and retained his leadership on the Southern Education Board.

One of the most important activities was his work as treasurer of the General Education Board. In addition to the first gift of $1,000,000 the Rockefellers had made a gift of $10,000,000 to the Board. They followed this with a gift of $32,000,000 in 1907, and added more later. The investment of these huge sums called for meticulous planning and for shrewd analysis of business trends. Peabody often conferred with Mr. Rockefeller's adviser, the Reverend F. T. Gates, and with other members of the board. In the main, he advised the board to buy bonds; on occasion he advised the purchase of preferred stocks.[1]

His association with Mr. John D. Rockefeller, Jr., was most pleasant. The younger Mr. Rockefeller and his wife had visited Yaddo and Lake George, and, as we have seen, the cordial relation already existing between them and

1. Peabody Papers, Yaddo files.

Peabody was further cemented at that time. On December 3, 1906, Mr. Peabody wrote:

> Dear Mr. Rockefeller
>
> I was glad to find you so evidently better and am encouraged thereby to suggest now and briefly to you the thought of the present condition of the Negro and his Educational prospects.
>
> And this in particular relation to the peculiar opportunity which I think is providentially within the power of the General Education Board either directly or through the Southern Education Board as conditions may determine.
>
> As a Southern man the condition of affairs in this respect has been upon my conscience heavily for many months, for I have realized that the State of feeling or indifference at the north as respects the negro was discouraging and not easy to improve—at the South it is distressing but easy I think with judgment to improve—I will not weary you as to details of how or why for those I can give to you if you desire after giving thought to the opportunity.
>
> It has seemed to me that few things could have result so large as a fund of not over Five Millions for Income or some one or two hundred thousand a year available— if any doubt still prevail as to continuity of use—which being at the disposal of the General Education Board without public knowledge—to bring an avalanche of persistent requests or to provoke loud antagonism from Tillman and such—would enable them in the many places they have knowledge of to strengthen existing work in a moderate way—that is from $100 to $3,000— to schools like Calhoun—the Walker Baptist and scores of those of which we have record—now doing much work which could be improved and enlarged by careful conditioning and oversight. We have a most excellent Negro Inspector—Mr. Williams.
>
> Then there are special lines of work as to farming which we could further as we are doing for the white farmers mainly in Mississippi and Alabama.
>
> But mainly by reason of our relations with true and earnest Christian Southern men in office and out who are moving forward by the organization of Christian Leagues (clippings from today's Post enclosed) to try and stir up the right minded people to the state of

apostasy as to a real Christianity that they have developed by the real neglect of these needy ones at their door—I am in correspondence with Rev. Dr. S. C. Mitchell of Richmond and Rev. Dr. John E. White of Atlanta—both true men (and fortunately Baptists as the largest of Southern Denominations) respecting the formulation of a program to put into practical effect this arousal of conscience and so be sure that it is a real revival of sound religion—My belief is that we can develop a great arousal of the neighborhood to the condition of the Negro public school—which is the only hope.

Hampton Spelman & Tuskegee are preparing teachers for them and their normal Schools also to be furthered—If we can get a Southern man to get after his School Supt. because no Industrial training is given in the Public School and at the right time and place help to get the equipment here and there to give a start with a trained teacher we can make more of a true revolution than in any other way and at the same time develop a splendid reaction that will greatly improve the white schools.

I should be glad when I am next down to talk this over with you at length some evening if I might. I believe it a notable opportunity for great and truly Christian service.

Sincerely yours,
George Foster Peabody[2]

There is no doubt that, so far as the educational needs of the South were concerned, Peabody was one of the best informed men in the country. And indeed his counsel at board meetings was an immense asset to every one of the philanthropic organizations which he served.

Here is the man who is his own executor, sitting at his large desk at Abenia with a pile of letters and papers fresh from the post office. He slits open the envelopes: a report from Hampton; an appeal for funds from some struggling institution; a call for advice from a puzzled

---

2. Courtesy of Mr. John D. Rockefeller, Jr.

school principal who is too steeped in immediate problems to get the larger view.

On and on Mr. Peabody worked, with his secretary at hand to take his dictation. When the mail was answered, he continued at his desk, far into the night. Only the small hours of the morning and exhaustion at length stopped him. He was doing the thing that was important to him—encouraging educational development.

In 1907, a few months after his retirement, he assumed a new responsibility: he became one of the executors of the Jeanes Fund, a large sum of money given for the education of Negroes.

A few years before, Peabody had learned of the gift made by Miss Anna T. Jeanes, a Philadelphia Quaker, to Fort Valley Normal and Industrial Institute. He had suggested that Dr. Hollis B. Frissell, Principal of Hampton, call on Miss Jeanes to seek a donation. Dr. Frissell did so, and received a check for $10,000. Afterwards, Principal Booker T. Washington appealed to Miss Jeanes, at Dr. Frissell's suggestion, and received a check for $10,000 for Tuskegee.

Mr. Peabody, as treasurer of both Hampton and Tuskegee, wrote letters to Miss Jeanes thanking her for the gifts. He then suggested that she also make a contribution to the General Education Board of which he was treasurer. She agreed and turned over $200,000 to the board.

Incurably ill, the aged benefactress now decided to give one million dollars to establish a Fund for "rudimentary education" in Negro rural schools. The day came when she was ready to hand over all her securities, and she summoned Dr. Frissell, Dr. Washington, and Mr. Peabody.[3] The three men were ushered into her room at

---

3. On April 22, 1907, she executed the deed of trust, turning over to Booker T. Washington and H. B. Frissell the sum of one million dollars. She stipulated that William Howard Taft, Andrew Carnegie, Hollis B.

the Quaker Home where she was staying. She greeted them and spoke of the pleasure she had had in making her gifts to Hampton and Tuskegee. Turning to Mr. Peabody she asked if he remembered writing her about the General Education Board. He did indeed, he said, expressing his appreciation of her generous reply. Whereupon she said he did not need to thank her—she should thank him. Thus the Negro Rural School Fund of a million dollars was established.[4]

A short time later, on September 3, 1907, Booker T. Washington wrote Peabody about seeing Miss Jeanes. Her swollen hands had drawn upon the muscles of her shoulder and neck so that she was no longer able to hold her head straight or to walk. She was anxious to see something done before she passed away. She seemed supremely happy over making her gift. Three weeks later she died.

The first meeting of the incorporators of the Negro Rural School Fund was held at the General Education Board Office on February 29, 1908. The officers elected were James H. Dillard, president; Walter H. Page, vice president; George Foster Peabody, treasurer;[5] and Robert R. Moton, secretary. Mr. Peabody was also made a member of the finance committee.

The Negro Rural School Fund had for its purpose the training of Southern Negroes for more satisfying rural life. Working through local public officials, it provided money for salaries of rural teachers. In some instances it provided buildings and equipment. After the first few

4. *Ibid.*
5. He was treasurer from 1908 to 1927; vice president, 1928 to 1931; chairman of the board, 1931.

Frissell, Booker T. Washington, George Foster Peabody and any others they selected should be the board of trustees. A. D. Wright, *The Negro Rural School Fund, Inc.* (Washington, 1933).

years the expenditures went largely for salaries of supervising industrial teachers, often called "Jeanes Teachers."

2.

In 1907, Mr. Peabody was called upon to face a critical situation. Business conditions had shown an upward trend since 1897, interrupted only by two mild recessions. During the early months of 1907, prosperity continued; but by spring, securities began to decline. Large speculation the previous year had created heavy demands upon banks, and discount rates had increased. The national banking system, weakened by the operations of trust companies in the field of commercial banking, was threatened.

The situation went from bad to worse, and in October, 1907, the great Knickerbocker Trust Company of New York failed. Crowds of fearful depositors milled about on the sidewalk outside the closed doors. On the heels of this incident, the Westinghouse Electric Manufacturing Company suspended operations. These failures caused a panic on the Stock Exchange. Many other banks and trust companies closed their doors.

On the eve of the banking crisis, Peabody was in Richmond, Virginia, at the General Convention of the Episcopal Church. The day before the convention closed, he announced that he would be glad to welcome any delegates and their wives as his guests on a trip to Hampton Institute. One hundred and twenty-five persons accepted, and he made arrangements to charter a special train.

That night, just before dinner, a long distance call from New York came to the hotel. He took the call in a booth in the lobby. A few minutes later he put the receiver down, turned from the telephone, and, quiet and white, gave directions to his secretary to complete arrangements for the Hampton trip and to take the party without him. He went upstairs, packed his bags and after a second long distance call, caught the night train back to New York.

Upon his return to the city, he found a critical state of affairs. Spencer Trask and Company was experiencing the worst strain in its history, with the possible exception of 1893. Moreover other banking companies through which he had investments in behalf of educational institutions were in a threatened position. It was apparent that he must act, and act quickly. He sent his secretary, Robert C. Beadle, with letters to two great financiers. Within a few hours one of the two had lent him a large sum. He was able, shortly afterwards, to repay it.

By the end of 1907, the acute financial crisis had passed, though business continued bad through a large part of 1908. While it lasted, the panic was severe. One can well imagine the strain under which Peabody, with his responsibility for the great funds entrusted to him, labored during the period of uncertainty.

3.

All this time Mr. Peabody's interest in public affairs was as strong as ever. He continued to urge an improved currency, calling the matter to the attention of various leaders and referring to the recommendations of the Indianapolis Monetary Convention. The business crisis of 1907 impressed upon his mind the urgency of the question, and he increased his efforts. Late in 1907 he corresponded with Hugh H. Hanna on the subject. He approved of the Aldrich-Vreeland Act of 1908 because it gave elasticity to the currency.[6] He did not think this

---

6. The Aldrich-Vreeland Act also authorized the appointment of a National Monetary Commission composed of 18 members. Under the Act experts were to be appointed to give their advice to the commission.

measure covered the situation, however, and continued to work for further reforms.

As the presidential campaign of 1908 approached, he discussed the issues of the day in letters to friends, General Palmer, Edward M. Shepard, John Moody, Louis Post, and others.[7] The letters indicate that about this time Peabody's views became distinctly more radical. Not only was he in favor of free trade—this, of course, was standard Democratic doctrine—but he also became more ardent than ever in his advocacy of the single tax and of government ownership of railroads. His disillusionment in connection with National Democratic Party affairs while he was treasurer may have influenced him to become further independent of the party. He wrote General Palmer that he favored the early dissolution of both the existing major parties, Republican and Democratic, and the organization of a radical party devoted to reforms for the benefit of the people.

4.

During the years 1907-1909 Mr. Peabody's health was a problem to him. He wrote to his friends saying that he was "nerve-tired."[8] Nevertheless, he enjoyed a rich and happy social life among his circle of friends and relatives. At Abenia he was the perfect host. He invited the boards of several organizations to meet at his home. The Southern Education Board held some of its annual conferences there. It was often said that Abenia's influence radiated to all parts of the country.

Among his close friends was small, shy Natalie Curtis, sister of George W. Curtis, Civil Service reformer. He enjoyed discussing literature and art with Natalie and encouraged her work of transcribing Indian folk legends.

---

7. Peabody Papers, Yaddo files.
8. *Ibid.*

Among his other friends were the Reverend J. Howard Melish; Thomas Mott Osborne, former Mayor of Auburn, New York, and later Warden of Sing Sing; Newton D. Baker; Louis Post; George U. Lunn. He had kept in touch with General W. J. Palmer and in 1909 was deeply saddened by this old friend's death. He also kept up his contact with Robert C. Ogden of the Southern Education Board. His wide circle of acquaintances included educators, churchmen, and statesmen.

His friend Edward Shepard lived on a beautiful estate called Erlowest, near Abenia, on Lake George. The two friends could often be seen enjoying a drive or a walk together. They had many common interests—business, politics, art, and, among special hobbies, the conservation of natural resources. At the end of the Southern Education Board Conference at Abenia each summer, Shepard entertained the guests at a farewell dinner at his home.

Peabody was very fond of his young cousins in the South. On September 28, 1908, two of them were married at his home at 28 Monroe Place, Brooklyn—Frances Mildred Shepperson to Willard E. Boileau, and Mary Clement Shepperson to George Arthur Crabb.

He had followed the education of his nephew Carlos, Charles S. Peabody, with great satisfaction. Carlos was graduated from Harvard in 1902. From there he went to Columbia. Later he studied at the Beaux-Arts, in Paris, where he won distinction as first in his class. Returning to the United States, he became an outstanding architect. His uncle procured his services in designing several campus buildings.

Peabody liked children and young people. He knew every child in Lake George by name, it was said, and he used to bow to these young friends on the street. He liked to escort some young guest on a walk about the grounds and would refer to fascinating ferns and wild flowers by their scientific names. One day he was striding along with a little girl whose parents were calling on him. He pointed out all the shrubs and trees. When they reached a certain beautiful spot, he turned to his young companion and said gravely, "And this is where the fairies were." That cemented their complete understanding and they continued their beguiling journey.

With the Trasks Peabody continued to enjoy an intimate and stimulating friendship. With them he was at his best. He visited them frequently at Yaddo; when he was not there, he had word from them at least once a day.

He and the Trasks discussed all kinds of topics of an educational or philanthropic nature. Although they did not always agree as to just what should be done, they were in fundamental accord in their humanitarian aims, and especially in their desire for the coming of peace on earth. At the dinner table, Katrina would expostulate with him, "Now, Foster . . .!"[9] Trask and Peabody often referred to her as the "senior partner."[10]

Katrina was forced to spend much of her time in a darkened room. The hemorrhage in one eye suffered in 1905 had caused failing sight. She was still busy, however, writing her plays. The theme was usually an heroic one dealing with matters of the spirit. Sometimes one of her characters would be a magnified representation of her husband or of Peabody. Her friend Peabody was often clearly in her mind's eye when she was drawing a word-portrait of a knight.

9. Interviews with the Reverend J. Howard Melish.
10. Interviews with Miss Allena Gilbert Pardee, July, 1944.

5.

Spencer Trask was now a man of sixty-five. Like Peabody, he had been somewhat inactive in business for the past several years. In the summer of 1909, he had suffered an accident which had caused him the loss of an eye. Otherwise, however, he was robust and in good shape.

Trask was a man of many interests. He was one of the founders of Teachers College, Columbia University, and he had continued to take a special interest in that institution and to aid in its development. He was a founder of the National Arts Club in New York City. He established St. Christina's Home for children at Saratoga and contributed large funds for its maintenance; this was but one of the many humanitarian works which he sponsored. At the same time he was a member of many social clubs and had an active social life.

Cheerful in spirit, he enjoyed life. He was deeply devoted to his family and friends. He took pride and pleasure in his wife's literary work. On January 22, 1909, he was a member of the fashionable audience at the German Theatre in New York City when Katrina's best known play, *The Little Town of Bethlehem*, was first presented at a benefit performance.

For several years he had been a member of the Saratoga Springs Commission to develop the healthful properties of the Spa. To this work he devoted much time.

At Christmas time in 1909 the Yaddo household enjoyed the usual festivities of the season. Carols rang out over the frosty air. The halls were decked with evergreens, and an atmosphere of joy pervaded the place. Spencer and Katrina and their household went through the usual activity of exchanging gifts and wishing all a Merry Christmas and a Happy New Year.

The days slipped by until New Year's Eve when there was again the exchange of felicitations and the spirit of good cheer and happiness. Late that day[11] Spencer received word that made it necessary for him to go to New York for a conference regarding the Saratoga Commission. He drove into town, boarded the Montreal Express, and retired to a drawing room. At eight o'clock the next morning, near Croton, a freight train, running at thirty miles an hour, crashed into the rear car in which Mr. Trask was riding. The train jerked to a halt and trainmen rushed back to the car. They made their way into the drawing room and found Mr. Trask, who had been dressing, fatally injured. He died within a few minutes. Near him lay his pocketbook in which they found the motto which he always carried with him, "A man's life consisteth not in the abundance of things which he possesseth."

His brother-in-law, Acosta Nichols, on receiving the tragic news, hurried to the scene of the accident, and took charge of arrangements. Mrs. Trask was in a state of collapse and physicians feared for her condition. Peabody showed a remarkable fortitude as he attended to the many details. His niece, Carlos's wife, who was visiting him at the time, said he sat at his desk with a white, mask-like face, taking care of messages. It seemed unbelievable to him that Spencer, who had been in the prime of life, was gone.

The body was cremated and the ashes were buried beside those of Trask's children and his father in Greenwood Cemetery, Brooklyn.[12] Memorial services were held at the Church of the Ascension in New York City under

---

11. He was in the habit of going to New York about twice a week, but he usually took a later train.
12. A memorial stone was later placed by the family in the Yaddo burial ground.

the auspices of the National Arts Club. The town of Saratoga Springs, wishing to honor the man who had done so much to revivify its healing waters, later placed a memorial fountain, "Spirit of Life," in the center of the public park.

CHAPTER XV

Saratoga Springs Commissioner; Shepard's Last Days

SPENCER TRASK LEFT HIS ENTIRE ESTATE IN TRUST FOR his wife. He named as executors Mrs. Trask, George Foster Peabody, and Kate's brother, George Nichols. Although he had made a large fortune, he had also spent lavishly. He did not leave great wealth, though the income was many thousands a year. He had numerous commitments to philanthropy and the arts. His wife also had her commitments to humanitarian causes, and their combined obligations of this nature ran to a large total. The Yaddo estate,[1] too, though partially productive, was costly.

Kate Trask had a clear head for business. Her husband and Peabody used to say that she had great acumen in meeting a financial problem. But she was ill and almost blind, and unable to meet the burdens of the estate. Peabody, as an executor and a friend, assumed heavy responsibilities. He accepted a temporary partnership at Spencer Trask and Company to carry on the business details, and assisted Mrs. Trask in making the many readjustments. He also, with some reluctance, consented to serve in Mr. Trask's stead on the Saratoga Springs Commission.

1. He left it in trust at his wife's request. They had decided to perpetuate Yaddo by the establishment of an artists' retreat after the death of both. This plan was not generally known at the time.

His new duties required him to be in Saratoga much of the time. He therefore took a house, which he later bought, at 19 Circular Street, Saratoga Springs. Here he set up what he called "headquarters."

His secretary at the time, Mr. L. W. Noland, describes Mr. Peabody's office.[2] The desk was piled high with correspondence, pamphlets, bulletins. How he found his way to the various pieces is a mystery; yet he could put his hand on any pamphlet without delay. He continued his practice of mailing copies of books, magazines and newspapers to friends, and at times the office looked like a parcel-mailing business. He would dictate letters far into the night, an average of about fifty a day, many of them two and three pages, single-spaced.

It was impossible for him to keep up his establishment at 28 Monroe Place, Brooklyn. In May, 1911, he leased the place. Later he sold it. He kept his estate on Lake George for a few years,[3] but never again entertained on the old lavish scale.

2.

Amid the pressure of duties following the death of Spencer Trask, Peabody was informed of a rumor that the government was bringing suit against him in connection with the sale, years before, of certain Western coal lands. The matter had to do with the question of validity of patents. Newspapers took up the rumor and carried a story. Peabody was indignant. On reading the newspaper story, he wrote a letter to *The World*, dated February 14, 1910. His statement was firm, denying that any suit had

---

2. Interview with Mr. L. W. Noland, President, Saratoga National Bank, June 24, 1940.
3. He sold Abenia in the winter of 1914-1915 and moved some of his belongings to a small bachelor-sized cottage at Lake George for the summer of 1915. (Letter to a London friend, Lord Moulton, July 15, 1915. A copy is in the Yaddo files.)

ever been brought against him by the United States. He said that in the past summer he had been informed by his counsel that an intimation had been made that unless the executors of General Palmer, Peabody, D. C. Dodge, and others were willing to make a payment of money, a suit would be brought. He had heard nothing further. He said that if the Government had not established, and had apparently not been able to establish, the invalidity of the patents issued by the Government, and if the patents were now in effect, he did not see the basis of any claim against the companies which had developed the mines in accord with the patents. He added, however, that if the representatives of the Government thought the Government had a claim they were entitled to present such a claim in the courts.

No action was taken against him in the courts, and the matter received no further review in the newspapers.

3.

At the time of Trask's death, plans were under way to re-establish Saratoga Springs as a health resort. A commission had been appointed to study the situation and make a report. Trask was chairman of the commission and had been giving the matter his careful attention. Serving with him were Edward M. Shepard and Frank N. Godfrey. At Governor Hughes's urgent request, Peabody accepted the chairmanship made vacant by Trask's death.

Under Peabody's chairmanship, the Saratoga Springs Commission made a detailed study of the situation, and several years later, it submitted a report. It found that the natural properties of the Springs had been exhausted through the draining off of certain gases, and that, if the State wished to restore the waters to their former condition, it would need to acquire various parcels of land in the neighborhood and develop these lands for the minerals they contained. This report was submitted to Governor Dix, who approved the findings and placed the matter before the legislature. Eventually an appropriation was made, a European expert was engaged to come over and test the waters, and the land needed for development[4] was purchased.

4.

Peabody and Edward Morse Shepard had been intimate friends for more than thirty years. They were neighbors in Brooklyn and at Lake George, and moved in the same circle of close friends. They were in almost daily contact. Peabody had a profound respect for Shepard's abilities. He liked the analytical quality of Shepard's mind. In his friend he always saw a potential leader in national politics. In 1910, he again promoted Shepard for office—this time, for that of senator. But opposition appeared within the party, and Shepard withdrew his name.

There was a plaintive note in Shepard's letter to Peabody in December, 1910. He had been depressed, he said, and had waited to write until he felt more cheerful. His friend reassured him as best he could.

The following summer, Shepard contracted pleurisy, and suffered complications. At first he rallied, and his family thought he was gaining ground. But a few hours later, a relapse occurred and on July 29, 1911, he died at Erlowest. Funeral services were held on Tuesday, August 2nd at St. James Church, Lake George. The following day services were held in Brooklyn at Holy Trinity, where he had been a vestryman, and he was laid to rest in Greenwood Cemetery.

---

4. This will be discussed later.

Thus, within two years, Peabody lost the companionship of three persons who had been very near to him in all his life and work—Spencer Trask, General Palmer, and now Edward M. Shepard.

During the time of readjustments after Spencer Trask's death, Peabody had found it necessary to give up some of his activities on various educational boards. He was unable to give the time that he wished to the American Church Institute. A period of two years went by between his visits to Hampton Institute. He regretted this situation keenly. Nevertheless, he was never far from any of these enterprises in spirit, and his contacts were maintained without serious interference.[5]

In 1909, before Trask's death, he had given up his office as treasurer of the General Education Board. He had continued his membership on the Board, however. From the beginning, he had enjoyed the association with men like Buttrick, Page, Shaw, and Rockefeller, Jr. He had had a long working relationship with F. T. Gates in connection with investments. The two men were friendly, though they did not always see eye to eye.

The General Education Board had been established upon a basis of help to existing organizations. It recognized the work of accredited agencies. Peabody's own benefactions were also made through accredited organizations, but essentially he was a pioneer, a promoter and builder, a man who enjoyed the personal relationship with the educational object which he was supporting. As time passed, he believed that the Board, now more and more channeling its work through organizations, no longer needed the kind of contribution that he had to make.[6]

5. Correspondence in Yaddo files.
6. *Ibid.*

An incident in February, 1912, may have hastened his resignation. He had hoped to interest Gates further in the work of the University of Georgia. One of the prominent alumni wrote Mr. Gates inviting him to visit the University while in the South. Gates replied, sending his regrets. Peabody was troubled, because he believed that the visit would have been an inspiration.[7]

On March 15, 1912, he tendered his resignation to the Chairman of the Board. He stated frankly that he believed the present policy of the Board called mainly for scrutiny by officials of the institutions of higher learning requesting funds, rather than for the sort of "special equipment" which he had. He thought others could do the work as well as he. At the same time, he expressed his appreciation for the honor and privilege of having served with the distinguished members of the Board.

His resignation was accepted with regret. Mr. Gates wrote a letter expressing his sense of personal loss and voicing the hope that they might continue to see each other often. Dr. Wallace Buttrick sent a message of warm appreciation.[8]

7. *Ibid.*
8. *Ibid.*

CHAPTER XVI

Peabody and Wilson

PEABODY'S LIFE AFTER 1912 IS MARKED BY A CLOSE RE-lationship with the Wilson Administration. In his role as "statesman without portfolio," it is believed that he had a considerable influence upon the country's affairs.

It is not indicated when Peabody first met Woodrow Wilson, but Wilson's name is prominent in his files from 1909 on. In the summer of 1909, the Southern Education Board was holding its annual meeting at Mr. Peabody's home on Lake George. One day the guests were in recess on the piazza. The discussion turned to the 1912 campaign possibilities. Conversation buzzed for a few minutes. Someone then turned to Walter H. Page, and asked him his opinion regarding the most suitable candidate. His reply was "Woodrow Wilson."[1]

Peabody's interest in Wilson, kindled by the discussion at Abenia, was intensified in the period between 1910 and 1912. The latter months of 1911 and the first months of 1912 found him in correspondence with Page, Henry Morgenthau, Oswald G. Villard, William G. McAdoo and others in the interest of the nomination of Wilson. During

1. Peabody Papers, Yaddo files. The group that day included David F. Houston; Chancellor Kirkland of Vanderbilt University; E. A. Alderman, President of the University of Virginia; Robert C. Ogden; Frank Chambers, executive of Rogers-Peet and Company; Philander Claxton, Commissioner of Education of the United States Office of Education. (Correspondence in Yaddo files.)

the spring of 1912, he was in touch with the Wilsons personally.

He awaited the Baltimore convention with eager concern. He had not felt such enthusiasm since the campaign of 1884. He hoped, but was not entirely confident that Wilson would be nominated. On June 12, 1912, he wrote Governor Wilson:[2]

> ... Mr. McCombs and Mr. McAdoo each write me they think I should be there and I am now trying to arrange it.
>
> The time is particularly awkward for me because I am to lose then the Secretary of this Commission and I must be in Washington July first. As to this latter also I hope for a chance to talk with you beforehand— I have been summoned by Senator Clapp as Chm. of Sub Comm. on Privileges & Elections respecting the funds for the 1904 campaign—when I was Treas'r of the Nat'l Comm.
>
> May I ask therefore if it will be convenient for you to see me on the 21st, 22d or 23d if I go to Princeton? I should like a fairly full conference if not asking too much—I want to post you a bit on some political inside history.
>
> I think I wrote to Mr. McAdoo to get in touch with Mr. Hollis. Will you kindly return his letter.
>
> I am Sincerely Yours
>
> *George Foster Peabody.*

At this time it was rumored that Peabody himself might be considered for high office, but he denied the truth of the reports. He told his brother Royal that he was too radical for the party, and that, furthermore, he did not wish to hold office.

On the eve of the convention Peabody had a talk with Wilson. He wrote later:

---

2. Woodrow Wilson Papers, File II, Library of Congress. Courtesy of Mrs. Woodrow Wilson.

Maryland Club
June 23, 1912

The Hon. Woodrow Wilson
Sea Girt, N. J.

My Dear Governor Wilson

    I must thank you for the honor of your so gracious hospitality to me and the confidence I appreciated.

    I must also thank you for the word of masterful apprehension which your telegram to Mr. Bryan gave forth as a true prelude to the leadership which he will I feel resign to your abler handling—I must congratulate the country on all it means to have one who can see and knowing has the courage to do and dare.

    I found a fine state of enthusiasm and courage aroused by it here altho Senator Gore was evidently not so ready to put away the idea of harmony expressed by having both sides speak their discordant words—he is loyal however—I feel that the lines will now be drawn clearly and you alone could have done that. It is an accomplishment worth while. I cannot but think you will in consequence be nominated and thus be the Leader but surely the country will now take your measure and call for your service.

    Sincerely yours,
George Foster Peabody

After the nomination of Wilson, Peabody was active in his support. He was an important factor in the New York State Campaign. His efforts brought letters of thanks from William F. McCombs, Chairman of the National Committee, and from William G. McAdoo, Vice-Chairman. McAdoo discussed matters with Peabody and referred to the latter's "sincerity of view and purpose."[3]

He received the news of the Election returns with deep satisfaction. Wilson had carried forty states. Roosevelt, the Progressive Party candidate, had won in six states; while Taft, the Republican nominee, had carried only two states.

Thinking that a rest would be good for Wilson after

---

3. Correspondence in Yaddo files.

the strenuous campaign, Peabody wrote to offer the hospitality of Abenia for the month of November. The place would be quiet and private, he said. His menage would be there, but he himself must be away. The Wilsons did not accept the invitation, however.[4]

The correspondence with Wilson continued. Peabody wrote the president-elect on a number of subjects with which he had long been familiar, such as the currency problem. He sent a copy of the report of the Indianapolis Monetary Convention. He wrote[5] on January 30, 1913:

> My dear Governor Wilson:
> I well know that your mind is constantly incubating on the question of the currency. I therefore venture to enclose to you copies of letters which I have just written to Professor Laughlin and Professor Willis . . . I am sending to you from my office a copy which I am glad to find of the full report of the Monetary Commission. I am sure that you have referred to it in your studies of the question. . . .
> . . . I am expecting to be in New York on Saturday evening and am hoping while there for a few days to have opportunity for some conference with Mr. McCombs and Mr. Morgenthau.
> I cannot even at the risk of too long a communication refrain from adding a few words respecting my unlimited admiration and enthusiasm for the marvelous insight and perspicacity with which you diagnose [the] situation. . .

One of Mr. Peabody's important contributions was his sponsorship of the publishing of Wilson's essays, under the title of *The New Freedom*. Arrangements were made with Doubleday, Page and Company. On January 21, 1913, William Bayard Hale, of the editorial staff, in sending Peabody a set of the page proofs, wrote that Wilson had made his final corrections and that the shop

---

4. Woodrow Wilson Papers, File II, Library of Congress. Courtesy of Mrs. Woodrow Wilson.
5. *Ibid.*

was straining every nerve to get the volume ready. The book was a re-affirmation of the principles of the president-elect; it was his pledge to the people on the eve of his inauguration.[6]

Mexico was at this time in a troubled state, and there was talk of this country's becoming involved in her affairs. Peabody, writing to Wilson, offered to put him in touch with D. C. Brown, a man prominent in Mexican railway and mining developments, who knew conditions in Mexico at first hand. There is nothing to indicate whether Wilson received from Peabody's acquaintances or from Peabody himself any information about Mexico.

Desirous that Wilson discuss the matter of peace policy in the inaugural, Peabody wrote:

> Feb. 17, 1913
>
> I venture the further intrusion of the most earnest hope that your inaugural may make reference to your complete sympathy with the peace view as opposed to the militaristic view. I venture this expression not that I have any doubt, for it is not so probable that there will be occasion for a special message relating to this question, but I merely want to do what I may to emphasize the great moral support which I am sure you will find coming to you from all over the country in connection with your announcement of such a position.
>
> I am sure Mr. Carnegie knows whereof he speaks in his reference to the organized effort for battleships and increased military expenditure.
>
> I am
> Very respectfully yours,
> *George Foster Peabody*

There are numerous notes of thanks from Wilson in the files of Yaddo. It is clear that Peabody's encouragement meant much to him.

It is interesting to observe these two friends. They were both products of the ante bellum South and its

---

6. Correspondence in Yaddo files.

traditions. In both were ingrained the tenets of Calvinism. While Woodrow Wilson had pursued his studies in college and university, Peabody had been unable, because of poverty, to enjoy these advantages. Through reading and practical experience, he had gained a broad knowledge of political science. Their chief common interest lay in political science; they shared the desire to further progressive ideas of government. As friends, they were reserved; but there was a warmth and graciousness in their relationship.

Peabody's files indicate much exchange of correspondence with other leaders prior to inauguration day. In answer to a letter from William Jennings Bryan, he wrote:

Jan. 28, 1913

My dear Mr. Bryan

It was good of you to take the time to write me and express to me your kind sympathy and interest. I feel greatly honored and I beg to assure you that I shall highly value any opportunity that I may have to confer with you when you are North.

I feel so deeply interested in the incoming administration and all that it means to the Country that I am led to regret that so many obligations which I have hereabout will prevent my spending the time at Washington, for I should so enjoy the opportunity of conferring with my many friends who would be associated in the work of assuring "The New Freedom" to the Country.

I share with many the glow of hope cast by the American's assertion respecting your being Secretary of State. I recognize, of course, that it was not authoritative, but I am sure that the general thrill that went throughout the Country was an influence for better politics. . . .

I am glad to believe from the indications that I have that Gov. Wilson is most hospitable to any thought I have respecting the situation and I assure you that I shall be glad at any time to express myself respecting any situation which might be helped thereby. . . .

I trust that Mrs. Bryan is getting the good rest which I fear you are not doing even in quiet Florida.
I am,
                    Very truly yours,[7]

March 4, 1913, was a significant day in the eyes of the country. Woodrow Wilson took the oath of office as President. Immediately thereafter, he was faced with staggering issues in both domestic and foreign affairs.

From Saratoga Springs, Peabody watched the new President with the keenest interest and was in frequent touch with him directly and through administration leaders. He was eager to know what cabinet members would be appointed. He was in favor of William Jennings Bryan for Secretary of State, and was glad when the appointment was made.

Early in the administration Peabody himself was offered the post of Secretary of the Treasury. He was troubled, and after deliberation, wrote in reply:[8]

March 20, 1913
Saratoga Springs
New York

His Excellency
The Honorable Woodrow Wilson
President
Washington, D. C.
My Dear Mr. President

I was deeply moved by the honor you did me in urging reasons for my acceptance of the post offered by the Secretary of the Treasury.

I was led by your forceful words to wonder whether there had been lack of loyalty to you as Leader in my prompt declination, even though it was in obedience to a life-long conviction that I could render my largest quota of Public service outside of the constraints of office.

7. Copy of Mr. Peabody's letter, Peabody Papers, Yaddo files.
8. Woodrow Wilson Papers, File II, Library of Congress. Courtesy of Mrs. Woodrow Wilson.

I therefore have given earnest thought to your so honoring suggestion that my experience, acquaintance and knowledge respecting financial matters, currency reform and progressive politics, gave me peculiar equipment to be the point of contact between Wall Street and this Administration.

I feel the thrill of interest which such opportunity would evoke. I realize that it would not be a sacrifice—in fact no true service could be I think—

I have been in quite excellent health for some time so I may not plead to be excused on that ground.

I am though bound to say to you that I do not believe there is the critical aspect to this call, that would justify my departing from a confirmed belief as to my true line of service—I have therefore advised the Secretary of the Treasury of my regret that I may not avail of the honor and pleasure which the personal association would bring—I trust that I am right in my conclusion that he will find someone to fill the position who by reason of the occupancy will bring an addition to the forces of alert interest to work with you.

I am more enthusiastic than ever respecting your splendid leadership and the great constructive program you have in mind. I am intensely and constantly interested in the furtherance of its every success.

I beg to assure you that I shall rejoice to be able to render any service for which I may have equipment, at any time, and in any way that you might deem helpful.

I trust that you will feel free to call upon me in the same manner that you would if I were officially associated.

I am with high respect
    Very truly yours
       George Foster Peabody[9]

It was with keen interest that he awaited news of the appointment of a Secretary of the Treasury, and he was glad to see Wilson turn to William G. MacAdoo for this post.

Peabody had known MacAdoo for a long time in connection with National Democratic Party matters. They

---

9. *Ibid.*

had worked together in support of Wilson in the recent campaign. He had respect for MacAdoo's abilities in finance and believed he was a good choice. Moreover, he liked MacAdoo and found contacts with him pleasant and genial.

The other cabinet appointments, too, were interesting to Peabody. Through long acquaintance in Democratic circles, he knew most, if not all, of the men appointed. He corresponded with most[10] of them and made it a practice to send them copies of reports, clippings from newspapers, and other material.

The date when Peabody first met Col. E. M. House, Wilson's confidential adviser, is not revealed in the files. It is clear that he knew House well in the early part of Wilson's first administration. He wrote to him in regard to the political standing and abilities of many upstate Democratic leaders. As time went on, the two men often exchanged letters and had conferences. It is true that House consulted many other prominent persons before drawing his own conclusions, but he certainly gave weight to Mr. Peabody's estimates of persons and measures.

Three outstanding problems faced the new administration—the tariff, banking and currency, and industrial abuses. Another issue, the international complication with Mexico, was soon added.

Peabody, who had long advocated free trade, hoped for sweeping tariff revision. Wilson was not a strong free trader, however. The Underwood tariff fell short of Peabody's hopes.

As for currency reform, this had been on the carpet through previous administrations; there had been, in particular, many attempts to make the currency more elastic. Wilson knew the political history of the question,

---

10. Peabody Papers, Yaddo files.

but he was anxious to have a fuller knowledge of its background and a more thorough grasp of the issues involved. Many economists and financiers sent him material and made suggestions; among them was Peabody. Under Wilson's leadership, a bill was drafted by Senator Robert L. Owen and Representative Carter Glass in behalf of banking and currency revision.[11] It was passed by Congress.

The Federal Reserve System, under the terms of the Federal Reserve Act, provided a decentralized system of banks under Federal control. Its aims were to provide elastic currency to stabilize bank reserves and to mobilize credit. In keeping with these aims, it authorized the setting up of regional banks which would pool reserves. It provided a device for re-discounting notes and called for the gradual retirement of national bank notes in favor of Federal Reserve Bank notes.

The Federal Reserve Act represented a culmination of the long controversy which had troubled bankers and business men for more than a generation. In a letter dated December 26, 1913, MacAdoo expressed to Peabody his jubilant belief that the measure would be accepted promptly by the leading bankers of the country.

Soon afterwards the Federal Reserve System was established and regional banks were opened in accordance with the plan. One of the regional banks was set up in New York. Wilson appointed Pierre Jay as chairman of the board of directors, and Peabody deputy chairman.

The heavy responsibilities of the New York Federal Reserve Bank officials required their presence at meetings at least every other week, and usually each week for several days at a time. The distinguished group of bankers

---

11. As presented to Congress, the bill was a joint product of many counsellors including William G. MacAdoo; H. Parker Willis, the economist; Paul Warburg, banker; Colonel House; and the President.

met in the conference room and discussed policies and procedures. Peabody made an important contribution to the discussions. As a result of his long experience with monetary reform in connection with the Indianapolis Monetary Convention, and later in relation to the Aldrich-Vreeland Commission, he had a great deal of information at his fingertips.[12] He served on several committees including the executive committee, the building committee, and the committee on welfare of the staff. During Pierre Jay's absence over extended periods, he served as chairman.

The task of the Federal Reserve Bank directors was a difficult one. From the day of opening, critical domestic and international issues affected the system. The European war, which began several months before the Federal Reserve went into operation, brought shifting financial conditions which called for the steadying influence of the banks and for keen penetration on the part of the Federal Reserve Bank directors. The entrance of the United States into World War I in 1917 necessitated the floating of war loans and bond issues amounting to billions of dollars. Public trust must be encouraged in the new system. New York being the financial center of the country, the New York Federal Reserve Bank had an enormous responsibility.

Peabody served on the board of the New York Federal Reserve Bank from 1914 until 1922. He made it one of his chief concerns. His membership made it necessary for him to give up his duties as chairman of the Saratoga Springs Commission. Every other week and sometimes oftener he took the trip from Saratoga Springs to New York to attend the board meetings.[13]

12. Interview with Mr. Pierre Jay, April 16, 1941.
13. Correspondence in his files.

2.

A third great issue tackled by Wilson was the problem of industrial abuses and monopolistic practices. Under his leadership, Congress instituted several reforms, among them the Federal Trade Commission and the Clayton Act. Peabody was offered an appointment on the Federal Trade Commission, but he declined. He was, however, glad to see these reforms inaugurated. He favored regulation of monopoly and the government control of public utilities, and thought the measures now taken were a step in the right direction.

A fourth problem of the Wilson administration, destined to be one of the most vexing, was a matter of particular concern to Peabody. This was the Mexican situation, which became acute just before Wilson took office.

For several decades foreign capital had exploited the natural resources of Mexico with the result that there was a great deal of unrest and discontent. A state of revolution existed. Eighty-year-old Diaz was deposed by Francisco Madero, who was in turn overthrown by his commander-in-chief, Huerta, in 1913. The stormy career of Huerta was ended in flight to Europe, and a new struggle for power began between his successor Carranza and the colorful Villa. Interests in the United States were threatened by these revolutionary activities. Wilson, faced with crisis, urged a policy of "watchful waiting." After Wilson authorized recognition by the United States of the de facto government of Carranza on October 9, 1915, the resentful Villa seized and shot a number of Americans traveling with passports. This called for a punitive expedition which brought the United States to the brink of war with Mexico. Troops massed on the border were withdrawn, however, on February 5, 1917, because the entrance of the United States into the World War seemed imminent.

Peabody's feelings regarding Wilson's policy in the matter were mixed. He had long felt a special interest in the people of Mexico and had sympathized with them in their desire for self-improvement. On the other hand the continued revolutions threatened devastation to his holdings. On January 16, 1914, in a letter to Congressman F. H. Gillett, he wrote:

> I am at present connected with large interests there which have some twenty-five different plants located in fourteen different states of Mexico—I have, myself, a large pecuniary interest in these investments. In fact the bulk of what I have not invested in Education and similar permanent work is still invested in these Mexican enterprises. . . .

Yet he believed that Wilson was right in taking the stand of "watchful waiting," and added,

> I believe that President Wilson has taken the only course that could possibly lead to the permanent security of investments and a course that will cost far less in life, almost infinitely less, than any other that he could have taken.[14]

Non-intervention was in keeping with his belief in neutrality and in peace, and he voiced his approval to Wilson and to other friends in government circles. The continued state of instability in Mexico through the early 1920's was to cause him serious personal losses.

---

14. Copies of Peabody's letters, Yaddo files.

CHAPTER XVII

The Busy War Years

GREATLY DISTURBED OVER THE EMBROILMENTS IN MEXICO and fearful lest the country be drawn into European War, Peabody now bent his energies to the cause of peace. From his office at 19 Circular Street, Saratoga Springs, he sent letter after letter to administration leaders and to his colleagues in the peace movement.

From boyhood he had been opposed to war. He had never forgotten the devastation in Columbus on that day in April, 1865. The Spanish-American War had further crystallized his convictions and had taught him to regard imperialism as a sure precursor of conflict. In fact, his denunciation of imperialistic war in 1898 had called down upon him a good deal of criticism. During the first few years of the century, he had identified himself with peace organizations. He had long been a member of the American Peace Society; like Carnegie, he was a vice president of that organization. He was a member[1] of the International Committee on a Durable Peace. He was in touch with such leading advocates of peace as Jane Addams, Dr. Nicholas Murray Butler, Mrs. Fannie Fern Andrews, and Andrew Carnegie.

His zeal in the cause of peace was no greater than that of Katrina Trask. For many years the central theme of her writings had been peace. Her play, *In the Vanguard*,

---

1. He was also a member of the New York Peace Society of which Andrew Carnegie was president.

came off the press in 1913, on the eve of the Mexican and European crises. It was like an omen; it sounded a warning to take heed before it was too late. Through arrangements made by Mr. Peabody, this little volume was sent to individuals and groups in all parts of the country. A few months later, the American Peace League awarded to Mrs. Trask the medal for the most notable effort of the year by an individual in behalf of peace.[2]

Everyone is familiar with the train of events between August, 1914, and April, 1917. Although the United States at first professed neutrality, she was increasingly enmeshed in the conflict in Europe as the days passed and as she attempted to keep the channels of trade open to her vessels. The dangerous state of affairs with Great Britain was matched in seriousness by Germany's submarine attacks on American vessels in reprisal against Great Britain's embargo.

Peabody hoped that Wilson would do everything in his power to curb the militarist spirit and keep the country at peace. In a letter to Colonel House dated November 20, 1914, he expressed himself to this effect. In reply, House wrote that he knew Wilson would in the end throw his influence in the desired direction.

The efforts of Peabody and other peace leaders served as some restraint against war, but they were vain in the face of developments. By the beginning of 1915, complications over the loss of American lives in ship sinkings had brought the United States near the brink of war. Nevertheless the pacifists kept up their work.

Peabody stated his views in a letter to the *Evening Post*. Laurence Godkin, commenting on this letter, wrote

2. Peabody wrote to J. H. Scattergood on May 24, 1924: "I have always felt that it (*In the Vanguard*) was a real factor in developing the sentiment which was back of President Wilson's delay in entering the war. . ." (Copy of his letter is in the Yaddo files.)

that it was inconceivable that a man as wise and sound as Peabody should express himself in such a way[3]—that if Peabody's views were carried to their logical conclusion, German militarism would control Europe.

Believing that one way to curb war would be to scrap the Navy, he wrote Franklin D. Roosevelt, Secretary of the Navy:[4]

Sept. 8, 1915

Dear Mr. Secretary:-

Thank you very much for the remembrance of me in ordering a copy of "The Economic World" containing your discussion of "The Cost of the United States Navy" mailed to me. I shall take pleasure in reading it at the earliest opportunity. I very much hope that someone will compile the data as to how much money the United States Government has spent on the Navy in the fifty years which have elapsed since the Civil War. My own strong conviction is, you know, that if we had not had the *Oregon* and other battleships, the stigma of the Spanish War would never have been laid upon this country. I am personally a believer in the obligation of non-resistance upon the man or woman who follows Christ's teachings, and also am completely convinced that it is the one way in which ultimate and true victory could be obtained from such war-mad countries as Germany and some others in Europe—I mean really, countries led by war-mad individuals in control of the government. I am quite clear that the early history of this country showed that the theory and practice of William Penn in Pennsylvania and General Oglethorpe in Georgia, proved that such methods were the only ones calculated to keep peaceful relations with our aboriginal inhabitants, who were continually driven back and compelled to give up the lands which had afforded them and their ancestors a living. . . .

It is not known when Wilson first became convinced that the United States must take part in the war. His

---

3. Peabody Papers, Yaddo files. Copy of his letter, dated January 15, 1915.
4. Copy of Mr. Peabody's letter is in Yaddo files.

THE BUSY WAR YEARS

secretary, Joseph P. Tumulty, said he believed it from the beginning. On July 21, 1915, he wrote to the Secretaries of War and Navy seeking their advice on a program of national defense. In January, 1916, he set out for the Middle West on a tour to speak in behalf of preparedness. In spite of Peabody's esteem for Wilson, he criticized the President's policy in this respect.

Early in 1916, an event occurred which placed a strain upon Peabody's credulity. On February 10, Lindley M. Garrison, Secretary of War, resigned. Shortly afterward, Wilson turned to Newton D. Baker, who was a pacifist, as a successor. An exchange of correspondence between Peabody and Baker clarified the situation. Baker said that the question now seemed to be "how much" rather than "whether" the country should arm. Since the United States had an army and a navy, they should be as good as military science could make them, he averred. He defended Wilson's position, asserting that the latter would not favor a military republic.

Baker's explanation appeared logical to Peabody, although he did not agree regarding a military program. He wrote to the Secretary of the Interior in February, 1916:[5]

> I shall be very glad if he [the President] should decide to ask Newton Baker to be Secretary of War, because I believe that would add to the "Counsel" which does seem desirable. I have never been able to understand why the President declined absolutely to meet and discuss with the strong peace advocates among his enthusiastic followers, when it was manifest to the whole country that he was continually getting the impress of the strong Army and Navy people, who were, most of them, at heart his bitter opponents under any conditions. I am personally confident that if he had continued to uphold the position taken in his speeches at Mobile, Swarthmore and Philadelphia instead of taking

5. Copy of his letter is in Yaddo files.

the new departure of his Manhattan Club speech, he could have rallied two thirds of the countryside to enthusiastic approval. . . .

War was narrowly averted early in 1916 when an American vessel was sunk by German U-boats in the English channel. An ultimatum was sent to Germany requesting her to desist from submarine warfare against the passenger and freight carrying vessels. She complied on May 4, and retained her pledge during the remainder of 1916. Meanwhile, however, President Wilson came out aggressively for preparedness. Marching in parades, speaking on important occasions, he urged a military and naval program adequate to national defense.

In the face of the preparedness program of the administration, the pacifists redoubled their efforts. Peabody himself spoke at a dinner, on March 8, 1916, in honor of Ambassador Morgenthau, recently returned from Europe. Addressing several hundred persons there gathered, he denounced a peace which rested upon arms.

On July 21, 1916, he wrote to an acquaintance:[6]

> I am utterly opposed to any Army or Navy and cannot co-operate as a voter and a taxpayer in furthering movements that may lead to support of Army and Navy. . . .

He endorsed the work of the League to Enforce Peace, but said he wanted peace without force. During the same period, he became a prominent member of the American Neutral Conference Committee, whose aims were to support the government in a move to call, or to co-operate in, a conference of neutral nations which should offer mediation to belligerents and help form the basis of a permanent peace. A few months later, as chairman, he gave a dinner to the members of the American Neutral Conference, and included among his guests Mrs. Henry

---

6. Copy of his letter is in Yaddo files.

Villard, Rabbi and Mrs. Stephen S. Wise, Frank W. Kelsey, Amos Pinchot, Rebecca Shelley, Angela Morgan, and many others.[7]

Through Mrs. Fannie Fern Andrews of the American School Peace League, Peabody kept up a barrage of circulars to schools and organizations throughout the country. He sent her a large number of copies of Mrs. Trask's peace play, *The Conquering Army*. Mrs. Andrews later reported the favorable comments on the poem which she had received.

Although Peabody's hope that Wilson would maintain peace was now dim, he retained his great admiration for the President. The difference over policy in this respect in no way lessened his esteem. He therefore regarded Wilson as the suitable candidate for nomination in the campaign of 1916. He endorsed the slogan of the Democratic Party—"He kept us out of war." Several times in the course of the summer Wilson wrote to thank him.

During the campaign he wrote letters, circulated literature, and was in personal contact with members of the Democratic Party. He contributed at least $10,000 to pay campaign expenses.[8] In November, with the re-election of Wilson, there was still hope, though a faint one, that peace might be maintained.

The first months of 1917 saw Peabody continuing his pacifist stand. On January 30, presiding at a meeting at Carnegie Hall, he spoke of the horrors of war.[9]

By the early spring of 1917, matters between the

---

7. During this period his long-standing friendship with Andrew Carnegie deepened. Peabody on several occasions had expressed to friends his appreciation for Carnegie. They had long worked together in the peace movement. On May 18, 1916, Carnegie autographed a photograph of himself and sent it to Peabody with his best wishes.
8. The receipt, dated December 21, 1916, is in his files.
9. Peabody Papers, Yaddo.

United States and Germany had reached an acute stage. There remained only the final steps. On April 2, at 8:30 in the evening, Wilson rode under armed guard to the Capitol, where he addressed the assembled throng in the House, summing up the situation and asking Congress to declare a state of belligerency. On April 6, Congress sent the declaration of war to the President, and he signed it the same day. Thus the United States entered the great conflict.

In spite of his support of Wilson, Peabody could not accept the policy of war as justifiable. On April 21 he wrote to Daniel Kiefer, of the National Single Tax League:[10]

> War [is] the wrong way to settle any great question, it being inhuman of necessity, and alas it is inherently and necessarily undemocratic. . . .
> I have believed that if England and France had had the grace to be truly democratic, and disarmed, and thus emphasized to the German people their lack of animosity and their confidence in the true basis of human brotherhood, that the German people would have restrained and finally overthrown Prussian militaristic dynastic power.

In further correspondence with Mr. Kiefer, he wrote:

> May 12, 1917
> I have the profoundest conviction as to the *wickedness* of war . . *defensive as well as offensive,* and I cannot justify the United States nor England nor France in killing others because Germany began to kill them, nor can I justify Germany in killing. . . .

Again, on June 16, 1917, he wrote to Mr. Kiefer:

> I personally still believe that if France and Belgium had had the *grace not to resist Germany* but allow the German devastators to march over them without resistance it would have been but a few weeks before, and with an expenditure of only a hundred thousand lives that the German soldiers thoroughly trained as they

---

10. Copy of Mr. Peabody's letter is in Yaddo files.

are to obey would have revolted, and instead of millions of lives and no results we should have had Permanent Peace because of the awakening of the German conscience and the dethronement of Hohenzollerns from within the Empire. I have to admit, however, that the President's indictment of Germany with the light we now have seems to be a marvelously concise and accurate one.[11]

Since Congress had actually declared war, however, Peabody believed that the Government should be supported in its undertaking. Mrs. Trask joined him in this view and was quoted in the *New York Times*[12] as saying that though her intellectual convictions against war remained the same, the face of the situation had changed and she would remain silent and abide by the act of Congress and the President, and she hoped others would do this in a hearty way.

On August 15, 1917, the *New York Times* carried a caption, "Council Aids Kaiser, Peabody Asserts." The article stated that the former pacifist leader had rebuked the peace body for what he termed abandonment of American methods. Peabody was quoted as favoring the selective service draft as the only democratic method of compulsory recruitment. The following day, an editorial in the *New York Times* carried the heading, "A Pacifist and Yet a Patriot." The editorial said that Peabody had a sense of where a citizen's duty lay when the government had determined upon a course of action.

All this time, Peabody was giving a considerable portion of his thought and time to the Federal Reserve Bank, which was now called upon to handle the Liberty Loan issues thrown open by the Treasury. The first of these issues, amounting to two billion dollars, was oversubscribed; a second, amounting to three billion dollars, was

---

11. Copies of Peabody's letters are in the Yaddo files.
12. *New York Times*, August 4, 1917.

also oversubscribed. Other large loans followed. In these transactions the New York Federal Reserve Bank took a leading part. In order to do his share of the work, Peabody found it necessary to go to New York frequently, remaining in the city for several days at a time.

In an article in the *New York Times*, published on November 28, Peabody urged the public to buy war savings certificates and give them for Christmas presents.

Peabody approved of Wilson's wartime domestic policies. On August 22, 1917, he wired the President:

> Heartiest congratulations on your most necessary action prescribing prices for coal. My experience with coal and railroad properties and their financing enables me to know the vital importance of the action you are taking. I rejoice with the multitudes because you thus are making Democracy safe for the consumers and producing masses.[13]

On November 12, in a speech at Buffalo, Wilson made some rather scathing remarks about pacifists. In answer to a letter from Peabody objecting to his speech, Wilson wrote that he had found it necessary to make a generalization at the time, but regretted that he was unable to single out particular cases of persons deserving consideration.

During the war, Peabody made large purchases of war bonds. Mrs. Trask also purchased bonds and gave liberally to war causes. She moved from the mansion to the smaller house on the place in order to curtail expenses, and devoted to war needs a good part of the proceeds which she received from the sale of the farm's produce.

Mr. Peabody's files for 1917 and 1918 contain many letters to and from cabinet members and congressmen. He had several interviews with the President in Washington, and was at all times in close touch with him. He often exchanged letters with Newton D. Baker. At his

---

13. He received a letter of warm appreciation in reply. (Correspondence in Yaddo files.)

sugggestion, Secretary of War Baker discussed some of the problems of Negro soldiers with the President.

Peabody continued to feel great concern for the problems of the Negro. One day in 1918, he received from Miss Grace B. House, Assistant Principal of Penn School, a letter containing a touching account of a school assembly. She wrote of the dimly lighted hall, gay with flags; of drafted Negroes, fresh from work, still wearing their overalls; of the voices raised in song. In the margin of the letter, Peabody wrote: "Is not this fine. It delights my heart, which however cannot get away from the pathos of it all." He added that the national crisis, when every man was needed, should insure the Negro opportunity.

2.

During the war, Peabody lived in simple style at his home in Saratoga Springs. He went to Yaddo often, and enjoyed assisting the "Ladye of Yaddo" with her benefactions.

In September, 1917, he suffered a great loss in the death of his brother, Royal.

3.

Although engaged in heavy war-time duties at the Federal Reserve Bank, helping to float loans, encouraging subscriptions in bond drives, Peabody was at heart a pacifist. He encouraged Wilson in his early efforts to negotiate peace. When, finally, the war came to an end, he was in hearty accord with the idea of a brotherhood of nations and with Wilson's plan for a League.

While President Wilson was at the Paris Peace Conference early in 1919, Peabody sent him a cablegram:

> Your cooperating leadership in wisely laying foundations Society of Nations has constant interest, sympathy of your friends. I venture congratulations as structure

rises to world view. My profound satisfaction and joy shared by millions, whose faithful prayers attend journey home.

George Foster Peabody

It troubled him to see the change in temper regarding Wilson, and the opposition of certain Senate leaders toward Wilson's proposals. He wrote to Colonel House, who was Commissioner Plenipotentiary at the Peace Conference:

> February 25, 1919
>
> The most pitiable part of it is that both Reed and Borah should have had any such response, not from the Senate, but from the gallery crowd. It means, of course, that many of the Republicans are financing a vigorous opposition, their fear being, in my judgment, the great prestige that President Wilson will achieve and be able to spread over for his Party's benefit. . . .
>
> I was struck with the fine temper of the letter from Mr. Robert R. Reed in the Evening Post of last Saturday, the 22nd, and venture to enclose it because it is the sort of thing you will desire to have in the way of criticism. . . . On the whole I think their stupid temper of attack will prove helpful to the President in gaining firm and steadfast public opinion . . .
>
> I am, with hearty appreciation, and ever increasing admiration for our great President and his right-hand man. . . .

To this letter House replied that the work had indeed been heart-breaking, especially during the past few weeks, when they had been pushing every hour toward the signing of a preliminary peace.

Peabody did everything he could to gather support for Wilson and the League of Nations. He wired Wilson, who was touring the country in behalf of the League:

> May I intrude an expression of my sense of the country's obligation to you for the wonderful series of addresses and for the development of a most valuable sentiment based on thoughtful consideration of the great issues you are presenting in unequalled style.

He was deeply troubled over Wilson's illness, and sent messages of cheer. In November, he heard from Baker that the President was improving but as yet was not able to see more than a few callers.

Peabody sent several letters to Senator Gilbert M. Hitchcock, a spokesman for President Wilson, regarding the League. On January 31, 1920, he wrote:[14]

> I cannot refrain from expressing to you my appreciation of your patience and persistence in your conduct of the Treaty conferences in the Senate. I have been satisfied from the beginning that Senator Lodge did not want the Treaty ratified even with his own extremist statements. I assume that you did not think very highly of Mr. Taft's reservation. It certainly never has appealed to me, but it served splendidly in this case for a demonstration of the true inwardness of this partisan personal performance.
>
> As far as Mr. Lodge is concerned I presume nothing would have made any difference, but as far as the "mild reservationists" are concerned I cannot but feel that Mr. Bryan very unskillfully "butted in" and that it may well be that he did serious harm by selecting the time and manner of his pronouncement . . . Mr. Bryan's irruption at the Jackson Day dinner served to make a great many feel that there should be pressure put upon the President as well as Senator Lodge. . . .

---

14. Copy of Mr. Peabody's letter is in Yaddo files.

CHAPTER XVIII

Post War Readjustments

THE COUNTRY WAS NOW FACED WITH THE DIFFICULTIES OF readjustment after the war. Problems of transportation, banking, tariff, industry, and labor were second only to the great international question of whether the United States should join the League of Nations.

As a part of the post war measures, the several states were invited to send representatives of Governors and Mayors to a conference at Washington. Governor Alfred E. Smith had appointed Peabody as a member of the New York State Reconstruction Commission and now asked him to be a representative at the Washington meeting.[1]

Among the post-war issues, none was more puzzling than the problem of the railroads and their future. As an emergency measure in war time, the government had taken over the railway system. This measure had been received with mixed feelings by the country, but had been generally acknowledged as proper to the conduct of the war. Now that the war was over, everyone had his own ideas as to what should be done. Opinions were expressed by those who favored continued government control, those who favored return to private hands, and those who suggested some form of compromise between the two.

As we have seen, Peabody had long sponsored government control of railroads. He again expressed his views

---

1. Governor Smith found Mr. Peabody's report very helpful. (Mr. Smith's statement to author.)

that public utilities should be in public hands. He favored a plan sponsored by Glenn E. Plumb, counsel for the railroad brotherhoods, which called for the purchase of the railroads by the government and subsequent lease to a national operating corporation made up of officials, labor members and members appointed by the President. He thought this plan had merits in helping to achieve Wilson's ideal of the democratization of industry. Early in May, 1919, he had a conference with Mr. Plumb to discuss the proposal.

In November and December Congress debated other proposals in regard to the railroads. During this time Peabody wrote a number of letters in which he stated his view of the matter. To Carter Glass, for example, he wrote that he would follow if the roads should be returned to private ownership. On November 29, he wrote to William G. MacAdoo urging consideration of a five-year extension of government control.[2]

The disposition of the railroads was settled in February, 1920, when the Esch-Cummins Act was passed. This act returned the railroads to private control, provided for adjustment of rates, prohibited interlocking directorates, and authorized a railway labor board to adjust labor disputes.

Peabody disapproved of the Esch-Cummins Act. He said he considered it the worst law ever placed upon the statute books. He viewed the return of the railroads to private ownership with regret, and continued to advocate public ownership.

2.

Another issue of concern to the public at this time was that of currency stabilization. The Federal Reserve

---

2. What influence Mr. Peabody's letter may have had upon what Mr. MacAdoo did is conjectural, but it is interesting to note that MacAdoo made such a proposal in his report of December 11, 1919.

Bank system, which had begun its life in the war era, had shown itself capable of leadership. It had held up well under the exigencies of war years—especially that of handling war loans and that of ensuring the continued elasticity of the currency. Its role in relation to readjustments in industry and commerce would need to be thought out.

As a Federal Reserve Bank director, Peabody had an important part in the deliberations regarding the Bank's policies. He considered that the Federal Reserve System would have more of a regulative influence than some believed, and expressed confidence that it would prevent too rapid a liquidation of debts.

3.

Among the urgent matters to be faced by the country was the problem of the Negro. In this matter so close to Mr. Peabody's heart, constructive ideas were sorely needed. While Colonel House was at the Peace Conference at Paris, Mr. Peabody asked him to receive Major Robert R. Moton, President of Tuskegee, to review some of the pressing issues.

A few months after the war, while Peabody was doing all he could to further the interests of the Negro, his attention was drawn to the efforts of a young Southerner, Will W. Alexander, who was working to promote interracial understanding. Will W. Alexander was serving on the War Work Council. It was one of his duties to make arrangements for Negro soldiers. He was in close touch with John J. Egan, an Atlanta industrialist, who, as Assistant Secretary of the Navy, was handling problems of Negro soldiers at Brest, the port of debarkation. Alexander talked with Egan about the need for considering the Negro soldier after the war was over. They discussed the rising tension apparent in the South on the race question.

Meanwhile, Mr. Alexander had been traveling in the

South, helping to sell war bonds. He had noticed the praise accorded to Negro men and women for their support in the war fund drive. It occurred to him that a plan could be devised to cultivate understanding and co-operation between the two races. He talked with Mr. Egan and several others, and the idea took shape.

The next step was to interest others in the plan, and their thoughts turned to Mr. Peabody. They wrote him and asked for an appointment, which he readily granted.

One morning, six months after the close of the war, Will W. Alexander and several other men alighted at the Pennsylvania Station, New York City. Mr. Peabody met them there. He shook hands and took them to the City Club for breakfast. All day they discussed the Negro problem. Five o'clock came and went, six, seven, and they were still intent. At seven-thirty, Mr. Peabody had to keep a dinner engagement, and the conference ended. They shook hands and parted, convinced that their plans would come to something. It was in this way that the idea of inter-racial co-operation became crystallized, taking the form of an inter-racial commission.

The work of the Inter-racial Commission is well-known. Conciliatory in character, aiming at mutual understanding and mutual help, the Commission appointed committees composed of white and Negro leaders. Alexander, whose devoted service had inspired confidence, became the director.

Will Alexander tells the story of his early acquaintance with Mr. Peabody.[3] At the New York conference, the day was devoted entirely to the purpose in hand. A short time afterward, Will Alexander says, he was at his home in Ansley Park, Atlanta. He was poor and unknown. Supper was over and the evening was well along, a cold evening,

---

3. Dr. Alexander to author.

with light snow falling. Suddenly a knock sounded, and Mr. Alexander rose and opened the door. He saw a tall figure "with long coat and handsome face." It was Mr. Peabody.

"I had an hour to spend between trains," he said. "And I came to spend it with you."

That evening was the beginning of their long friendship. Mr. Peabody listened intently to Alexander's plans and dreams. They followed the occasion with frequent correspondence and interviews. Their mutual interests were not confined to the Commission on Inter-racial Cooperation, but extended to the entire social and economic picture of the South.

4.

The busy war years had not crowded out Peabody's interest in education. In 1915 he became a member of the Board of Trustees of Skidmore College. Of his work for the college, President Henry T. Moore later wrote:[4]

> When Mr. Peabody joined the Skidmore Board of Trustees in 1915, it was a struggling young institution full of promise but greatly in need of strong support. By his personal distinction, by his generous material help and above all by his constructive thought he was to become at once a tower of friendly aid. Few were the visitors to this campus who had not heard of his great personal reputation, few were the donors whose gifts equalled his contributions, and no single person contributed more to discussions of educational policy and of the development of our buildings and grounds. His wide range of experience and personal acquaintance were a never failing source of wise interpretation of every matter brought to him, and the hospitality of his open door at Yaddo has meant more to me than I can express.

---

4. Letter from Dr. Moore printed in the Skidmore *News*, March 9, 1938. Courtesy of Dr. Moore and Miss Starbuck.

To this tribute, Miss Kathryn R. Starbuck, later Secretary of the College, adds:[5]

> Mr. Peabody was an active trustee of Skidmore College from 1915 through 1935. He was a trustee emeritus from 1935 to the time of his death in 1938.
> Most of his gifts to the college were made anonymously so that it is somewhat difficult to give the exact amount. A conservative estimate of his financial help would be $20,000 to $25,000. In addition to his personal contributions, Mr. Peabody was instrumental in securing gifts from others. In the early days of the college, when it was still Skidmore School of Arts, he was always associated with the group of Saratogans who helped to acquire property to expand the campus. . . .
> During his years as trustee he constantly extended hospitality to the students and faculty of the college. He believed firmly that a college should be a part of the community life. I have heard him say on many occasions that one of the drawbacks of college life was that it took young people, for four of the most formative years of their lives, out of normal community living and set them in the somewhat artificial environment of a college campus. . . .

He continued as a trustee of the American Church Institute for Negroes. He also continued as a Trustee of Hampton Normal and Industrial Institute and was Treasurer of its Investment Committee. He was a trustee of Colorado College and of the University of Georgia, and retained his connection as a trustee of Penn School and connections with other institutions.

5.

For many years he had been interested in the movement for woman suffrage. He had served as president of the Men's League for Woman Suffrage. Of the encouragement he gave to persons interested in the movement Miss Starbuck writes:[6]

---

5. Letter from Miss Starbuck to author, Sept. 8, 1944.
6. Letter from Miss Kathryn Starbuck to author, Sept. 8, 1944.

My friendship with Mr. Peabody dates back to 1911 when, as a young college graduate, I came back to my native city and became actively interested in woman suffrage. He was, as you know, an ardent believer in absolute equality of women with men. He supported me in my work in every way. Later when I became active in work for peace, I again had his interest and support. Scarcely a week passed that he did not send me a newspaper clipping in which he thought I might be interested. Whenever he had guests whom he thought it would be useful for me to meet, he would invite me to lunch or dinner. As he was constantly entertaining most interesting people, he made many valuable contacts for me. I count friendship with him as one of the richest experiences of my life. I know that to be true of many others. . . . His interest in good causes was always vital and active . . . and he never missed an opportunity to help toward the end that women might be given an opportunity to use their abilities in professional and political life. . . .

6.

During the war and in the following years, Peabody's business affairs gave him serious concern. Conditions in Mexico continued unstable. The coup of Obregon, Calles and de la Huerta in 1920 led to strained relations with the United States.[7] Peabody's holdings were affected. He attended meetings of the boards of directors of the numerous companies with which he was affiliated, and helped to direct the reorganization of some of the enterprises.[8]

His scale of living had been simplified for many years, though he lived comfortably and was still a

---

7. It was not until the later 1920's that, partly through the diplomacy of Ambassador Dwight W. Morrow, the situation was eased.
8. The business enterprises with which he was connected in May, 1919, as director, officer, or both, were: President, Treasurer and Director, Compania Metalurgica Mexicana; Vice-President and Director, Mexican Coal and Coke Company; President and Director, Mexican Lead Company; Director, Mexican Northern Railway Company; Director, Southern Improvement Company; Director, Teziutlan Copper Smelting and Refining Company; Director and Vice-President, Fresnillo Mining Company; President and Director, Potosi & Rio Verde Railway

generous host. At retirement, he had carefully laid aside enough to provide for his needs, but the philanthropic commitments were a constant drain upon his resources. The uncertainties of the Mexican enterprises gave him some fear for his benefactions. Nevertheless, from his various investments, he was able to make some large contributions in the 1920's and to keep the steady stream of small gifts going.

On moving to 19 Circular Street, Saratoga, Mr. Peabody became a member of Bethesda Church. From that time on, the distinguished white-haired man sitting in a front pew was a familiar sight to the Skidmore College girls on a Sunday morning. It happened, by the way, that the pastor of the church had been, as a young man, Mr. Peabody's secretary. Each of the two had pleasant recollections of this early contact—recollections that helped to enrich the mutually helpful relation which now grew up between them.

An amusing incident at Yaddo is recalled by those who witnessed it. One day the officials of a large film company came to Mrs. Trask with an odd request—they were filming one of their masterpieces, and they wished to lay some of the scenes in the Yaddo gardens. She consented, and an army of camera-men, movie stars and satellites, descended upon the quiet estate.[9] Stately women

---

9. Interviews with Miss Pardee and Mrs. Waite, summer, 1940.

Company; President, Treasurer and Director, Montezuma Lead Company; President and Director, Broadway Realty Company; Director and Chairman of Board, Combustion Engineering Corporation (List in his files).
The Combustion Engineering Corporation connection was one that he had made about 1910 as a result of prior connections with its forerunner, the American Stoker Company. At the time Peabody owned stock in it, the Combustion Engineering Company was a profitable enterprise.
This was in addition to his office as a director and Vice-Chairman of the New York Federal Reserve Bank.

in flowing robes, attended by Ethiopian servants adorned the benches of the rose gardens, and posed against the Greek pergola. Peabody, arriving for a call at Yaddo, was surprised to find himself transported back to ancient times. He turned to and assisted Mrs. Trask and Miss Pardee in extending hospitality to the guests on their three-day "location."

7.

With the war over, the thoughts of many Americans turned to the approaching 1920 campaign. Some wished Wilson to run for a third term. Though his advocacy of the League of Nations had lessened his popularity, it was believed that he had a chance of re-election. Peabody thought it would be a mistake for Wilson to run again. He wrote Baker his views as early as April 3, 1919. Wilson had achieved the "pinnacle of Fame," he said; moreover, a third term would be contrary to the American tradition.

Among the possible candidates, Peabody favored MacAdoo. He did not see Baker as presidential timber at this time. He thought MacAdoo, with Murdock as running mate, would make an excellent choice, and was confident that he could be elected.[10]

At the convention, MacAdoo and Palmer led on the first ballot. Spirited voting continued. At the end, James M. Cox of Ohio was nominated for President, with Franklin D. Roosevelt as his running-mate for Vice President. Their opponents in the Republican party were Warren G. Harding of Ohio for President and Calvin Coolidge of Massachusetts for Vice President.

10. When the Democratic Convention met at San Francisco on June 28, 1920, Peabody sent to the party leaders some suggestions for planks to be included in the campaign platform. One of the suggestions was for a statement on the race issue.

Although Peabody's preference had been for MacAdoo, he readily supported Cox, with whom he had become pleasantly acquainted at the Governors' and Mayors' Conference at Washington. Writing to Professor Irving Fisher, Peabody said:[11]

> The more the campaign develops the more appalling seems the evil that would follow the election of a man of Senator Harding's extraordinary calibre. The fact that he has a polite and well-meaning personality only makes it worse. The prospect is of a modern revival of the Doges of Venice and the Council of Ten. . . .

The letter severely criticized the Republican Party for its choice of a candidate.

During the campaign, Peabody tried to encourage pro-League sentiment. He supported the "Match the President" fund to disseminate information on the League of Nations. Mrs. Trask, too, contributed to this fund. In a letter dated October 28, 1920, Ray Stannard Baker, who was traveling with the pro-League party, told Peabody that he was pleased over the results of the tour. League sentiment was strong, he wrote, in Indiana, Missouri, Iowa, Nebraska, and Colorado. He believed, however, that Taft, Root, Hughes, Wickersham and Hoover had confused the issue in the minds of many—even of many who believed in the League.

Despite the efforts of pro-League advocates, the Republican Party won in November. Warren G. Harding was the successful candidate for President.

---

11. Cited in the *New York Times*, October 31, 1920.

CHAPTER XIX

The Wedding at Yaddo; The "Ladye" at Rest

AT 19 CIRCULAR STREET, SARATOGA SPRINGS, PEABODY toiled at his letter-writing. Often he would go to New York to attend Federal Reserve Bank meetings, or South to visit a school. He had long ago given up Abenia.

It was his greatest pleasure to call on his friend Katrina Trask at Yaddo. They had maintained the easy informality of the early years, and Peabody was a welcome sight as he appeared in the doorway of the farmhouse.

The mansion was still closed, and Katrina lived in the smaller house, known as West House, or Mansell Alsaada, which, in Arabic, means House of Happiness. The place was done over to make it more comfortable. It had a large living room, upholstered and decorated in gold; a big dining room, beautifully furnished with rich, dark woods; and rambling wings. On the second floor were bedrooms and Kate's studio, looking far out through a clearing in the pines to Saratoga Lake.

In this upstairs living room, decorated in rose with white touches, Kate, ill and almost without sight, propped herself up on her large Empire divan. About her were objects to recall old memories, a little shrine to Christina with the child's picture framed above it, paintings and portraits of her husband and friends, books everywhere.

On the window was etched a poem dedicated to Yaddo and Kate by her friend Henry Van Dyke. Her eyes could see scarcely any of the surroundings, however, for heavy portieres shielded her imperiled sight. Here she dictated her writing to Miss Pardee, who read the lines over to her. Here she discussed with Mr. Peabody the business matters of the estate, the philanthropies, the cause of peace.

Other friends came when she was able to receive them. Among them was the Reverend Germanos, metropolitan of the Syrian church. It was he who named the house Mansell Alsaada, and the burying ground, a short distance from the house, the "Holy Hill."

Years before, after Spencer Trask's death, friends had wondered whether Kate would marry Peabody. It was clear that she was the center of Peabody's life. She had said no when he had eventually asked her, saying she did not want him to have an invalid on his hands.

As an executor, he had helped her to administer Spencer Trask's will. With increasing burdens, and more ill, she needed him now more than ever. Once again he asked her, and this time she gave her consent. They would be married, and if her health permitted, they would return to the mansion to open the big home to their friends.

Preparations were made for a quiet wedding. They asked the Reverend Edwin Knox Mitchell of Hartford to perform the ceremony. Because of Kate's frail health, the clergyman's wife, who was Spencer Trask's niece, was the only guest.

The ceremony took place on Saturday morning, February 5, 1921, in the Rose Room at West House.[1] Flowers sent by friends were banked against the walls.

1. Newspapers of the day. Interviews with Miss Pardee, June, 1940; July, 1944.

At the appointed time, the Reverend Mitchell opened his book and Kate Trask, frail, yet still attractive, stood beside the tall, distinguished Peabody, to take the vows. Thus these two dear friends, Kate, sixty-eight, and Foster, sixty-nine, became husband and wife.

That evening they had their wedding supper alone. Two dainty trays were placed on small white tables, in the Rose Room. It was all very quiet and peaceful.

Peabody was astonished at the shower of letters and telegrams which arrived. Friends from every part of the country and from abroad sent their best wishes.

All spring, they made their plans for a "picnic occupancy" at the mansion that summer.[2] They would invite a few old friends. They were especially desirous of having Mrs. Fannie Fern Andrews, the pacifist leader, as their guest in August.

Mr. Peabody and Miss Pardee spared Katrina in every way, but she suffered from any exertion. In June, they removed from West House to the mansion. It was only a stone's throw away, but Katrina had to be carried part way on a stretcher. She suffered heart exhaustion after the trip.

On June 2, 1921, Peabody wrote to a friend:[3]

> My dear Mrs. Dashiell:
> I know you will forgive my dictating again when you hear that Mrs. Peabody and I have just moved over from the farmhouse, where she has been living for five years to the old house, which has been put in shape for picnic occupancy this summer. Miss Pardee and others, as well as myself somewhat, are a bit busy. . . .

The following day, he wrote to Fannie Fern Andrews in reply to her letter suggesting that the play *Without the*

---

2. *Ibid.*
3. Peabody Papers, Yaddo.

Walls be presented and asking permission. He said Mrs. Peabody gladly consented, and that he would himself underwrite the $300 necessary for the performance. His letter continues:[4]

> She wishes me to say that you are one of the people whom she very much wishes to have here, hoping that she will get stronger as the summer progresses. Will you not let us know whether, perhaps, some time in August it might be convenient for you. . . . It will be a great pleasure to me, of course, to have the honor of welcoming you in my new relation to the Yaddo home. . . .

Natalie Curtis, now married to Paul Burlin, the artist, and living in Paris, wrote him that much interest had been shown in another of Katrina's peace plays, *In the Vanguard*. On August 4, 1921, Peabody wrote in reply:

> The Ladye of course was deeply interested, as I was . . . I am sending you two copies . . . I was interested to find that Pavolozky is willing to put up one half the cost of printing.

A few days later, on August 11, 1921, he wrote Natalie:

> Unfortunately she has been much more ill for several weeks past and only hears letters that have the personal touch and refer to things close to her heart, such as peace work. . . .

A few weeks later came the sad news of Natalie's death, on October 23, 1921. Thus ended a warm and understanding friendship of many years' duration—a friendship strengthened by shared tastes in music and in art and by a common devotion to the cause of peace and of humanitarian reform.

2.

Because of Katrina's frail health, Mr. Peabody cur-

---

4. *Ibid.*

tailed his activities during the summer and fall of that year. Nevertheless, he kept up his correspondence on educational matters, and on the peace movement. In July, he attended several meetings of the Federal Reserve Bank, but in August he had to be absent. He always followed the work of the Bank with close attention, and was in constant touch with the officials. He felt called upon on several occasions to defend the Bank's policies.

During 1920 and 1921 the Federal Reserve System was the target of some criticism. This was probably to be expected in the days of readjustment. As we have noted, Peabody had served on several committees of the New York Federal Reserve Bank, among them the Executive Committee, the Building Committee, the Real Estate Committee, and the Committee on Welfare of Staff. For a long time he had been chairman of the Committee on Salaries.

On one occasion, when the Bank had been under attack on the ground that it paid unnecessarily high salaries, Peabody wrote a letter to the *Times* in which he said that the directors, after a thorough study of the subject, had found that the salaries paid by the Bank were no higher than necessary in order to secure and retain able persons.

In the fall of 1921, Peabody entered the controversy further. At that time, John Skelton Williams, former Comptroller of the Currency, make an attack on some of the Bank's policies. An article on the subject appeared in the *New York Evening Post*, November 11, 1921. Mr. Peabody not only answered the charges made about the high salaries, but also made it a point to explain[5] the Bank's general policies. Peabody realized that the question of what course the Federal Reserve Banks should follow in the post-war period was one of crucial importance.

5. As did the other directors.

To his colleagues on the board in New York, he expressed the view that it was important to make ample resources available for the small business man so that he might carry on his function in the community. He had some exchange of correspondence with Adolph C. Miller, official on the Federal Reserve Board at Washington, regarding methods of re-discounting.

His fellow directors at the Federal Reserve Bank had a warm feeling for the tall silver-haired man. Though he was not, perhaps, the most outstanding of the men around the conference table, he had a capacity for penetrating to the heart of whatever matter was under discussion. Moreover, he had a fund of information on the currency issues of the past.

3.

Though haunted by anxiety for Kate's health, he had hope that she might regain her strength. He enjoyed his role as her husband, and devoted himself to her needs with tenderness and pride.

She spent most of her days in the Rose Room now, at the West House. Mr. Peabody read her mail to her. Once or twice she was strong enough to play a few airs on the white piano in the corner, but otherwise she reclined on the divan in the subdued light. When strong enough, she would dictate a few passages to Miss Pardee or would discuss some humanitarian interest with her husband.

Christmas that year brought them the usual greetings from old friends. Wreaths and boughs, fresh-picked from the grounds, decorated the living room. The fire glowed warm. On December 31, Peabody sat at his desk sending felicitations, among them a note to W. P. G. Harding, Governor of the Federal Reserve Board:

> A Happy New Year
> To You, Dear Governor Harding, I wish this with utmost heartiness and the prayer that the New Year

may bring some measure of the peace so sadly needed by this sorely stricken world. . . .

This holiday season was their last one together. Early in January, Kate's strength failed and she grew more ill. On January 8, 1922, less than a year after their marriage, she passed away.

Only one who has suffered a comparable loss can understand Peabody's sorrow at this time. For fifty years his life had revolved around Kate. Hardly a day had gone by when he had not been in touch with her. In the months since their marriage, he had cared for her with the tender devotion of a husband.

The funeral service was private, attended only by members of the household and a few close friends. Prayers were read at the house by the Reverend Irving G. Rouillard, rector of Bethesda Church. A burial ground had been selected on the Yaddo estate some years before by his Eminence Germanos, and there, at the top of the knoll, the family gathered for the final rites. Burial took place in a heavy snow storm. In Saratoga Springs, two miles away, all business was suspended for the afternoon out of respect for her who had died.

In the hard days following Kate's death, Peabody was a sad and lonely figure. He received comfort from the condolences of their many friends. He sat long at his desk each day attending to the details. Letters must be answered, business matters attended to.

Kate's personality had been so identified with the place that it seemed as though she were there still. They wished the illusion to continue. Miss Pardee kept fresh roses in front of her friend's picture and spoke as if Kate were still present.

In Kate's will, she had said, "No mourning shall be worn for me, as the incident of mortal death is but the passing on into a larger sphere of a more abundant life." Her sorrowing family bore her wish in mind.

In her will, Mrs. Peabody provided that her husband was to have the use of West House and five acres of land and approaches during his lifetime. She provided that Miss Pardee was to continue to make her home at Yaddo and that a piece of property on the estate was to be given her. She also left Miss Pardee a substantial sum of money. She made other bequests to friends and philanthropies. In accordance with plans made by Spencer and Kate Trask years before, Yaddo was to be a guest home for artists.

As the weeks slipped by, he filled his lonely hours with activities. He busied himself with his numerous educational and philanthropic interests. His resignation from the Federal Reserve Board left him free to give more time to other matters.

With some of his old hospitality, he invited friends to West House to discuss various causes. Miss Pardee and the household staff assisted him in making his guests comfortable. Kate was with him in spirit.

CHAPTER XX

Warm Springs and Roosevelt

AT THE TIME OF HIS MARRIAGE TO MRS. TRASK, PEABODY ceased to make his home at 19 Circular Street, Saratoga Springs, and moved to Yaddo. It now occurred to him that he might donate the Circular Street property as a memorial to Kate. The house was turned over for this purpose and became the home of the Katrina Trask Alliance. In June 1922, Peabody gave the money to install a gymnasium in the building.

In planning further developments at the Center, he procured the services of Mrs. Majorie Knappen Waite to make a comprehensive survey of needs in the town. Her report recommended the establishment of a community center for young working women. Mr. Peabody was so favorably impressed with Mrs. Waite's report that he suggested her appointment as Welfare Director of the center. A short time later she accepted the post.

Mrs. Waite was a graduate of the University of Minnesota. Prior to her marriage, she was a member of the faculty at the Hollywood School for Girls in Los Angeles. Shortly after the war, she became secretary of the Knox School for Girls, a school with which Mr. Peabody had some connections.

Mrs. Waite began her new duties with enthusiasm. Under her capable leadership, the house on Circular Street opened up many new opportunities for its members.

Classes were held, and a program of other activities was set up.

Peabody watched with keen interest the development of this project. The new call upon his time was a boon in the lonely days after his wife's death. Finding that Mrs. Waite's views on philanthropy coincided remarkably with his own, he made it more and more of a habit to talk things over with her. He went to the community house often and Mrs. Waite called often at Yaddo.

Later, Mrs. Waite's sister, Mrs. Elizabeth Ames, came to visit at Saratoga Springs. Peabody found her, too, congenial. A graduate of the University of Minnesota, she was a young woman of cosmopolitan interests with a keen literary sense and an appreciation of music and of art.

The friendship of these two young women opened up a new life for Peabody. The pain of his loss of Kate would never wear away—with her death went the shared experience of fifty years. His aim for the rest of his life would be to bring nearer to fulfilment all that he and she had planned and labored for. But he thought of Mrs. Waite as a daughter, and indeed sometimes began to speak of her as a spiritual child of himself and Katrina. He liked and admired her gifted sister, Mrs. Ames. And so, from 1922 on, his life was lived in company with young life; his spirit was refreshed by new enthusiasms.

On November 15, 1922, a memorial gateway at Congress Park, given by the men and women of the Yaddo estate, was dedicated to Katrina Trask. In December, the Albany players presented her play *The Little Town of Bethlehem*. Requests continued to come in for permission to give this play and others from her pen. Thus her influence in the cause of peace did not cease with her death.

Having given up his connection with the Federal Reserve Bank, Peabody now made fewer trips to New York. Nevertheless he was in touch with friends by letter. On December 4, 1922, he wrote to John D. Rockefeller, Jr.:[1]

My Dear Mr. Rockefeller:
My infrequent and brief visits to New York City do not allow me the pleasure of meeting many friends and associates of former years, but here in my continued interest in educational matters, I have the pleasure of observing their activities.

I often recall in conversation my good fortune in coming to know you and your earnestness of devotion and fine character, but now I must write a line expressing to you my personal pleasure and real satisfaction in the large service you are rendering to the country in so clearly and frankly expressing your convictions that humanity is the first consideration in the industrial relations which men and women must have together. As the educational work to which you have so nobly given your energies has emphasized, one of the real problems is to secure the "open mind." You are in position, fortunately, to open the minds of many to the truth of this issue in which you are now dealing and I rejoice greatly.

I am struck with the passage of time as I observe references to your daughter's having now entered upon her social life and think of the early days when you were the charming young couple who were so eager to find occasions of service. Will you kindly present my regards to Mrs. Rockefeller and believe me,
Faithfully yours,
George Foster Peabody

Mr. Rockefeller wrote him in reply:

December 18, 1922
My dear Mr. Peabody:
Your kind note of December 4th is received with genuine appreciation. I value your friendly expressions in regard to what I am trying to do.

How rapidly the years slip by! I remember well the delightful visit which Mrs. Rockefeller and I made at Yaddo and your home on Lake George. It must have

---

[1] Letter by courtesy of Mr. John D. Rockefeller, Jr.

been fifteen or twenty years ago.

The addresses in connection with the gateway at Yaddo I have read with much interest, and thank you for sending them to me. It must have been a very impressive service.

Thank you for your letter, and with cordial regards, in which Mrs. Rockefeller joins, I am

Very sincerely,
John D. Rockefeller, Jr.

2.

Within two years after his wife's death, Mr. Peabody had resumed many of his activities. He had new interests, too, among them the development of Warm Springs, Georgia.

As a boy, he had enjoyed vacations with his family at the Springs, a few miles distant from Columbus. At that time the place was a favorite summer resort; years afterwards, it was extensively developed, and became the site of three large schools and a few smaller ones. In 1923, the property immediately around the Springs was owned by Tom Loyless, a former newspaper editor, who wished to sell it. The matter was brought to Mr. Peabody's attention, and shortly thereafter he bought the Springs and the surrounding land.

As at Saratoga Springs, he wished to have expert opinion, and arranged to have the waters tested. A chemical analysis convinced him of the therapeutic values of the water. He now sought to interest friends in a plan to develop the Springs as a health center.

It was a coincidence that at this time Franklin D. Roosevelt was struggling to overcome the handicap of paralysis with which he had been afflicted for several years. Peabody had known Roosevelt for many years in upstate New York. He had followed the latter's career as Assistant Secretary of the Navy. As a personal friend, he wrote Roosevelt suggesting that he go to Warm Springs and try the Baths.

In October, 1924, Roosevelt followed Peabody's suggestion and spent three weeks at Warm Springs. At the end of the first week, he wrote an enthusiastic letter. He had spent two hours every morning in the pool, which he described as "wonderful." The muscles of his legs had improved to a noticeable degree.[2]

A conference between Peabody and Roosevelt followed. The result was a plan for the development of Warm Springs into a therapeutic center. Bathing facilities would be enlarged, new buildings constructed, and a staff of physicians and physiotherapists procured for the treatment of paralysis patients.

The rest of the story is well known. Roosevelt became President of the Warm Springs Foundation, formed in 1926. Peabody was one of the trustees. Roosevelt bought some land and built a cottage on the side of Pine Mountain near the pools.[3] Peabody reserved some of the property for his own use, and later built a winter home there.

Apart from the therapeutic aspects of this great center, the venture is interesting because it led to a closer association with Roosevelt, and also because it led to Roosevelt's becoming better acquainted with the people of the deep South.

3.

Early in January, 1924,[4] Peabody was grieved over the loss of his grandnephew, Royal Peabody, Carlos's thirteen-year-old only son. On February 24, he suf-

2. Peabody Papers, Yaddo files.
3. After Mr. Roosevelt became President the cottage was called "The Little White House."
4. January 5, 1924.

fered another blow in the death of his brother, Charles J. Peabody—the only one remaining, besides himself, of the original home circle. The two brothers had been devotedly attached to each other. Partners at Spencer Trask and Company for years, neighbors at Lake George, affiliated in various civic enterprises and philanthropies, they were never far apart.

Wishing to honor the memory of Charles, George Foster, with members of the family, gave a new organ to Holy Trinity Church in Brooklyn. A few months later, the Church held a memorial service of music on the organ.

In 1924 Peabody suffered another great personal loss. On February 3 his good friend Woodrow Wilson passed away. All through the years of the former President's illness, Peabody had written to him frequently, sending messages of cheer and encouragement. He had been in constant touch with Mr. Wilson's brother-in-law, Mr. Bolling.

Wilson saw few callers in his last days, but Newton D. Baker had a brief, pathetic interview, about which he wrote to Peabody. Peabody, too, was admitted to the sick room for a few minutes.

The sense of loss which Peabody felt when Wilson died was great indeed. He had loved Wilson as a friend and had revered him as a President. His hopes for the country and for the world were bound up with Wilson's struggle to bring about permanent peace through a League of Nations.

4.

As the campaign of 1924 approached, Peabody had an active correspondence with Newton D. Baker and was in frequent contact with William G. MacAdoo and other Democratic leaders. His first choice for President would have been Baker, but he feared that labor would not support him because of his opposition to the closed shop. He could not support MacAdoo because of the latter's advocacy of a bond issue for the bonus and because of his failure to support government ownership of railroads. Peabody would have liked to see Franklin D. Roosevelt as Vice President.

In June, the Democratic National Convention met in New York City, and Peabody appeared at the meetings with his delegate's badge. When John W. Davis was nominated, he wired his congratulations, adding that what the country needed was a leader to follow the path of progress which Woodrow Wilson had so clearly outlined. He was active in the campaign that fall.

Asked to state his views regarding the Socialist platform, Peabody wrote to Norman Thomas:[5]

> I cannot . . . accept the Marxian doctrines as either wise or practical or founded on what I believe to be the only principle of life conduct—the teachings and example of Jesus Christ. I have always been most sympathetic, however, to individual Socialist aspirations . . . I have particularly observed the Fabian System of England with hopeful anticipations.

In a letter to Miss Roberta Hodgson, Athens, Georgia, he discussed the campaign and, in particular, gave his views on LaFollette, the Independent candidate:[6]

> Personally, I shall be in no wise sorry to see him have a very large vote, hoping that our Conservatives and particularly our Southern Industrial Conservatives may be so shocked as to take account of stock of public sentiment. I like the Republican course at Cleveland of driving out the conservative protectionists who are in the Democratic Party, particularly in the South. Therefore I should like to see a live Republican Party in the South which would give the Negro his vote when two shall compete for it. . . .

5. Peabody Papers, Yaddo files.
6. *Ibid.*

Writing to Daniel Roper in support of John W. Davis Peabody said:[7]

> It is pleasant to hear from you again. I communicated with Mr. Davis at once upon his nomination and had some communication and made a remittance to Mr. Hull who turned it over to Mr. Shaver. I also have had some communication with Mr. Frank Polk and Mr. Spellacy respecting my thought as to the campaign in New York State. As far as I can discover, nothing has been done to deal effectively with the independent vote which usually decides the direction in this state. I think it is a rather lamentable situation. . . .
> I think myself, that LaFollette will carry enough Northwestern states to prevent the election of Coolidge. . . .
> I have known Mr. Davis, of course, for many years and know of his high character. As I believe the League of Nations issue is the one supreme issue, I am well content to support him.

During the fall of 1924 Peabody was also busy with New York State political affairs. Alfred E. Smith had long been a friend. As we have noted, Smith while Governor, had appointed Peabody as a member of the Reconstruction Commission after the first World War.

After Smith had withdrawn as candidate for the Vice-Presidential nomination at the 1924 Convention, Peabody wrote him a letter urging him to run again for Governor of New York State. The people needed Smith's services, he said. Smith wrote him in reply stating that because of personal interests connected with his family, he did not feel he could run. Peabody's answer was published in the *New York Times*.[8] After expressing sympathy with the former governor's desire to make provision for the future of his family, Mr. Peabody wrote:

> There is, of course, the question as to how much of public service one ought to render and there is a limit as to the particular sacrifices that can be made or

---

7. Letter dated Sept. 6, 1924, Yaddo files.
8. October 19, 1924.

called for. However, it seems to me that is covered by the result in the way of permanent welfare of a community and the body politic and . . . humanity as well.

Yielding[9] to this persuasion, and perhaps influenced by other motives also, Smith decided to run again for the office of Governor.

5.

Peabody was still very active in the development of Saratoga Springs. In 1924, having been appointed by Governor Smith as a member of a special commission to recommend a program for the further expansion of the reservation, he was instrumental in bringing over Dr. Paul Haertl, of Kissengen, Bavaria, an able engineer and biologist, to study the water and make suggestions. In writing to Dr. Haertl on December 24, 1924, he said:

> Mr. Bernard Baruch, son of the late Dr. Baruch and one of the members of the Governor's Commission, is also desirous that you should come and join me in the risk of the advance. . . .
>
> The Governor desires to have the fullest knowledge possible and the Commission, acting in his behalf, deem it necessary to have your resurvey of present conditions and the output and use of the waters since you were here. . . .
>
> I very greatly appreciate the high courtesy of the Government of Bavaria in granting the request of the Gov. of the State of N. Y. for this leave of absence for you to come as a representative of your government.[10]

Desiring to promote a conservation program, Peabody gave the State large tracts of land on Lake George so as to extend the State Park system beyond Saratoga. He was also instrumental in the establishment at Saratoga Springs of the State Forest Nursery, from which millions

---

9. Mr. Alfred E. Smith affirmed this to the author, June 30, 1940.
10. Dr. Simon Baruch, Bernard Baruch's father, had made a trip for the Saratoga Springs Commission while Peabody was chairman some years before, and had recommended Dr. Haertl. (Copy of Mr. Peabody's letter to Robert Moses, March 24, 1924, Yaddo files.)

of seedling trees were distributed each year for reforestation.[11]

In the field of education Peabody's efforts were intensified in the 1920's. After the first World War, the alumni of the University of Georgia decided to raise a million dollar fund as a memorial to the students who had died in the war. The campaign was launched in the early 1920's.

Mr. Peabody was deeply interested in this fund. His nephew Carlos was selected as the architect to design the Memorial Hall. Peabody told the chairman of the campaign committee he would pledge $15,000. A few months afterwards he lost heavy sums in his Mexican investments and at first thought he would have to reduce his pledge. On the day when the campaign opened, the chairman wired him in New York to learn his decision. Requesting that his gift be kept anonymous, he replied that he was transferring to the fund stocks estimated at $50,000. As matters turned out, his gift was actually worth $60,000. In making the gift, he stipulated that his money was to be used to keep the building in repair and also to pay part of the salary of the secretary for religious work.

When the campaign was over, and the Memorial Hall was being constructed, Mr. Peabody was especially anxious to have a swimming pool built also. One day he was discussing the matter with Mrs. Trask. What would such a pool cost, she inquired. If made of tile, instead of concrete, the cost would be $3,000, he estimated. At that, Mrs. Trask drew a sapphire ring from her finger, handed it to him, and asked him to sell it to pay the cost of a tiled pool.[12]

In the spring of 1925 Peabody went to Georgia in

---

11. Associated Press sketch of Mr. Peabody, 1926.
12. He later referred to it as the "sapphire pool."

order to talk over, with leaders in various fields, the possibility of a state-wide movement for a better educational system. He succeeded in arousing a great deal of enthusiasm for the aims he had in view. Dr. Charles McMurry of the Peabody School of Education wrote an article with the caption—"Peabody Starts Citizens' Movement for Greater Educational System." Referring to the issue of who would be appointed as the next Chancellor of the University of Georgia, he said that under Peabody's quiet leadership, the issue was no longer the question of who should be Chancellor, but rather of how a University System could be financed to challenge a great Chancellor.[13]

In regard to this citizens' movement, Mr. Peabody wrote to Adolph S. Ochs, publisher of the *New York Times*:[14]

> I hope to be able to run up and see you before I have to go South but I am not certain as I may be called at an early date. We have to elect a new Chancellor in the University of Georgia and in that connection we have a Citizens Education Movement on hand. I had the privilege of really starting this movement when I was in Georgia in April and, therefore, I feel rather bound to heed the suggestion of Governor Walker that I go to Georgia to address the Legislature and to do what I can to further this most necessary movement. . . .

While interested in the general educational needs of the South, Peabody was especially mindful of the needs of the Southern Negro. On July 17, 1925, the *New York Times* quoted him as saying:

> One-third of the population are Negroes. The South is entitled to have the most generous aid from the wealth of the North and West, to help it educate the negro to an understanding of agriculture and the coincident production of wealth. . . .

---

13. The article was printed in a pamphlet entitled: *Home, School and Community*, May, 1925. Courtesy of Mr. John D. Rockefeller, Jr.
14. Peabody Papers, Yaddo files.

> James B. Duke has made an emphatic beginning in dealing with the situation, but his contribution for negro education was only about 5 per cent of his total gift, whereas the negro is 30 per cent of the population of the South and more than 40 per cent of this educational program. . . .
> There is an immediate way for people not living in the South to help effectively, to help wisely, to help prudently—that is, by helping to educate teachers for the tens of thousands of negro public schools which the South is supporting through taxation.
> I venture to call upon all having funds to follow the example of George Eastman and Mr. Rockefeller in studying the opportunity for the wisest of educational investments.

Two large campaigns to raise funds for education of Negroes in the South were conducted in the period 1924-1926. One was the campaign to raise $8,000,000 for Hampton and Tuskegee Institutes; the other was the campaign of the American Church Institute to raise $20,000,000 in behalf of the schools under its guidance—St. Paul's, St. Augustine's, Fort Valley, and others. Peabody wrote a great many letters to wealthy persons soliciting contributions for both campaigns. He had some correspondence on the subject with John D. Rockefeller, Jr. On August 10, 1925, he wrote to Mr. Rockefeller:

> My reason for asking you to inform yourself is that Georgia is the largest State east of the Mississippi, physically, has more negroes than any State, has more population than any Southern State excepting Texas, is the strategic centre of the South, Atlanta being the Chicago of the South—but only a quarter of a million people—the next largest four cities having less than 30,000 population. The South represents 30 per cent of the U.S.A., and negroes over 30 per cent of that. . . .
> In helping to educate negro teachers you are doing the most effective thing in my opinion to stir up whites to vote more money for schools.

It is interesting to note that five of the eight million dollars for Hampton and Tuskegee came from three sources—the General Education Board, which started the campaign with one million dollars; John D. Rockefeller, Jr., who gave one million; and George Eastman, who gave three millions. It is possible that Mr. Peabody's efforts had a good deal to do with persuading the General Education Board and Mr. Rockefeller to make their contributions.

In regard to the fund being raised by the American Church Institute, Peabody wrote to an acquaintance:[15]

> I am endeavoring to lay foundations for a movement in the Church to raise from ten to twenty millions for the American Church Insitute for Negroes during the coming five years, to enlarge the present schools and to take over other schools in the South, and perhaps, build new ones in some of the dioceses. I am Assistant Treasurer, having been the original Treasurer, and am very fully informed respecting this Institute. . . . I consider this organization potentially the most important with reference to future service of which I know. . . .
> I should, therefore, place first, I think in recommending to a man who wished to devise wisely funds to aid the education of the Negro . . . the giving of a considerable portion and with entire safety—all of such legacy to the American Church Institute.
> I am President of the Board of Trustees of the Penn Normal School.[16]

He wrote a long letter to the trustees of the American Church Institute, setting forth conditions in the South and discussing the work of several of the schools for Negroes. He advised the board to take twenty million

---

15. Copy of Mr. Peabody's letter to W. Sheppard, Denver, Colo., Aug. 24, 1925.
16. In a letter to Miss Isabella Curtis, dated June 3, 1926, Peabody wrote: "Mr. Cope, Mr. Maule, Mr. Wood and I spent some three hours today discussing the situation of Penn School. Dr. Thomas Jesse Jones . . . sat with us, and strongly emphasized his judgment as to the peculiar and special importance of Penn School in relation to education in this country. . . ." (Copy of his letter is in Yaddo files.)

rather than ten as its goal, and outlined a plan of campaign, which, he said, might begin with a survey by the General Education Board.

CHAPTER XXI

Yaddo, A Retreat for Artists

THE LONELINESS WHICH PEABODY FELT AFTER THE DEATH of his wife had been relieved to some extent by his many activities. He had been cheered and stimulated by his new-found interest in the Katrina Trask Alliance and by his discussions with Mrs. Waite. He found her a cheerful companion, interesting and vivacious. He looked forward to the occasions when she came with her sister to enjoy the hospitality of Yaddo. Informal picnics under the skilful hand of Miss Pardee were arranged, and the little party of friends would have a day of pleasant fun on some quiet hilltop of the estate. He had come to accept Marjorie Waite as a part of his life.

There had been some speculation as to whether he might, in time, marry again. He did not wish this, however. His tie with Kate remained dominant. Yet he craved affection in his loneliness, and it was natural for him to turn to the young woman who had brought so much cheer into his life. Moreover, he wished to have a successor who would carry on his philanthropies sympathetically. For several years he had referred to Mrs. Waite as his daughter, and he desired to make a legal adoption.

On her part Mrs. Marjorie Waite had found her acquaintance with Mr. Peabody a happy experience. Sadness in her own life had left her in need of just such a friendship. Although well educated already, she told friends she received a liberal education from his broader experience. As the months passed by, she was happy, interested in her work at the Center, and in new philanthropic activities, and increasingly fond of the man who was like a father to her.

After her husband's death in 1924, Mrs. Waite decided to remain in the East. She thought, naturally, of living in Saratoga Springs, for it was here that she had been so happy during the past few years. When Mr. Peabody asked her to become his adopted daughter, she hesitated for a long time. The idea seemed logical, however, in the light of all the circumstances, and she finally gave her consent.

On May 4, 1926, the adoption papers were signed at Ballston Spa, the county seat of Saratoga County. In becoming Peabody's adopted daughter, Mrs. Waite took his name. She was now Mrs. Marjorie Peabody Waite. She referred to him affectionately as "Mon Pere."

Mr. Peabody brought his adopted daughter to Yaddo, where she was welcomed by Miss Pardee and the members of the household. Everyone was agog with the excitement and novelty of having young life in the house. A jolly atmosphere began to pervade the place. Mr. Peabody, for perhaps the first time in his life, unbent from his customary rather stiff courtesy and became more informal.

Miss Pardee tells of the cheerful breakfasts at West House. The mail, brought from Saratoga by car, was heaped at Mr. Peabody's plate. Neglecting his food, he would open letter after letter, stopping now and then to read some bit that particularly appealed to him. Much hearty laughter accompanied these breakfasts.

The memory of Kate was everywhere about the house; they spoke of her as if she were in the next room. But he was now a man at ease from strain. He enjoyed a measure of light-heartedness in the complete acceptance by his women folk—Miss Pardee, like a sister; Marjorie, his daughter.

2.

The converting of Yaddo into a retreat for artists was a major undertaking after Katrina's death. The idea of the retreat was first conceived by Spencer and Katrina in 1900; directors had been appointed, and the organization, with Katrina Trask as president, had been incorporated under the name of Pine Garde. This corporation was now replaced by the Corporation of Yaddo, of which Mr. Peabody became president, and Miss Pardee, secretary. The other members of the board of directors, continued from the previous board, were Daniel Chester French, Henry Van Dyke, John H. Finley, the Reverend Edwin Knox Mitchell, Acosta Nichols, Thomas Mott Osborne, and Mrs. Mia Potter Sturges.

First the question of tax liability had to be cleared. In 1923 Yaddo was granted tax exemption as the site of a philanthropic institution. Under Mr. Peabody's leadership, the Corporation then went about converting the estate to its intended purpose.

The first step was the taking of an inventory of the contents of the mansion. In July, 1923, Mrs. Elizabeth Ames, Mrs. Waite's sister, directed this work. That fall, the Corporation asked Mrs. Ames to be the executive director of Yaddo, and she accepted.

It was a big task to convert the mansion and the other buildings into a place suitable for the artist guests. Alterations were needed, and, in making them, the utmost care must be taken to preserve the atmosphere of the old Yaddo. Gracious hospitality must be the dominant note, as in the days when Spencer and Katrina Trask had opened their home to friends. Aided by the suggestions of Mr. Peabody and Miss Pardee, Mrs. Ames proceeded to restore the mansion to its old charm. The rich furnishings were set in place. Life-sized portraits of Spencer Trask; of blue-eyed Mrs. Trask, gowned in shimmering satin and carrying her pink roses; of Mr. Peabody, with the dark beard of his younger days; of Miss Pardee, graced the walls of the great entrance hall. The portraits of little Christina and Spencer, Jr., hung in the library.

On the grounds various smaller buildings were converted into studios where guests could work without interruption. Everything was put in order.

The selection of guests was made with care. Yaddo could accommodate ten or twelve persons the first summer, more later, for periods ranging from two weeks to the whole summer. A few could remain through the winter in one of the smaller houses. In keeping with the plans of the Trasks, guests were to include painters, sculptors, writers, and musicians; all were to be persons whose work had received commendation and who showed promise of further creativeness. Mrs. Ames conducted the correspondence. She placed the names before the board of directors, who made the final choice. As a rule, an individual was not accepted through his own application, but through the recommendation of some recognized person or group. Invitations were sent to the prospective guests.

After months of planning and hard work, Yaddo was scheduled to open. On June 1, 1926, an atmosphere of quiet excitement prevailed at West House, where Mr. Peabody, Miss Pardee, Mrs. Waite, and Mrs. Ames were conferring over last details.

On their arrival, guests were welcomed at the mansion by Mrs. Ames, the director. She showed them to their individual suites and made them feel at home.

The order of the day in this first summer was followed year after year. At eight o'clock, the artists enjoyed a leisurely breakfast, served in buffet style in the spacious dining room. After breakfast they sauntered away to their various studios to work. Printed signs about the grounds requested silence, and only the whistling of birds or the whir of an occasional car in the driveway interrupted the quiet of the scene. At noontime the guests returned to the mansion, or ate picnic luncheons on the grounds. As the sun sank low, one figure after another reappeared along the pine-needled driveway. Dinner was a pleasant affair. The guests, dressed informally in cool cottons and linens, seated themselves at will at the large tables in the dining room and enjoyed a delicious meal, served on the lovely old china of the Trasks. After dinner, demi-tasse was served in the great hall, and conversation ran to works of art, to a symphony, or to a chapter just completed in someone's book. Many a young artist found stimulation in this pleasant company.

Mr. Peabody and Mrs. Waite would often join Mrs. Ames and the guests in the evening. Occasionally, Mrs. Waite would sing for them in her rich contralto voice. Each year at the end of the summer, a concert was given—guests who were musicians presented their work to an audience assembled in the library[1] and the great hall.

As time went on and finances permitted, Yaddo increased the number of its guests. Some of the well known artists of the country have found inspiration amid these beautiful and peaceful scenes. Mr. Peabody and the other members of the family fostered in every way the spirit of the founders, Spencer and Kate Trask.

Family and friends tell us that Peabody was no musician. Though his voice was rich and pleasing, his ear was untrained, and he could not sing. He loved music, however,

---

1. The library was converted into a concert hall by Mrs. Trask in memory of Spencer Trask.

and enjoyed various forms of musical expression. In the late 1860's, when Wagner's operas were being introduced into this country, he heard *Tannhauser* and was thrilled by it. He soon learned to enjoy Bach[2] and Beethoven; these composers, with Wagner, were his favorites. In later years, he took pleasure also in the works of Russian composers.

Peabody loved the Negro spirituals, not only because they were a part of his early childhood in the South, but even more for their intrinsic beauty and pathos. He did what he could to promote the singing of spirituals, being convinced that this was a good way of teaching people to appreciate the Negro's contribution to the rich pattern of American life.

Through his contacts with Miss Rossa Cooley, principal of the Penn School, he had become acquainted with the Negroes on St. Helena Island, South Carolina. He had heard them sing spirituals at their work in the cotton fields, and at school festivals. In the middle 1920's he sponsored a study of the St. Helena spirituals by a Negro musician, Nicholas H. G. Ballanta (Taylor)[3] of Gold Coast Colony who was in this country on a scholarship. The musician's research work at Penn School resulted in the discovery that, in the old spirituals which went back to early slave days in this country, seventeen tones were used within the limits of our octave. Mr. Peabody subsidized the publication of a little volume of one hundred and three of the spirituals.

He had long sponsored musical developments at Hampton, and had encouraged the work of the gifted composer Nathaniel Dett, director of the Hampton choir.

---

2. He was one of the founders of the Bach Festival.
3. Dr. Frank Damrosch sent Ballanta (Taylor) to Peabody, who in turn put him in touch with Hampton and Tuskegee, and later with Penn School.

In the late 1920's Mr. Peabody and other friends underwrote the expense of sending the Hampton choir to England in the interest of inter-racial understanding. Mrs. Waite went to Europe while the choir was there and sent reports of the favorable reception to her father.

3.

Though forced to take care of his health because of a heart condition and complications, Mr. Peabody was constantly on the go. His daughter often accompanied him. The courtly, white-haired man was a familiar figure on the train trip from Saratoga Springs to New York. He frequently visited the many schools in the South with which he was affiliated as trustee; he was present regularly at board meetings of Penn School, Hampton, and the University of Georgia.

He kept up his correspondence with friends. To Mr. John D. Rockefeller, Jr., he wrote:

July 20, 1928

Dear Mr. Rockefeller

I cannot refrain, even at the risk of intrusion into your summer recreation time, sending you this word of warmest congratulation on the noble gift for the University project in Paris. The thoughtful discrimination which you continue to manifest in these wise provisions for the rational growth and evolution of humanity in its climb up the ladder is a great inspiration. It is a joy to have the real satisfaction of being among your debtors as a citizen deeply interested in world affairs as well as Education in general.

Since I first had the privilege of knowing you twenty-five years and more ago, I have again and again thought of the profound satisfaction that your Father and Mother had every cause to feel in your continual growth and development in grace and truth in accord with their hopes and prayers. I, also, think of you as emphasizing to the world a continuing manifestation of achieving the "durable satisfaction" of life which President Eliot so finely phrased.

I am, with kind remembrances to your gracious Lady,
                    Faithfully yours,
                    George Foster Peabody

Mr. Rockefeller replied on July 23, 1928:

Dear Mr. Peabody:

How can I adequately express my appreciation of your charming note of July 20th, speaking specifically of my recent gift to the Cite Universitaire of Paris, and, generally, of other benefactions which it has been my privilege to make. You must understand, as few others do, how great are the opportunities which lie before me, and what a deep satisfaction it is to me to be able to avail myself of at least some of them. But all of this is possible only through the unprecedented generosity of my father, while for the will to do these things I am indebted to the heritage received from my parents.

With truest thanks for your letter and for the warm friendship which it breathes, I am
                    Very sincerely,
                    John D. Rockefeller, Jr.

In 1928, when his friend, Alfred E. Smith, ran against Herbert Hoover for the presidency, Peabody swung once again into action. His daughter, too, took part in the campaign, thereby winning his enthusiastic approval.

He was in touch with party leaders. To Newton D. Baker he sent the following night letter:

Hon. Newton D. Baker
Cleveland
Ohio.

Women's Democratic Committee wanted you for the great mass meeting held here last night in Convention Hall where you captivated all Saratoga in 1916. I was distressed to learn from New York Headquarters you were ill and all appointments cancelled. I hope not too serious and that you are recovering your strength.

Lunn was chief attraction, a near neighbor, and well known but they overflowed that great hall and sat for three hours deeply interested. I consider this demonstration in a Republican centre most significant and warrants confident expectation of New York's leading the procession which the New England ovation indicates may be a landslide to put another Governor in the White House to follow Governor Wilson and Governor Cleveland in the work of reconstruction so greatly needed.

Your letter on Prohibition today's World most important. Am having 10,000 copies of the page struck off to send to colleges and other influential centres in the South mainly. Thank you, it is just what was needed. As always you clarify the question completely and prove yourself our great Statesman.

Our greetings to Mrs. Baker and family,
George Foster Peabody

To an acquaintance he wired:[4]

With only our neighbor Lunn and Harriet Mills as a drawing card the Women's Committee of Saratoga gathered nearly 4,000 in our Convention Hall to ratify nominations Smith and Roosevelt. I consider this in a Republican Centre most significant and warranting confidence New York will lead procession which your New England ovation to our great Governor warrants us in believing now will land Governor Smith in succession to Governors Wilson and Cleveland to do the constructive work so greatly needed.

My congratulations to you and my greetings to Mrs. Sayre, if you will, please, whose voice on radio here was reported to me as most lovely.
George Foster Peabody

To Walter Lippmann, editor of *The World*, he wrote on October 24, 1928:

Thank you for your letter of congratulation. I am feeling more like myself and moving around but am still delimited by the Doctors keeping on the brakes. I find myself, however, deeply interested in the Campaign and greatly appreciative of The World's fine treatment of the issues. I had the feeling yesterday that if I could get space on The Times editorial page for a review of Mr. Hoover's speech, I might strengthen a bit the criticism they had made. I venture to enclose you carbon of what I hope they may find space to print tomorrow or the

---

4. Peabody Papers. Copy of his telegram.

next day but I realize that it is getting late in the Campaign.

I have the feeling that perhaps no one can tell until after Election Day what the outcome may be. The great registration and the great activity of the women on both sides—my daughter is out on the Cavalcade today with Mrs. O'Day and others in Republican counties hereabouts—impress upon me the fact that many votes may be decided at the last minute but the influence of bigotry and snobbishness is, I fear, widespread and also beyond calculation. Somehow I have the feeling, as well as the hope, that we shall be rid of having to endure for four years . . . with I am convinced a not successful leader.

I think Mr. Jerome Green's analysis of the qualities of Mr. Hoover and Mr. Smith admirable. It accords with my own observation of the lack of breadth of engineers and most professionals who come to deal with business, and the Presidency requires dealing with politics as well as business.

I am,

Faithfully yours,

For a long time he had wanted to make some recognition of General Palmer's contribution to the development of the Southwest and Mexico. With this in view, he commissioned Evelyn Longmans Batchelder to design a memorial tablet with a profile of Palmer's head upon it, and an inscription. On February 12, 1929, the tablet was placed in the Union Railway Station at Denver. Copies were struck off; one was placed in the Mexico City Railway Station, and one at Hampton Institute. He also compiled a small volume of addresses made at the dedication and included a short biographical sketch of Palmer.

Shortly after the 1928 campaign Peabody left for the South. While there he became ill; he then went to Baltimore for an operation at the Johns Hopkins Hospital. An amusing incident occurred at the hospital. It was the day before Christmas and he was being wheeled along the corridor toward the operating room. A little girl who was being wheeled past him, noticing the white hair and beard of the elderly gentleman, cried, "Oh, are they going to operate on Santa Claus, too?"[5]

The operation was successful, but it was followed by a heart attack, with symptoms of angina pectoris. On May 17, after returning to Saratoga, he wrote to Mr. Bernard M. Baruch:

> . . . I am to be extremely cautious for some time to come . . . I have no question but that I shall gradually overcome this but recognize that, in view of my soon completing my seventy-seventh year, I should be cautious and so I shall be.

One of Mr. Roosevelt's first acts when he became Governor was to appoint Peabody chairman of a commission to make a report and recommendations in regard to Saratoga Springs. Peabody wrote as follows to Mr. Baruch, who was prominently connected with the commission:[6]

> . . . I am really most sorry to have had to forego the privilege of a good talk with you in New York. I am deeply concerned as to the future outcome here and think it of the first importance that you have someone get to the bottom of the whole situation so that you will know the facts in detail respecting the past ten years' management. . . .
>
> I trust that the representatives of the legislature on the committee have been selected with care and that you can arrange that they shall soon go to Europe with some competent advisor respecting an effective program of inspection. . . .

The commission made a thorough study of the Saratoga Springs situation. In February, 1930, it made its report to the legislature. It recommended that the State develop Saratoga Springs intensively and efficiently so as to make it a health resort equal to any in Europe. In the course

---

5. Members of the family.
6. Copy of Mr. Peabody's letter of May 17, 1929, Yaddo files.

of the next few years, the Saratoga Springs Spa was developed into one of the finest health resorts in the world. Each year thousands of persons from all parts of the country came to the Springs to take the medicinal baths.

CHAPTER XXII

Peabody and the New Deal

WITH ALERT STEP THAT BELIED HIS YEARS, PEABODY ARrived at his eightieth birthday. Except that his health required watching, he was as briskly active as in the old days at Spencer Trask and Company.

When the day came, the *New York Times* honored him with an editorial, "Not Measured by Years," in which he was described as a man of "cheerful yesterdays and confident tomorrows" who "keeps himself in vigor because he is alive with human sympathy." The editorial further pointed out that he was as forceful as ever and praised him for his judgments of parties and candidates.

His mind at eighty retained its old clarity. There was no impairment of faculties. Peabody seldom indulged in reminiscences—seldom referred to past happenings unless they served to throw light upon some issue of current interest. No one thought of speaking of him as a "grand old man" for, though snowy-haired, he kept his youthful outlook. It was only when his physicians warned him to slow down that one thought of the passage of time and of the fact that he was no longer young.

2.

Like millions of other Americans, Peabody viewed with grave concern the problems that beset the country after the business slump of 1929. As a result of the critical state of affairs in Mexico, his own income had already for many years before that been seriously threatened. After 1929 he felt still more anxiety for his holdings. On March 8, 1930, he wrote Frank Tannenbaum, an authority on Latin America, that he was profoundly disturbed by the decline in prices of silver, lead and zinc. All his interests in Mexico were practically bankrupt, including coal mines, railroad holdings, and the large metal production plant at Fresnillo, a three million dollar investment. To add to his problems, the office building at 11 Broadway from which came the bulk of the money necessary for maintaining Yaddo was partly depopulated by the building of new skyscrapers uptown, and the income from this source was diminished to a threatening degree.

Ever since his retirement in 1906, Peabody had been drawing upon his accumulated wealth, as well as upon his income, for the support of educational and philanthropic enterprises; what he had left now after meeting his pledges was only a few thousands a year. He was actually hard put to it to meet the many calls upon his generosity and often had to decline a request for help. He was by no means submerged by these financial losses, however; accepting the situation, he attended meetings of the boards of directors on which he served, and made many able suggestions.

He believed that President Hoover had no conception of the true nature of the problems which faced him. In his opinion, the President should have exercised leadership as early as March, 1931, by presenting Congress with a balanced budget and a non-partisan sales tax plan.[1] Steps should be taken at once, Peabody urged. In letters to newspapers and to friends he made a number of suggestions; among other things, he advised railroad reforms.

---

1. Peabody Papers, Yaddo files.

He endorsed the housing program outlined by Alfred E. Smith as a means of providing large scale employment.

As the time for nomination of Presidential candidates approached, he considered the timber within the Democratic Party. Newton D. Baker was his first choice, but Baker was not likely to be elected even if nominated, for certain prejudices had continued to militate against him. His thoughts next turned to Franklin D. Roosevelt, whose personality already had a strong appeal.

Before the time of the Democratic National Convention at Chicago, Peabody was in touch with party leaders in New York State. In the spirit of his early days of political activity, he invited a group of influential party men to Saratoga Springs for a conference. Mr. Roosevelt came to talk with them. Though the session went on in private and the files give scant information, acquaintances of Mr. Peabody consider that plans for the nomination were shaped at this meeting.

While Peabody's relationship with Roosevelt was very different from that which he had had with Wilson, he had confidence in Roosevelt's abilities. He had watched him in state politics in 1911 and had corresponded with him on several occasions when Roosevelt was Assistant Secretary of the Navy. Their common interest in Saratoga Springs developments and in the Warm Springs Foundation had furthered their friendship. If he detected less of Wilson's lofty idealism in Roosevelt, he saw abilities for intelligent leadership which he believed promised well for the country. During the campaign he gave Roosevelt his hearty support.

Peabody's activities took on increased vigor and intensity with the coming of the New Deal. He has sometimes been referred to as a "Brain Truster," and there is evidence that his counsels bore weight. Since many of the files and documents are not yet available, it is difficult to assess his contribution; but several of his activities stand out in clear outline.²

For many years he had known Roosevelt well; their close relations were continued when Mr. Roosevelt went to the White House. Mr. Roosevelt had a real admiration and affection for Mr. Peabody and had confidence in his judgments of men and situations. He was quick to recognize Peabody's comprehensive knowledge of Southern conditions, and his broad acquaintance with national problems.

Peabody praised President Roosevelt's prompt action in meeting the banking crisis which came to a head on Inauguration Day, March 4, 1933. He spoke on the subject of the currency at the Rotary Club in Saratoga Springs and endorsed the banking bill pending in Congress. Later in the year, he expressed himself in favor of developing a commodity standard to take the place of the gold standard. In a letter to Oswald Garrison Villard on November 27, 1933, he wrote:

> It was a lamentable reflection upon our modern thought and consequent action that no sound basis for a commodity standard had been developed. It is beyond doubt, even, that if all the gold in the world were to disappear through some alchemy, commerce would quickly re-adjust itself to some basis for clearing the necessary barter between producers as such, and consumers as such.
>
> I could not but feel a bit ashamed of myself as one of the building committee of the New York Bank in the amount we expended to go down five stories below ground level, and three below the level of the

2. Peabody Papers, Yaddo files. There are letters from Louis McHenry Howe, the President's Secretary, to Mr. Peabody dated Feb. 10, 1933; Mar. 17, 21, 25, 1933; Apr. 5, 21, referring to several matters under consideration. There are letters from Daniel C. Roper, Secretary of the Interior, dated April 14 and 24, 1933, and also notes of thanks for his letters from Frances Perkins, Secretary of Labor, dated Mar. 21 and Apr. 17, 1933, and correspondence with numerous other Government officials.

Atlantic Ocean in order to store gold, and make it practically useless as regards any true utilization, its main use being to ship it back and forth between banks and Washington and across the Ocean, a quite absurd performance for truly intelligent people. . . .[3]

Railroad problems continued to concern Peabody deeply. He advocated Federal authority over the railroads and was critical of the President for not dealing with the situation promptly. In March he sent copies of an article on railroads to his friends. On March 29, 1933, he wrote[4] to Mr. Eugene Koop, a member of the firm of Spencer Trask and Company:

> Dear Mr. Koop:
> Thank you for your kind letter respecting my article on railroad matter. I think you may be interested in seeing copy of letter I have just written to Mr. Moulton, President of the Brookings Institution, which made the elaborate study for the Baruch Committee, a book of nine hundred pages.
> Mr. Brookings was a warm friend of mine, and I have known Mr. Moulton as one of our leading Research students.
> My convictions are only strengthened by more experience as to the now vital necessity for a distinction by the voters in modern democracy. Therefore, I think we can only look forward to better conditions through Government control of the Utilities through which alone modern life is made possible with any sort of satisfaction.
> I am, with appreciation,
> Faithfully yours,
> *George Foster Peabody*
> I hope you read Lippman's Charter Day address at Univ. of California published in Herald-Tribune of March 24.

In April, 1933, the *Survey Graphic* published an article by Mr. Peabody on "Public Railroads and Bond-Holders." He proposed that shippers and investors be dealt

---

3. *Ibid.*
4. Courtesy of Mr. Eugene Koop.

with even-handedly and that a single publicly owned system of transportation be developed in this country.

Realizing, however, that the Government was not going to take over the railroads, he did what he could to promote the adoption of remedies. For instance, in a statement published in the *World Telegram* on April 20, 1933, he discussed the question of securities, concluding with a strong plea for the recognition of the claims of the holders of railroad stocks and bonds.

Peabody was in accord with the administration's industrial recovery program. In a letter to Mr. Roosevelt, he said he had believed from the beginning that the ultimate purpose of the National Industrial Recovery Act was to deal in the large with issues that had been raised many years before by the Industrial Workers of the World.

Regarding government responsibility for meeting business conditions, he wrote his views. On January 11, 1935, the *New York Times* published a letter from Peabody which ran to one and one-fourth columns. Peabody wrote, in part:

> I have read with much interest and provocation to thought your editorial "In Plainer Language" . . .
> First I venture to say that your statement "Big business, as a separate entity, does not exist", is not justified, and the general public will be misled by your statement. My clear conviction is that there is nothing more practically substantial than what is generally understood today by Big Business; that is, the temper of control and the elaborate organization of many agencies relating to legislation as well as statistical data by a few dozen dominant men in great banking organizations and the vast corporations which today exert an influence that is out of proportion to their financial magnitude even.
> While it is true, as you say, that business "is made up of hundreds and thousands of little businesses", it is true as never before in history, I think, that their subordination in many ways to the influence I have

referred to is as powerful as it is subtle. . . .

I wish that they might after reading your editorial, read some portions, at any rate, of Secretary Ickes's book "The New Democracy". While I think that he, as perhaps the administration in general, fails to deal with the fundamental economics of the situation as to rightful ownership of land and all that evolves from the privileges of eminent domain which government has granted; yet the facts as to the situation in large which he sets forth are of vital importance to this country in working out its great experiment in democracy.

All thinkers have realized for generations that from 1776 on we have been making the experiment. Therefore that word is not new by reason of President Roosevelt's use of it, but is an effective assertion of the truth of the situation and of the purpose to deal drastically with the dangers that threaten this experiment. . . . If the people of this country are in need of "rails, bridges, houses, &c" and no corporations or individuals are supplying that need, the government, representing all the people, would be faithless to its trust if, having the best credit in the world and the most thorough understanding of the need, it did not go forward to supply that need. Our President has made it clear again and again, and more particularly to Big Business leaders, that conditions justify in his judgment—which should be the best to be had—the investment of wealth controlled by individuals and corporations in these necessities of the time. . . .

I submit that such conditions as this country has experienced during the last fifteen years warrant efforts to employ labor in manufacture and in purchasing and selling where the margin of profit may seem slight or even doubtful. It is beyond question that, as labor is employed, consumers' purchases are developed. . . .

As time passed, Peabody became increasingly enthusiastic over Roosevelt's leadership. He spoke at meetings, giving arguments in favor of the President's measures. On February 4, 1935, he wrote to Dr. James H. Dillard: "I am kept more or less busy talking to various groups hereabouts." The same day, he wrote to Dr. Will W.

Alexander "I found a very responsive group of Kiwanians interested in my talk last week at Columbus on 'Roosevelt the Man'." In a letter to the *New York Times*, which appeared on May 30, 1935, he declared:

> Franklin Roosevelt not only knows what the people think they need, but he knows what it may be possible for them to have under conditions existing with the minimum of harm and the most of advantage . . . his heart is ever keeping pace with his mind. . . .

One cannot help wondering whether the whole-hearted endorsement of a man of Peabody's long-established reputation may not have had a good deal to do with winning approval for President Roosevelt's policies in circles that might have been expected to oppose them.

It was probably in relation to the agricultural program that Peabody's efforts for New Deal policies were most effective. Here his knowledge of the South and of rural conditions generally made him a valuable source of information and suggestion. He was a consultant without portfolio, to whom the President and many of the administration officials turned for help in ascertaining farmers' needs and formulating a program for farm relief and development.

In spite of efforts already made by the Roosevelt Administration to aid the depressed farmer, farm prices had continued to drop, and values of farm property had reached new lows. Debts had brought many farmers to a state of bankruptcy. To meet the critical situation, the Administration, under the guidance of Secretary of Agriculture Henry A. Wallace, proposed measures of which the two most important were direct aid to farmers and the raising of agricultural prices by the curtailment of agricultural production. These proposals were accepted and put into effect by a series of acts.

The Agricultural Adjustment Act of May 12, 1933,

was designed to prevent wasteful production of crops and to stabilize farm income through a system of marketing quotas. The result was an increase in the farmer's income between 1933 and 1935. But crop reduction brought a reduction of labor on the farm, with the result that many tenant farmers and share croppers found themselves without work and dispossessed.

Mr. Peabody followed these developments with concern. He desired to see more comprehensive measures taken for relief and rehabilitation of the South. At this time he was in touch with Professor Frank Tannenbaum, who had been asked to study rural problems and to write a book incorporating his findings, and who upon making his study, found the situation so urgent that he said: "What we need is not a book, but a program." The Bankhead Bill, later the Bankhead-Jones Bill, incorporated the main suggestions made by Professor Tannenbaum—among them the suggestion that a farm tenant homes corporation be created.[5]

Mr. Peabody received a copy of Dr. Tannenbaum's suggestions. He was so impressed that he assembled a committee of influential persons to advocate the proposed program. He went to Washington and lobbied in behalf of the Bill.

Dr. Tannenbaum tells us of the vivid picture made by Peabody at Washington. Erect as a tall tree, snowy-haired, he stepped from office to office speaking to Congressmen, many of whom he knew well personally.

Mr. Peabody made further efforts in behalf of the Bankhead Bill. In a letter to the *New York Times* published on March 16, 1935, he wrote:

> I feel warranted in saying that perhaps no move in the Congress has been more significant or offers greater

---

5. Dr. Frank Tannenbaum to author, Oct. 30, 1944.

promise for the future of the country than this wise effort to eliminate the homeless and practically peripatetic classes of our population who are more widely scattered through the country than is realized by those who have not studied the question. . . .
It will always be true that the livelihood of our citizenship will be dependent upon the farmer, the lumberjack and the miner, without whose efforts there would be no food nor clothing nor provision for necessary shelter. . . .

He communicated with Clark Howell, publisher of the *Atlanta Constitution* regarding the Bankhead Bill.[6]

March 25, 1935

The Hon. Clark Howell
Atlanta, Georgia.
Dear Mr. Howell:

Many thanks to you for your prompt advice to me by telegraph of your public temper *and willingness to help on in the matter of the farm movement.*

It would really be a very great thing to have the million and three-quarters of Southern tenant and sharecropper folk so located that their children can have a continuity of school opportunity. It is, I think, rather difficult to calculate the gain that will come to these Southern States.

I hope we shall have the opportunity to talk over the great importance that these Southern States have to the future of the country—more than is at all realized by even our Southern leaders in my judgment. And, as for the North and West, they are as densely ignorant on this question as alas are some of these farmer folk whom we hope to have enlightened.

In connection with this question "enlightenment", I venture to hope that you will read, if you have not already, 'The American Way' just published by Dr. Studebaker, the new United States Commissioner of Education.

I am very happy to think the President has been at hand for the vital needs of our Recovery decade. He is a most attractive personality and when he next comes to

---

6. Dr. Will W. Alexander had wired Mr. Peabody urging him to send a telegram to Mr. Howell in an effort to bring the Bankhead Bill to the Senate (May 22, 1935). Peabody Papers, Yaddo files.

Georgia, I hope that you will meet him.

The present one-quarter of our population, *dominantly Anglo-Saxon*, largely influences the action of Congress at all times and rather completely so with the Democratic Administration.

My friend, Fred Osborn, author of *'Dynamics of Population,'* published last fall, tells me that it is possible, perhaps probable,—from a study of the census returns that within twenty-five years a majority of the Continental population of the United States will reside in our fifteen Southern States. The present educational status continuing, that, as you will realize, is an appalling prospect. Therefore, the President was quite right when he said to me 'I think Education is the way out'.

Probably you have seen, but I am sending to you copy of Embree's pamphlets and the study made by Rosenwald Fund. I am

                Faithfully yours,

GFP/AWD

                George Foster Peabody

Because of the critical conditions among the tenant farmers, the Rosenwald Fund made an appropriation for a study of the farm situation. The study was made by Dr. Charles S. Johnson of Fisk University, Dr. Will W. Alexander and Professor Edwin R. Embree; their conclusions were presented in a little book, *The Collapse of Farm Tenancy*.

The authors were anxious that the results of their study should be brought to the attention of the public in the most effective possible way. They communicated with Mr. Peabody and asked his advice. He agreed to do what he could, and asked them to meet him in the lobby of the Hotel Chatham in New York. They were glad to do so. When the time came, he arrived promptly, accompanied by a man whom he introduced as a newspaper reporter formerly with the *World*. Will Alexander had a few misgivings at the thought of having an ex-*World* reporter do the work, but he was ready to take Mr. Peabody's suggestion. The conference resulted in wide publicity for the book, and wide dissemination of its material.

One of the best examples of Peabody's tireless energy is given by Alexander. A short time after *The Collapse of Farm Tenancy* was published, Dr. Alexander was visiting Mr. Peabody at the latter's Warm Springs home, Pine Glade. Peabody listened intently to his friend's discussion of the farm problem. "I want you to talk with the President," he said.

He stepped to the telephone and gave the "Little White House" number. The President's secretary, Mr. MacIntyre, came to the phone. Mr. Peabody told him he would like to make an appointment for Dr. Alexander to talk with Mr. Roosevelt. It would not be possible, said Mr. MacIntyre—the President's calendar was full for the day. Mr. Peabody used his powers of persuasion, but without result. He finally gave it up and came back to Dr. Alexander. They resumed their conversation.

A few minutes later, Mr. Peabody again rose and stepped to the telephone. This time he asked for Miss LeHand, the President's private secretary. She said the President was tied up. Mr. Peabody told her how urgent it was that the President talk with Dr. Alexander. She left the phone; after a few minutes, she returned. The President would see Dr. Alexander at 12:30.

At the appointed time, Dr. Alexander was ushered into the living room at the "Little White House." The President was sitting alone in front of the fire. After a brief greeting they talked of rural problems. At the end Dr. Alexander feared that he had not covered a great deal of ground. On leaving, however, he placed a copy of the book on the table beside Mr. Roosevelt's chair. Some time later, he heard the President refer to the contents of the book.

The above incident is only one of many illustrating Peabody's ingenuity in arranging conferences on vital issues.[7] In Dr. Alexander's opinion, much credit should be given to him for his help in meeting the farm crisis; his tireless work and unflagging enthusiasm were among the chief factors in bringing about the establishment of the Farm Security Administration.

Peabody's interest in the agricultural program and in the conservation measures of the New Deal led him to take an active part in the Tennessee Valley development. This program was established a few days after the enactment of the Agricultural Adjustment Act. The Tennessee Valley Authority, established by Act of Congress on May 18, 1933, was empowered to carry out a conservation program which included the acquisition of land, the construction and maintenance of dams, the selling of surplus power, and the re-settlement of persons displaced by the new development. Peabody, who had for years been an advocate of conservation of the natural resources of the country, was heartily in sympathy with this development. It was his particular wish that the Negro residents of the Tennessee Valley be given consideration in the planning. To this end he had a number of meetings with Will W. Alexander of the Resettlement Administration. He was also in touch with Dr. Arthur Morgan, and in this connection wrote to Will Alexander on October 31, 1934:[8]

> We are leaving here November 8th, meaning to stop over at Knoxville and see my friend, Dr. Morgan. We certainly have plenty of complexes to deal with. . . .

On November 28, 1934, Dr. Morgan sent him an outline of the integrated rural program of the T.V.A., showing the proposed improvements in two counties. Later, in a letter

7. On November 30, 1935, Peabody wrote to Will W. Alexander: "The President kindly called on me the other day at his own suggestion, and we had a forty-five minute talk." (Copy of his letter is in Peabody Papers, Yaddo files.)
8. Copy of letter, Peabody Papers, Yaddo files.

PEABODY AND THE NEW DEAL

to acquaintances, Peabody writes:[9] "We came down through the Norris Dam country this year."

He was cheered by the efforts under way to meet rural needs. In a letter to Will W. Alexander on December 28, 1934, he wrote:

> It was good to have seen you yesterday and to have met Mr. Raper of your office for the first time. He made an excellent impression upon me. . . .
> I have jokingly said to the President, "when you wear all these youngsters out, send for me and I will help you out." But I am often tempted to think that he would be helped by the sort of presentation of the whole situation which I have indicated above. . . .

In 1936 the agricultural program received a blow when the Supreme Court declared unconstitutional several parts of the Agricultural Adjustment Act. However, several acts which had come in the wake of the A.A.A., including provisions for resettlement of farmers and conservation, were now established policy. Instead of the A.A.A. several laws were enacted between 1936 and 1938 culminating in the Agricultural Adjustment Act of 1938, which drew together previous enactments in modified form and called for a broadened farm program. Peabody lived to see a new day of agricultural development dawning in the South. His tireless work of publicizing, his letters, his newspaper articles, his telephone calls and trips to Washington, were undoubtedly a notable factor in bringing about this new day.[10]

Though Peabody's activities in the early years of the New Deal were mostly concerned with domestic affairs, he also played a part in the development of territorial and foreign policies, chiefly those affecting the Caribbean region. On one occasion, he went to Hyde Park for a talk

---

9. *Ibid.*
10. This is the consensus of all with whom the matter was discussed by the author.

with the President about the Virgin Islands.[11] Harold L. Ickes, Secretary of the Interior, was present at the conference. Writing to Mr. Ickes on March 1, 1934, Mr. Peabody said:

> You, of course, know of my deep interest in the outcome of the work which I had the high privilege of advancing through the Commission which kindly accepted my invitation to make the study which resulted in a report to the Navy department which so fortunately Governor Pearson has called his "Bible" in connection with the work he has undertaken.

Peabody's long interest in Mexican affairs and in Latin American relationships with the United States, led him to be one of the prime movers in the establishment of the "Good Neighbor League," under the leadership of Stanley High in the early years of the New Deal.

---

11. He was a member of the Virgin Islands Council. The appointment was made on February 3, 1934, when he was nearly eighty-two.

CHAPTER XXIII

At Warm Springs

PEABODY AND HIS DAUGHTER, MRS. WAITE, HAD BEEN PLANning for some time to make their winter home at Warm Springs. The place appealed to them; they enjoyed especially the invigorating air of Pine Mountain. Here they finally built a cottage which they intended to use as their home for six months of the year. Set among the pine trees and shrubs, with dark-shingled roof and soft-tone boards, the cottage blended well with the scenery.

They enjoyed planning the furnishings, Mrs. Waite taking the lead, to Peabody's amusement at times. He wrote to friends telling them of busy days getting the new house ready and received jolly letters in reply.

In March, 1934, Miss Pardee went to Warm Springs to assist them in making the house ready for occupancy. In April the task was completed and Mr. Peabody and Mrs. Waite moved in.

Only Mr. Peabody's failing health cast a shadow on life in the new home. They had thought that winter spent in this milder climate might safeguard him, but recurring heart attacks warned him to slow down. He kept up as much of his correspondence as possible, however, and received callers who wished to discuss social problems with him.

For many months he had been troubled and saddened by the ill health of his nephew, Carlos, always so close to him. Carlos had been suffering from a heart condition which left him little confidence in his own ability. Peabody wrote his nephew letters of fatherly advice and encouragement but his extreme concern was thinly veiled. On September 10, 1935, Carlos passed away.

Little of the old life was left now. Parents, sister, brothers, Carlos, the Trasks, Edward M. Shepard, Ogden, Palmer, Natalie Curtis, Wilson,—all were only memories. But far from spending his days in repining, Peabody was still absorbed in the struggle to obtain reforms, and in discharging his responsibilities in connection with Hampton, Penn School, and other institutions. The pleasure of his daughter's company and her assistance in all his undertakings meant much to him.

In 1935, upon his return from the winter spent at Warm Springs, he was honored at the opening of the stated-owned Spa at Saratoga. Governor Herbert H. Lehman, in introducing him as a speaker, referred to him as "that splendid pioneer of Saratoga as a health resort."

By force of will, he kept himself going. Through much of the year 1936 he was ill. Doctors and nurses restricted him to brief interviews with persons who sought his time, or for whom he had sent. It was difficult for him to become resigned to a life without usefulness. On one occasion,[1] hearing that Dr. Will Alexander had recently been in Atlanta on business, he wrote expressing a wistful regret at not seeing him. Dr. Alexander, who had wished to spare his friend any exertion, immediately wired Mr. Peabody and took the next train South. Mr. Peabody was so feeble that the physician would permit only a fifteen-minute talk. When Will Alexander rose to go after their brief discussion, Peabody said, "If they will let me see you one fifteen minutes, they will do so again after I am

---

1. Interview with Dr. Will W. Alexander, May 13, 1944.

rested."[2] Thus the two friends had several fifteen-minute talks interspersed by rest periods; by the end of the day, they had gone over many matters that were of vital significance in the New Deal agricultural program.

One day when he was very ill, an incident occurred which made a deep impression upon Mr. Peabody. Life was ebbing away, and he appeared to be sinking into a final coma. He believed, as he later said, that he was dead and that he saw the shadowy figures of the other world. His daughter, who was sitting beside the bed, called to him, beseeching him to live. With uncanny force, he pulled himself out of the enveloping shadows and exerted enough strength to return to reality.

In December, 1936, and early in 1937, he was confined to his bed with an attack of influenza. This left him in a weakened condition, but by the time summer came he had recovered sufficiently to return to Saratoga Springs.

That summer his daughter invited a few close friends to remember his eighty-fifth birthday with them. A recital was given in his honor at Yaddo by members of the Music Departments of Smith and Vassar. That very evening, announcement came from Georgia that a new highway was being constructed which was to bear the name of the George Foster Peabody Memorial Highway.[3]

In the autumn of 1937, the family returned to Warm Springs for the winter. Though failing in strength, he kept up some of his correspondence and was able to see a few visitors. He said he hoped to live long enough to see the 1940 Presidential election; he believed Roosevelt would win, if nominated.

Early in March he grew worse. He believed the end was near and sent for his household staff in order to sug-

---

2. Statements made by Mrs. Marjorie Peabody Waite, Dr. Will W. Alexander, and Dr. Arthur D. Wright.
3. *New York Times*, July 28, 1937.

gest to them that they be looking for employment elsewhere. Doctors and nurses knew it was a question of only a few days, for his heart was weakening. On March 4, 1938, he passed away. At his bedside when the end came was his daughter. Near him also were his devoted friends, Miss Pardee and Mrs. Ames.

With the simplicity which he had liked, they made the last arrangements. Many years before in talking with his mother, he had expressed a desire to have his body cremated. His wishes were followed. By request of his family, flowers were omitted, and friends were asked to give to philanthropic objects instead. His body was removed to a chapel in Jacksonville, Florida, where, on March 5, 1938, the services of the Episcopal Church were read and cremation took place. His ashes were later removed to Yaddo and buried in a grave near that of his wife.

Messages of condolence arrived from all parts of the country—from friends in educational work, in government, in business, and in philanthropy. There were many public testimonials to Peabody's character and work. The *New York Times* said that few Americans had had a career of public service more devoted than his.

Memorial services were arranged at Warm Springs by his friends. President Roosevelt was unable to attend, but he wrote to Mrs. Waite that Peabody's memory would always be honored at Warm Springs, since he had given his efforts unsparingly to the work of the Foundation. He wrote of the wide range of Mr. Peabody's activities and the depth and warmth of his sympathy.

In the afternoon of March 11, 1938, his friends gathered at Warm Springs to pay tribute to him. After a reading of the Lord's Prayer, the Fort Valley singers sang "Every Time I Feel the Spirit Moving in My Heart, I Will

Pray," "Roll, Jordan, Roll," "Go Down, Moses," and "Swing Low, Sweet Chariot." The Reverend H. A. Hunt of the Fort Valley School followed those with a reading of Isaiah: 61. The speakers were President Arthur Howe, of Hampton Institute; Dr. Roland B. Daniel, retired superintendent of the Columbus public schools; and President Harmon W. Caldwell of the University of Georgia. All testified to the worth of Peabody as humanitarian and statesman.

Memorial services were also held at Holy Trinity Church in Brooklyn, on April 24, 1938; selections were played on the organ which he, with his family, had given as a memorial to his brother. The musical program included Widor's *Adagio,* Beethoven's *Sixth Symphony,* Wagner's *Prelude to Parsifal,* and several anthems by the choir. The speakers were John H. Finley of the *New York Times,* the Right Reverend Ernest M. Stires, Bishop of the diocese, and Roscoe C. E. Brown, member of the vestry of Holy Trinity and prominent in the civic life of Brooklyn. Tributes were paid to Peabody's public service and to his consecration of spirit.

Other testimonials followed. The schools with which he had had a long connection passed resolutions expressing their loss. The May issue of *The Southern Workman* was devoted to him; it carried the dedication, "To George Foster Peabody 'Lover of Men' this number is a memorial." Thus Peabody passed from this life mourned and honored.

CHAPTER XXIV

In Conclusion

LOOKING BACK OVER THE LIFE OF GEORGE FOSTER PEAbody one is impressed by the multitude of his interests. Although certain causes were nearest to his heart, he gave his time and attention to a great many. Through his life one increasing purpose ran, while he pursued now one immediate goal, now another. Dominating his thought was the ideal of an enlightened democracy, of which each citizen should be a responsible member—a democracy in which each element should be so well adjusted to the rest that there would be no occasion for dissension; a state which should have no thought or fear of war with any other state.

Peabody had faith in America—in her potentialities as a leader among nations. With the same orderliness with which he would have mapped out a business enterprise, he set about formulating his ideas for a practical program that should help the country to fill its optimum role. Education became the central feature of his planning. Schools must be multiplied and broadened; other educational undertakings must be encouraged; every citizen must be both informed and inspired in the interest of a responsible community. His activities in education, in politics, in the peace movement, in religion, all came to a focus at this point.

He tried to understand the needs of the whole country. At his study table at Lake George or at Saratoga Springs, he drew upon the practical experiences of his early years, and, with the benefit of that perspective, charted the course which he thought the country should follow. His inculcation of his ideas through correspondence, personal conferences, putting leaders in touch with one another, bears the stamp of a benign Jove. His assurance in regard to his convictions, though obvious, was not objectionable, for he deported himself with unfailing courtesy in a group. Though capable of a cutting word, he seldom resorted to one, preferring instead the reasonable exposition of his views and a dispassionate argument on their merits.

He loved the South with the devoted intensity of a native who has been uprooted. He was not an expatriate, for he kept touch; as soon as he had railroad fare, he returned to visit the state of his birth and his childhood, and here, years later, he died. His pride in the South had no taint of sentimentality. But he believed sincerely in the future of the South; he considered that it had resources, both material and spiritual, which would enrich the nation more and more in the years to come.

Yet one remembers that he was a Northerner too. Of New England ancestry and conditioned to the North from boyhood, he was at home in this region. He liked the correctness of life on Brooklyn Heights. He enjoyed the dynamics of New York business and the Stock Exchange. He liked the scenery of upstate New York with its gracious rolling countryside, its tracery of mountains in the distance. Most of all, the ties of family and his closest personal friends bound him to his adopted region.

It would be hard to name Peabody's activities in brief compass. Two or three stand out in the boldest outline. Among these is his connection with railroad development. Entering the investment and banking business at the age of twenty-eight, he was an important figure in the reorganizing of old roads and the building of new lines, particularly in the Rocky Mountain region. Though less gigantic in his enterprises than James J. Hill, Collis P. Huntington, the Morgans and the Goulds, he was an indispensable part of the transportation epic in the late nineteenth and early twentieth centuries. In pursuing this work he was also one of the exploiters of natural resources, an activity which has won both praise and blame from the American public. He was one of the outstanding figures in the development of the electric illuminating industry. A more definitive account of his business career should in time be written.

As a business man, he was one of the paradoxical figures of history. At the height of his reputation as financier, he retired from business in order to give away the fortune he had made. Moreover, though he made his money through the intense competition of private enterprise, and though he retained important stock and directorships in railroad companies, he was a staunch and tireless advocate of government ownership of railroads.

Important as were his activities in business, they are matched, or surpassed, by his efforts in other fields. Always actively concerned with national politics, he took part in presidential campaigns from 1884 through 1936. At the same time he was a force in state, county, and municipal affairs. He had a personal acquaintance with most of the men who were successively, in that period, governors of New York, and he was often consulted by them.

As a conservationist, his name is remembered in several connections: the preservation of trees on his own thousand acre estate at Lake George; the development of Saratoga Springs and Warm Springs; the growth of the school of forestry at the University of Georgia; and, not least, the mapping out of the Tennessee Valley project, to the leaders of which he gave much wise counsel and encouragement.

He was a friend of Woodrow Wilson and of Newton D. Baker; it is known that his suggestions carried weight with Wilson and with Wilson's unofficial adviser, Colonel House. It is also known that his varied experience, his good judgment, and his enthusiastic support were valuable to leaders in the Franklin D. Roosevelt administration, particularly in connection with the agricultural and conservation programs; the extent of his influence on these developments cannot now be established because of the recency of the history and the unavailability of some of the official files.

He is perhaps best known as a humanitarian—one who did much to further the causes of education, of religion, of charity, of peace, and of inter-racial understanding. Many Negroes have said that they have had no better friend than Mr. Peabody.

One remembers, too, his services to arts and letters— his gifts of organs to churches and of art collections to museums, his aid in the establishment of the Bach festival, his encouragement of the study of Negro and Indian folk culture.

His activities as publicist constitute one of his chief contributions. His indefatigable energy in writing letters to newspapers and to individuals, his circulation of pamphlets and books, his arranging of conferences at his home, all were of incalculable value in the clarification of issues. As a propagandist for peace, Peabody belongs in the front rank.

He was a distinguished host in the old tradition. Dinners at his home were occasions to remember for their epicurean fare, as well as for the distinguished company there gathered. He delighted in hospitality and spared no pains to entertain his guests.

Peabody's life was marked by rich friendships with both men and women. In his letters, he rarely unbent from his customary reserve, but one senses a warmth behind the words. Particularly was this true when he wrote to a young person or to a child.

Peabody's love for Katrina Trask is one of the interesting romances of American life. Here was the material of a great novel: three persons involved in what might have been an impossible triangle, hostile and painful, but achieving, nevertheless, comradeship and mutual trust. The atmosphere of medieval romance which surrounded Yaddo is almost incredible to a matter-of-fact mind, yet it actually existed. Katrina Trask, an amazing personality, part visionary, part realist, was the chief source of Peabody's inspiration. His natural striving to make the world a better place was intensified by her conception of him as a knight with feats to perform. What he would have done without her influence would no doubt have been considerable, for he was a man of energy and of clear and alert mind, and he loved his fellow-man. But what he might have done without Katrina Trask is idle speculation, for she was the central figure of his life.

Friends have indicated that they saw a change in Mr. Peabody as he grew older. He retained the clarity of mind and the balanced judgment which he had had as a young man, but he mellowed and lived in a more informal way. Some say that he began a new phase of his life when he adopted a daughter—that the presence of younger folk about the house gave him a sense of fun that he had not had in the stern days of his own youth.

The total effect and worth of one person's striving for human advancement is always a difficult matter to determine. The case of Mr. Peabody is no exception. He was one of a number of pioneers who built fortunes, and then contributed large sums for good causes. We have indicated some of his specific contributions as philanthropist and publicist; the intangibles of his influence cannot be measured.

The general public remembers him as a tall, picturesque, white-haired man, benefactor of Hampton, friend of the South. His family thinks of his gentleness, of his kindness, and of a certain dynamic quality that made life in his company always interesting and worthwhile. Posterity will think of him as a banker, philanthropist, and publicist.

Bibliography

PERSONAL CONTACTS

INTERVIEWS

Dr. Will W. Alexander, May 13, 1944.
Mrs. Elizabeth Ames, Director of Yaddo, summers 1940 and 1941; July 9, 1944.
Mr. Everett C. Bacon, partner, Spencer Trask and Company, April 2, 1940.
Mr. Robert C. Beadle, former secretary to Mr. Peabody, March 29, 1940; July, 1944.
Mr. W. W. Brierley, member of the staff of the General Education Board, June 11, 1940.
Mr. Donald C. Brown, president of the Mexican Northern Railway, July 25, 1940.
Mr. Edwin W. Bulkley, partner, Spencer Trask and Company, April 2, 1940.
Dr. Nicholas Murray Butler, president of Columbia University.
Dr. Roscoe C. E. Brown, professor of Journalism, emeritus, Columbia University, April 5, 1940.
Dr. George Washington Carver, Tuskegee Institute.
Miss Rossa B. Cooley, principal of Penn Normal Industrial and Agricultural School, Summer, 1940.
Mr. Jackson Davis, staff member of the General Education Board, June 11, 1940.
Dr. Lewis B. Franklin, April 20, 1944.
Mrs. Hollis B. Frissell, Hampton Institute, August, 1941.
Mr. Harry Hodgson, Athens, Georgia, June 14, 1940.
Miss Grace B. House, assistant principal of Penn Normal Industrial and Agricultural School, June, 1940.
Mr. Pierre Jay, former chairman of the Federal Reserve Bank Board of New York, April 16, 1941.
Dr. Thomas Jesse Jones, director of the Phelps-Stokes Fund, April 23, 1940.
Mr. Eugene J. Koop, member of the firm of Spencer Trask and Company, April 7, 1945.
The Reverend J. Howard Melish, rector of Holy Trinity Church, Brooklyn, March 26, 1940; May, 1944.

Mr. Henry Morgenthau, Sr., May 17, 1940.
Mr. Acosta Nichols, partner, Spencer Trask and Company, April 2, 1940.
Mr. L. W. Noland, president, Saratoga National Bank, June 24, 1940.
Miss Allena Gilbert Pardee, summers 1940, 1941; July 8, 9, 1944.
The Reverend Edward M. Parrott, rector of St. James Episcopal Church, Lake George, June, 1940.
Mr. and Mrs. James Paul, June 26, 1940.
Mrs. Charles S. Peabody, May 10, 1940.
Mr. T. K. Peabody, Columbus, Georgia, August, 1942.
Mrs. Helen Ogden (Mrs. Alexander) Purves, May 30, 1941.
Mr. Robert Ogden Purves, August, 1941.
Mr. John D. Rockefeller, Jr., June 10, 1940.
The Reverend Irving G. Rouillard, rector of Bethesda Episcopal Church, Saratoga Springs, New York, June 24, 1940.
Mr. R. E. Safford, secretary of the Mexican Northern Railway, April 12, 1940.
Mr. William J. Schieffelin, April 19, 1940.
Mr. James Shannon, June 29, 1940.
Mr. F. A. Sills, manager Broadway Realty Company, March 29, 1940.
Mr. Alfred E. Smith, former governor of New York, June 3, 1940.
Mr. William Mason Smith, April, 1941.
Mrs. Adele Ochs (Mrs. A. H.) Sulzberger, June 4, 1940.
Dr. Frank Tannenbaum, educator and author, October 30, 1944.
Mrs. Marjorie Peabody Waite, spring, summer, 1940; summer, 1941.

Visits

Yaddo, Saratoga Springs, New York, summers of 1940, 1941, 1944.
Hampton Institute, Hampton Virginia, summer, 1941.
Penn Normal Industrial and Agricultural School, St. Helena Island, South Carolina, summer, 1941.
Saratoga Springs Reservation, summer, 1940.
Skidmore College, summer, 1941.
Warm Springs Foundation, Warm Springs, Georgia, August, 1941.
Tuskegee Institute, Tuskegee, Alabama, Dr. F. D. Patterson, president.

MANUSCRIPT MATERIALS

George Foster Peabody Papers. At Yaddo. Letters, documents, pamphlets, clippings. (About 120 letter files.) Courtesy of Mrs. Marjorie Peabody Waite.

BIBLIOGRAPHY

George Foster Peabody Correspondence with Mr. John D. Rockefeller, Jr. A number of letters in Rockefeller's files. Courtesy of Mr. John D. Rockefeller, Jr.
George Foster Peabody Papers. (Several letters at the New York Public Library, manuscript room.)
Hampton Institute Collection. Correspondence with Mr. Peabody.
Tuskegee Institute Collection. Correspondence with Mr. Peabody.
Letter from President Ralph P. Bridgman, Hampton Institute, Hampton, Virginia, to author, March 15, 1944.
Letter from Miss Rossa B. Cooley to author, June 26, 1944.
Letters from Miss Eleanor A. Gilman, Hampton Institute, Hampton, Virginia, to author, April 6, May 31, 1944.
Letter from Mr. Charles G. Gomillion, Director, Department of Records and Research, Tuskegee Institute, Tuskegee, Alabama, to author, May 18, 1944.
Letter from Mr. C. B. Hershey, Acting President, Colorado College, Colorado Springs, Colorado, to author, May 24, 1944.
Letter from Mr. I. C. Moyer, General Secretary, Young Men's Christian Association, Columbus, Georgia, to author, May 19, 1944.
Robert C. Ogden Papers. Library of Congress. Courtesy of Mrs. Helen Ogden Purves.
Letter from Mr. W. W. Postlethwaite, Director of Museum, to Acting President C. B. Hershey, Colorado College, May 15, 1944.
Letter from Mr. R. E. Safford, Secretary of the Mexican Northern Railway Company, to author, April 18, 1940.
Letter (and other materials) from Miss Kathryn H. Starbuck, Secretary of Skidmore College, to author, September 8, 1944.
Booker T. Washington Papers. Library of Congress.
Woodrow Wilson Papers. Library of Congress. Courtesy of Mrs. Woodrow Wilson.

SPECIAL REPORTS, PAMPHLETS, ETC.

Annual Reports of the American Church Institute for Negroes, 1906-1912: 1917-1918.
Annual Reports of the Federal Reserve Bank of New York, 1915-1919. Washington, Government Printing Office.
Annual Report of the Surgeon-in-Chief, Georgia Warm Springs Foundation. Warm Springs, Georgia, 1930.
Appeal by the Reverend Algernon S. Crapsey, S. T. D. To the Court of Review of the Protestant Episcopal Church. New York, 1906.

Citizens' Union Campaign Scrap-Book, 1901. New York Public Library, Room 328.
Educational Conditions in Tennessee, Bulletin of the Southern Education Board, December, 1902, Vol. I. No. 3.
The Edison Electric Light Company, Fourth Bulletin. New York, Feb. 24, 1882.
The Edison Electric Light Company, Seventh Bulletin. New York, April 17, 1882.
The Edison Electric Light Company, Eighth Bulletin. New York, April 27, 1882.
Edison Electric Illuminating Co. of Brooklyn. Annual Reports of the Board of Directors to the Stockholders at their Annual Meeting, 1896; 1897.
Edison Electric Illuminating Companies of Greater New York. Spencer Trask & Co. Bankers, New York City, 1898.
Edison Electric Illuminating Co. of New York. Report of the Board of Trustees to the Stockholders at Their Annual Meeting, January 19, 1886.
Edison Electric Illuminating Co. of New York. Report of Trustees to the Stockholders at their Annual Meeting, January 28, 1890.
History of the Central Y. M. C. A. of Columbus, Georgia. Columbus, Georgia, 1941.
The History of the Movement for the Monetary Convention at Indianapolis, January 12 and 13, 1897. Also the Report of Its Proceedings.
Johnson, Joseph F., "The Crisis and Panic of 1907." Reprinted from *Political Science Quarterly,* XXIII. Boston: Ginn and Company, 1908.
National Democratic Platform Adopted at the Convention of the National Democratic Party at Indianapolis, Indiana, September, 1896.
Palmer, T. A., *Beet Sugar—A Brief History of Its Origin and Development,* March 2, 1903. Fifty-seventh Congress, Second Session, Senate Document, Number 204.
Proceedings at Conference Called by New York City Committee of Fifty. Albany, February 22, 1892.
Proceedings of the Second Capon Springs Conference for Education in the South, 1899.
Report of the Monetary Commission of the Indianapolis Convention of Boards of Trade, Chambers of Commerce, Commercial Clubs, and Other Similar Bodies of the United States. Indianapolis, 1900.
Report of the Re-Organization Committee of the Denver & Rio Grande Western Railway Company. To the Bond and

Stockholders of the Rio Grande Western Railway Company Upon the Conclusion of their Work, May, 1891.

Reports of the Commissioners on the state of Saratoga Springs, 1910 through 1916.

Syracuse Movement, Kings County. Proceedings on Dissolution of Central Committee, November 11, 1892.

Pursuant to Senate Resolutions 79,386, and 418. Vol. II. United States Senate, Sixty-Second Congress, Third Session. Washington, 1913.

Wiley, H. W., *The Sugar Beet: Culture, Seed Development, Manufacture and Statistics.* United States Department of Agriculture, Farmers' Bulletin, Number 52. Washington, 1897.

NEWSPAPERS

Athens Banner
 June 16, 1904, "George Foster Peabody" (editorial).

The Brooklyn Daily Eagle
 May 2, 1906, "George Foster Peabody."
 May 12, 1911, "Heights House Leased."
 Oct. 2, 1912, "Mr. Melish for Mr. Peabody."
 Feb. 5, 1921, "Widow of Spencer Trask Married to George F. Peabody."

The Charlotte News
 Aug. 4, 1904, "George Foster Peabody." (editorial).

Christian Science Monitor
 Oct. 15, 1930, "Mexicans Honor American Rail Builder's Name."
 May 23, 1933, "Morgan Holds Private Banker Fills Big Need."

New York Daily Tribune
 Oct. 7, 1901, "Mr. Peabody's Defection."
 Oct. 10, 1901, "Peabody as a Reformer."
 Oct. 10, 1901, "Peabody Resigns From C. U."
 Oct. 16. 1901, "Peabody With the Boss."
 Oct. 25, 1901, "Mr. Peabody in a Debate."
 March 23, 1902, "Sketch."
 May 2, 1906, "George Foster Peabody Retires."
 May 13, 1906, "Abandoning Business For a Life of Humanitarian Effort."
 Jan. 21, 1910, "Mr. Trask's Will."

New York Herald
 Jan. 24, 1899, "Electric Light Trust Forming."

New York Herald Tribune
    May 26, 1933, "Today and To-morrow: The Investigation of Private Bankers," by Walter Lippmann.
    Sept. 22, 1934, "R. F. Cutting, 82, Dies; Reformer of Government."

New York Post
    March 20, 1914, "Private Bank Law Wanted."

New York Sun
    May 6, 1906, "Many Sided George F. Peabody."

The New York Times
    Sept. 24, 1895, "It Looks Like a Democratic Year."
    Jan. 21, 1899, "Light Trust's Big Deal."
    Nov. 13, 1901, "Gift to Montgomery Y. M. C. A."
    May 30, 1902, "Peabody Not a Candidate."
    Jan. 6, 1906, "G. F. Peabody on Railway Ownership."
    Jan. 2, 1910, "Mr. Trask's Funeral Monday."
    Jan. 30, 1910, "High Tribute Paid to Spencer Trask."
    Feb. 14, 1910, "No Basis For Suit, Says G. F. Peabody."
    Mar. 15, 1913, "Talk of George Foster Peabody for Port Collector."
    April 27, 1913, "Yaddo, The Trask Estate, Devoted to Public's Use."
    May 19, 1913, "Peabody Declines Renomination."
    Oct. 1, 1914, "Name Class C. Directors."
    Jan. 2, 1915, "Three Men Chosen for Trade Board."
    Jan. 15, 1915, "Need of Defense."
    Jan. 28, 1915, "Peabody Will Not Accept."
    Feb. 14, 1915, "George Foster Peabody Asks Five Definite Questions and Suggests the Answers."
    Mar. 8, 1916, "America Noah's Ark to Warring Nations."
    Nov. 30, 1916, "Bryan the Guest of Peabody."
    Jan. 4, 1917, " 'Neutral Conference' Now Moves for Peace."
    Jan . 31, 1917, "Praise Wilson Peace Idea."
    Mar. 2, 1917, "Heads Campaign to Aid Negroes."
    Mar. 29, 1917, "Negroes Invading North."
    Aug. 4, 1917, "An Example for Pacifists."
    Aug. 15, 1917, "Council Aids Kaiser, Peabody Asserts."
    Aug. 16, 1917, "A Pacifist and Yet a Patriot."
    Aug. 30, 1917, "Finds 'Majesty of Purpose'."
    Nov. 28, 1917, "War Savings Certificates."
    Oct. 9, 1918, "Loan Creeps Up; Total $1,600,000,000."
    Oct. 9, 1918, "New Yorkers Laud President's Move."
    Oct. 10, 1920, "Democracy Personified."
    Oct. 10, 1920, "Peabody Joins Cox Ranks."

BIBLIOGRAPHY

Oct. 20, 1920, " 'Match the President' Fund Now $91,500."
Oct. 21, 1920, "Peabody Replies to Dabney."
Oct. 31, 1920, "Peabody Condemns 'Atrocious' Cartoon."
Feb. 6, 1921, "Mrs. Trask Weds Geo. Foster Peabody."
Jan. 9, 1922, "Mrs. G. F. Peabody Dies of Pneumonia."
Jan. 12, 1922, "Mrs. Peabody Buried on Hill at Yaddo."
Jan. 15, 1922, "To Carry Out Plan For 'Art Retreat'."
July 2, 1924, "Baker and Roosevelt."
July 12, 1924, "McAdoo Visits Davis; Will Back Ticket; Smith Also Calls."
Oct. 19, 1924, "Plea For the State Led Smith To Run."
Feb. 19, 1925, "Gives More Land to State."
July 5, 1925, "Definition of Taxation." (Letter).
July 17, 1925, "Needs of the South." (Letter).
Nov. 24, 1925, "Urges Bancroft Memorial."
Nov. 30, 1925, "Peabody Organ Dedicated."
Apr. 27, 1926, "F. D. Roosevelt Buys Spa."
Apr. 28, 1926, "Buys a Georgia Resort."
May 5, 1926, "George F. Peabody Adopts a Daughter."
May 6, 1926, "3,000 Join in Tribute To Oscar S. Straus."
Feb. 24, 1927, "The Monetary Commission."
Mar. 13, 1929, "Memorial to Palmer Unveiled in Colorado."
May 1, 1931, "Spencer Trask & Co. 50 Years Old Today."
July 26, 1931, "George Foster Peabody Reviews An Active Career."
July 18, 1932, "Government Leadership."
July 26, 1932, "G. F. Peabody Reaches 80."
July 27, 1932, "Peabody, 80, Affirms Faith In Democracy."
July 27, 1932, "Not Measured By Years."
Dec. 25, 1932, "Right Use of Nation's Wealth Held to be Government's Duty."
Feb. 9, 1933, "Banks and Railroads."
Mar. 6. 1933, "Thought on Vital Issues Our Great Need."
Mar. 9, 1933, "Control of Railroads."
Mar. 9, 1933, "Wages and Cost of Living."
May 18, 1933, "Peabody Honored at Skidmore."
July 28, 1933, "Gov. Lehman Honors George F. Peabody, 81."
Dec. 10, 1933, "Commodity Base Urged By Peabody."
Oct. 5, 1934, "Our President's Experience."
Jan. 1, 1935, "Saratoga Honors Memory of Trask."
Jan. 11, 1935, "Government and Business."
Mar. 16, 1935, "Bankhead Bill Approved."

May 10, 1935, "President May Visit Spa."
May 30, 1935, "The President's Composure."
May 3, 1936, "Help Is Needed."
Aug. 25, 1936, "Wife of President a Saratoga Visitor."
Dec. 14, 1936, "The Capital Gains Tax."
Mar. 16, 1937, "Roosevelt On Air Tomorrow Night."
Mar. 17, 1937, "A Friend at Warm Springs." (editorial).
Aug. 18, 1937, "Layman on the Court."
Dec. 26, 1937, "Newton D. Baker Dies in Cleveland."
Mar. 5 1938, "G. F. Peabody Dead."
Mar. 6. 1938, "Peabody Funeral is Held in Florida."
Mar. 6, 1938, "Praised by Governor Lehman."
Mar. 6, 1938, "George Foster Peabody."
Aug. 12, 1938, "Texts of Two Addresses Made by President Roosevelt in Georgia."

The Philadelphia Press
Aug. 9, 1884, "Colorado's Iron Giant."
San Francisco Chronicle
Nov. 13, 1891, "Railway Extension."
Saratoga Sun
Jan. 20, 1910, "Will of Mr. Trask Is Admitted To Probate Today."
Feb. 14, 1910, "George Foster Peabody Makes Dignified Reply."
The Saratogian
July 2, 1935, "Mr. Peabody Outlines Bankhead Bill's Purpose."
The Sun
July 10, 1914, "Peace Medal For Mrs. Katrina Trask."
The World
Jan. 22, 1909, "Mrs. Trask Ill, Fails To See Her New Play."

MAGAZINE ARTICLES

Aery, W. A., "Hollis Burke Frissell and Penn School," *The Southern Workman*, LIV, 9 (September, 1925).
Brown, Roscoe C. E., "George Foster Peabody," *The New Christianity*, IV (Autumn, 1938).
"Charles Peabody Passes," *The Southern Workman*, LXIV (November, 1935).
The Commercial and Financial Chronicle (Formerly the *Financial Chronicle and Hunt's Merchants' Magazine*):
XXX (June 12, 1880).

BIBLIOGRAPHY

XXXII (January 1, 1881).
XLVIII (March 23, 1889; May 11, 1889; June 1, 1889; June 29, 1889).
XLIX (July 27, 1889; August 24, 1889).
LVI (April, 1893).
LVII (November, 1893; December 2, 1893).
LVII (November, 1893), Investors' Supplement.
LXIII (October 17, 1896; December 5, 1896).
LXIV (January 16, 1897).
LXVII (July 9, 1898).
LXVII (July, 1898), Supplement.
LXVII (July-December, 1898; September 3, 1898; October 15, 1898; December 10, 1898).
LXVIII (February 11, 1899; March 11, 1899; April 15, 1899).
LXIX (September 30, 1899; October 28, 1899; December 2, 1899; December 16, 1899).
LXX (January, 1900), Investors' Supplement.
LXX (January 13, 1900; March 10, 1900; March 31, 1900; May 19, 1900).
LXXI (November 24, 1900).
LXXII (May 11, 1901; May 18, 1901; May 25, 1901).
LXXIII (July 27, 1901, Investors' Supplement; August 3, 1901; October, 1901).
LXXV (September 13, 1902).
LXXVI (April 4, 1903; April 11, 1903).

Dooly, Isma, "The Most Striking Figure in the Southern Education Conference," *Leslie's Weekly* (May 15, 1902).

"Frissell of Hampton" (editorial from the *New York Times*), *The Southern Workman*, LX (June, 1931).

Hodgson, Harry, "Tribute to a Great American: George Foster Peabody," *Georgia Alumni Record*, XVII (September, 1937).

"Hampton Builder Passes" (editorial), *The Southern Workman*, LXIV (November, 1935).

Jones, T. J., "Frissell of Hampton," *The Southern Workman*, LX (January, 1931).

"Katrina Trask Peabody" (editorial), *The Southern Workman*, LI (February, 1922).

"Memorial Bronze to General William J. Palmer," *The Southern Workman*, LVIII (July, 1929).

"Memorial to Dr. Frissell" (editorial), *The Southern Workman*, LX (January, 1931).

"Messages From Well-Known People," *The Southern Workman*, LXVII (May, 1938).

Moody's Manual of Industrial and Miscellaneous Securities, No. 12 (New York, 1900).
"Mr. Peabody's Address" (on the death of George Perley Phenix), *The Southern Workman*, LIX (December, 1930).
"Mr. Peabody's Gift," *The Southern Workman*, XLIV (December, 1915).
"The Nature and The Field of Trust Companies," *The World's Work* (August, 1902).
"Negro Collections in American Libraries," *The Southern Workman*, XLV (April, 1916).
Peabody, G. F., "For Negro Education," *The Southern Workman*, LIX (March, 1930).
Peabody, G. F., "A Plea For a Beneficent Industrial Justice," *New York Times Magazine* (Dec. 10, 1916).
"Warm Springs Memorial Service," *The Southern Workman*, LXVII (May, 1938).
Wolf, S. J., "G. F. Peabody Reviews an Active Career," *New York Times Magazine* (July 26, 1931).
"The World's Sugar," *Bradstreet's* (December 23, 1899).
"Yaddo's Gates Open to the Talented," *New York Times Magazine* (June 6, 1926).

BOOKS

Allen, F. L., *The Lords of Creation*. New York: Harper and Brothers, 1935.
Baker, Ray S., *Woodrow Wilson, Life and Letters*. Vols. IV-VIII. Garden City: Doubleday, Doran and Company, 1931-1939.
Bining, A. C., *The Rise of American Economic Life*. New York: Charles Scribner's Sons, 1943.
Bradford, F. A., "Investment Banking," *Dictionary of American History*. J. T. Adams, editor. New York: Charles Scribner's Sons, 1940.
Bradford, F. A., "The National Monetary Commission," *Dictionary of American History*. Vol. IV. J. T. Adams, editor. New York: Charles Scribner's Sons, 1940.
Carnegie, A., *Autobiography of Andrew Carnegie*. Boston: Houghton, Mifflin Company, 1920.
Chase, S., *A New Deal*. New York: The Macmillan Company, 1932.
Chase, Stuart, *Rich Land, Poor Land*. New York: McGraw-Hill Book Company, Inc., 1936.
Clark, V. S., "Sugar Industry," *Dictionary of American History*. J. T. Adams, editor. New York: Charles Scribner's Sons, 1940.

Collins, F. L., *Consolidated Gas Company of New York—A History*. New York, 1934.
Cooley, Rossa B., *Homes of the Freed*. New York: New Republic, Inc., 1926.
Cooley, Rossa B., *School Acres, An Adventure in Rural Education*. New Haven: Yale University Press, 1930.
Coulter, E. M., *A Short History of Georgia*. Chapel Hill: University of North Carolina Press, 1933.
Curti, Merle, *Peace or War, The American Struggle, 1636-1936*. New York: W. W. Norton and Company, 1936.
Dabney, C. W., *Universal Education in the South*. 2 Vols. Chapel Hill: University of North Carolina Press, 1936.
Dau's New York Blue Book. New York: Dau Publishing Company, 1907.
Davis, A., Gardner, B. B., and Gardner, M. R., *Deep South: A Social Anthropological Study of Caste and Class*. Chicago: The University of Chicago Press, 1941.
Day, Richard E., "Robert Curtis Ogden," *Dictionary of American Biography*. Vol XIII. New York: Charles Scribner's Sons, 1934.
Dewey, D. R., *Financial History of the United States*, American Citizen Series (12th edition). New York: Longmans, Green and Company, 1934.
Dumond, Dwight L., *Roosevelt to Roosevelt, The United States in the Twentieth Century*. New York: Henry Holt and Company, 1937.
Educational Progress in the South, A Review of Five Years. Field Reports of the Southern Education Board. Published by direction of the Board. Richmond: Richmond Press, Inc., 1907.
Eliot, Samuel A., "Samuel Chapman Armstrong," *Dictionary of American Biography*. Vol. I. New York: Charles Scribner's Sons, 1928.
Faulkner, H. U., *The Quest For Social Justice, 1898-1914*. A History of American Life, Vol. XI. New York: The Macmillan Company, 1931.
Flick, A. C. (ed.), *The History of the State of New York*. Vol. VII. New York: Columbia University Press, 1935.
Galloway, G. B. and Associates, *Planning For America*. New York: Henry Holt and Company, 1941.
The General Education Board, An Account of Its Activities 1902-1914. New York: General Education Board, 1915.
George, Henry, *Progress and Poverty, An Inquiry Into the Cause of Industrial Depressions and of Increase of Want With*

Increase of Wealth—The Remedy. New York: Robert Schalkenbach Foundation, edition 1929.

Hacker, L. M., *A Short History of the New Deal.* New York: F. S. Crofts, 1934.

Hendrick, B. J., *The Life of Andrew Carnegie,* 2 vols. Garden City: Doubleday, Doran and Company, 1932.

Hepburn, A. Barton, *A History of Currency in the United States.* New York: The Macmillian Company, 1924.

Hill, Ella Godwin, *The History of Warm Springs, Georgia.* Chastain, Arkansas: The Hillcroft Press, 1934.

Hutchins, M. C. (ed.), *The New York Red Book, 1938.* Albany: J. B. Lyon Company, 1938.

In Memory of Robert Curtis Ogden. True Friend, Patriotic Citizen, Unofficial Statesman, Christian Gentleman. Privately published, 1916.

Johnson, Charles S., *The Negro in American Civilization; A Study of Negro Life and Race Relations in the Light of Social Research.* New York: Henry Holt and Company, 1930.

Johnson, Charles S., Embree, Edwin R., and Alexander, W. W., *The Collapse of Cotton Tenancy.* Chapel Hill: University of North Carolina Press, 1935.

"Johnson, Tom Loftin," *Dictionary of American Biography.* Vol. X. New York: Charles Scribner's Sons, 1933.

Kemmerer, E. W., *The ABC of the Federal Reserve System.* Princeton: Princeton University Press, 1932.

Kirkland, E. C., *A History of American Economic Life.* (rev. ed.) New York: F. S. Crofts Company, 1939.

Klineberg, Otto, editor, *Characteristics of the American Negro.* New York: Harper and Brothers, 1944.

Koop, E. J., *History of Spencer Trask and Company.* New York: 1941.

Laughlin, J. Laurence, *The Federal Reserve Act: Its Origin and Problems.* New York: The Macmillan Company, 1933.

Lorenz, Carl, *Tom L. Johnson, Mayor of Cleveland.* New York: A. S. Barnes & Co., 1911.

MacIver, R. M., *Society, A Textbook of Sociology.* New York: Farrar and Rinehart, 1937.

Martin, J. H., compiler, *Columbus, Geo. From Its Selection as a "Trading Town" in 1827 To Its Partial Destruction by Wilson's Raid in 1865.* Columbus, Georgia: Thomas Gilbert, 1874.

Martin, T. C., *Edisonia, A Survey of the Edison Light and Power Industries.* Reprinted from *The Electrical Engineer.* New York, August 12, 1891.

BIBLIOGRAPHY

Mitchell, S. C., "Jabez Lamar Monroe Curry," *Dictionary of American Biography.* Vol. IV. New York: Charles Scribner's Sons,, 1930.
Moody, John, *The Masters of Capital. A Chronicle of Wall Street.* New Haven: Yale University Press, 1919.
Morison, S. E. and Commager, H. S., *The Growth of the American Republic.* Vol. II. New York: Oxford University Press, 1937.
Moton, R. R., *What the Negro Thinks.* Garden City: Doubleday, Doran and Company, 1929.
Muzzey, David S., *The United States of America.* (New Edition) Vol. II. New York: Ginn and Company, 1933.
Myers, Gustavus, *History of the Great American Fortunes.* New York: Random House, 1937.
Negro Education, A Study of the Private and Higher Schools For Colored People in the United States, Bulletins 1916, Nos. 38, 39. (Prepared in co-operation with the Phelps-Stokes Fund under the direction of Thomas Jesse Jones, specialist in the Education of Racial Groups, Bureau of Education, Washington, 1917.)
Nevins, Allan, *The Emergence of Modern America, 1865-1878.* A History of American Life. Vol. VIII. New York: The Macmillan Company, 1932.
Nevins, Allan, *Grover Cleveland, A Study in Courage.* New York: Dodd, Mead and Company, 1932.
Nevins, Allan, *John D. Rockefeller; The Heroic Age of American Enterprise.* New York: Charles Scribner's Sons, 1940.
Nichols, J. P., "The Gold Democrats," *Dictionary of American History,* J. T. Adams, editor. New York: Charles Scribner's Sons, 1940.
Ogg, F. A., *National Progress, 1907-1917.* The American Nation: A History. Vol. XXVII. New York: Harper and Brothers, 1918.
Peabody, Francis G., *Education for Life. The Story of Hampton Institute.* Garden City: Doubleday, Page and Company, 1918.
"Peabody, George Foster," *The New International Encyclopaedia.* Vol. XVIII. New York: Dodd, Mead and Company, 1916.
"Peabody, George Foster," *Who's Who in America, 1936-1937,* Vol. XIX.
Peabody, George Foster, editor, *William Jackson Palmer, Pathfinder and Builder.* Saratoga Springs, 1931.
Peabody, Selim Hobart, *Peabody Genealogy.* Boston: Charles H. Pope, editor, 1909.

Peck, H. T., *Twenty Years of the Republic.* New York: Dodd, Mead and Company, 1929.
Peterson, A. E., "Hollis Burke Frissell," *Dictionary of American Biography.* Vol VII. New York: Charles Scribner's Sons, 1931.
Pound, Arthur and Moore, S. T., editors, *They Told Barron.* New York: Harper and Brothers, 1930.
Pringle, H. F., *Theodore Roosevelt: A Biography.* New York: Harcourt, Brace and Company, 1931.
Ray, P. O., "Sugar Trust," *Dictionary of American History,* J. T. Adams, editor. New York: Charles Scribner's Sons, 1940.
Recent Social Trends in the United States. Report of the President's Research Committee on Social Trends. 2 vols. New York: McGraw-Hill Company, Inc., 1933-1938.
Rhodes, J. F., *The McKinley and Roosevelt Administrations, 1897-1909.* New York: The Macmillan Company, 1927.
Riegel, R. E., "William Jackson Palmer," *Dictionary of American Biography.* Vol. XIV. New York: Charles Scribner's Sons, 1934.
Roberts, D. A., "Edward Morse Shepard," *Dictionary of American Biography.* Vol. XVII. New York: Charles Scribner's Sons, 1935.
Satterlee, H. L., *J. Pierpont Morgan, An Intimate Portrait.* New York: The Macmillan Company, 1939.
Schlesinger, A. M., *The Rise of the City, 1878-1898.* A History of American Life. Vol. X. New York: The Macmillan Company, 1933.
Seymour, Charles, *Woodrow Wilson and the World War; A Chronicle of our Own Times.* New Haven: Yale University Press, 1921.
Slosson, P. W., *The Great Crusade and After, 1914-1928.* A History of American Life. Vol. XII. New York: The Macmillan Company, 1937.
"Southern Education Board, Activities and Results 1904 to 1910." Publication No. 7. Washington: Southern Education Board, 1911.
Stanwood, E., *A History of the Presidency from 1788 to 1897.* Vol. II. Boston: Houghton Mifflin Company, 1928.
Stiles, H. R., *A History of the City of Brooklyn, etc.* 3 Vols. Brooklyn, N. Y.: Published by subscription, 1867-1870.
Tarbell, Ida M., *The Nationalizing of Business, 1878-1898.* A History of American Life. Vol. IX. New York: The Macmillan Company, 1936.
Taylor, Fred G., *A Saga of Sugar, Being a Story of the Romance and Development of Beet Sugar In The Rocky Mountain*

BIBLIOGRAPHY

West. Salt Lake City: Utah-Idaho Sugar Company, 1944.
Telfair, Nancy, *A History of Columbus, Georgia, 1828-1928.* Columbus: Historical Publishing Company, 1929.
Thirty Years of New York, 1882-1912. Being a History of Electrical Development in Manhattan and the Bronx. New York: New York Edison Company, 1913.
Thompson, C. Mildred, *Reconstruction in Georgia, Economic, Social, Political, 1865-1872.* Columbia University Studies in History, Economics and Public Law. New York: Columbia University Press, 1915.
Thompson, Warren S., *Population Problems.* New York: McGraw-Hill Company, Inc., 1942.
Trask, Katrina, *Christalan.* New York: G. P. Putnam's Sons, 1903.
———, *Chronicles of Yaddo 1888.* Privately printed. A copy is in the New York Public Library.
———, *In The Vanguard.* New York: The Macmillan Company, 1913.
———, *The Little Town of Bethlehem.* New York: Samuel French, 1929.
———, *Sonnets and Lyrics.* (3rd ed.) Boston: R. G. Badger, 1903.
———, *Under King Constantine.* (5th. ed.) New York: G. P. Putnam's Sons, 1899.
Trask, Spencer, "Bowling Green." Paper in *Historic New York*, edited by Maud Wilder Goodwin and others. New York: G. P. Putnam's Sons, 1899.
"Trask, Spencer," *The Encyclopedia Americana.* Vol. XXVII. New York: Americana Corporation, 1938.
"Trask, Spencer," *The New International Encyclopaedia.* Vol. XXII. New York, 1916.
Trow's New York City Directory, 1881-82, 1898, 1899, 1900, 1901, 1903-04, 1904-05, 1905-06, 1908-09.
Tumulty, Joseph P., *Woodrow Wilson As I Know Him.* Garden City: Doubleday, Page and Company, 1921.
Vance, Rupert, *Human Geography of the South: A Study in Regional Resources and Human Adequacy.* Chapel Hill: University of North Carolina Press, 1932.
Waite, Marjorie P., *Seeing Saratoga. A Scenic and Historic Guide in Twenty-Two Trips.* Saratoga Springs: Business and Professional Women's Club, 1935.
———, *Yaddo, Yesterday and Today.* Saratoga Springs, 1933.
Washington, B. T., *Tuskegee and Its People: Their Ideals and Achievements.* New York: D. Appleton and Company, 1905.

Washington, Booker T., *Up From Slavery: An Autobiography*, Garden City: Doubleday, Doran and Company, 1928.
Weberg, F. P., *The Background of the Panic of 1893*. Washington, D. C.: The Catholic University of America, 1929.
Willis, H. Parker, and Bogen, J. I., *Investment Banking*. New York: Harper and Brothers, 1936.
Wilson, P. W., *An Unofficial Statesman—Robert C. Ogden*. Garden City: Doubleday, Page and Company, 1924.
Woofter, T. J., Jr., and associates, *Black Yeomanry; Life on St. Helena Island*. New York: Henry Holt and Company, 1930.
Wright, Arthur D., with the assistance of Redcay, E. E., *The Negro Rural School Fund, Inc.—Anna T. Jeanes Foundation 1907-1933*. Washington, 1933.

Index

Abenia, 45, 46, 88, 101, 106, 129, 132, 133, 149, 150, 161, 164
Abbott, Dr. Edward, 97
Agricultural Adjustment Act of 1933, 237
Agricultural Adjustment Act of 1938, 243
Akerman, Alfred, 112
Alderman, Dr. Edwin A., 91, 101, 161
Aldrich-Vreeland Act of 1908, 148
Alexander, Will W., 188, 189, 190, 236, 239, 240, 241, 242, 243, 246, 247
Allen, F. L., 134
American Beet Sugar Company, 80-82
American Church Institute for Negroes, 131, 159, 191, 215, 216
American Neutral Conference Committee, 178
Ames, Mrs. Elizabeth, 206, 220, 221, 222
Andrews, Fannie Fern, 198
"Anti-Snaps," 58
Armstrong, General Samuel C., 13, 33, 34, 35, 36, 115
Atlanta, Georgia, in Civil War time, 6, 7
Aycock, Governor, 98

Baker, Newton D., 68, 150, 177, 182, 183, 209, 225
Baldwin, William H., Jr., 103
Ballanta (Taylor), Nicholas H. G., 223
Bankhead Bill, 238, 239
Banking, investment, 17-19, 27
Barrow, David C., 110, 114
Baruch, Bernard, 212, 228
Batchelder, Evelyn Longmans, 227
Bayard, Thomas F., 32
Beadle, Robert C., 148
Beecher, Henry Ward, 10
Belmont, August, 122, 124

Bethesda Church, 202
Boileau, W. E., 150
Bowker, R. R., 127
Bradstreet's, 79
Brady, Anthony N., 76, 77, 78, 79, 134
Broadway Realty Company, 56, 133
Brooklyn Bureau of Charities, 139
Brooklyn Democratic Club, 32
Brooklyn, after Civil War, 10, 11
Brown, D. C., 24, 165
Brown, Roscoe C. E., 249
Bryan, W. J., 122, 123, 166, 167
Bulkley, Edwin M., 20, 76
Bureau of Corporations, 124
Business codes and practices, 28, 29
Buttrick, Dr. Wallace, 103, 104, 159, 160

Callaway, Judge, 110
Campaign contributions, 123-126
Campaign of 1896, 62
Campaign of 1904, 121
Campaign of 1920, 194
Campaign of 1928, 225, 227
Capon Springs, West Virginia, 97
Carnegie, Andrew, 70, 109, 133, 145, 165, 174, 179
Carver, Dr. George Washington, 117
Christ of the Andes, 139
Citizens' Union, 57, 93
Clayton Act, 172
Cleveland, Grover, 32, 58, 226
Cleveland, Cincinnati, Chicago and St. Louis Railroad, 52-53
Cleveland Electric Illuminating Company, 27
The Collapse of Farm Tenancy, 240
Colorado College, 69, 114, 136, 191
Colorado Springs, 22
Columbia University, 138
Columbus, Georgia, 1, 2, 3, 4, 5, 6, 7, 8
Compania Metalurgica Mexicana, 47, 82

273

Conservation, 112
Consolidated Gas Company, 78
Cooley, Rossa B., 115, 129, 137, 140, 223
Cornell University, 112
Cortelyou, George B., 124
Crabb, George Arthur, 150
Crapsey, the Reverend Algernon, 129, 130
Croker, Richard, 93
Curry, J. L. M., 97-99, 103, 110
Curtis, George W., 149
Curtis, Natalie, 149, 199, 246
Cutting, R. Fulton, 81
Cutting, W. Bayard, 81

Dabney, Charles W., 98
Damrosch, Frank, 223
Danbury, Connecticut, 8
Daniels, W. W., 45
Davis, Henry G., 122
Davis, John W., 210, 211
Deer Hill Institute, 8, 10
Denver and Rio Grande Railroad, 22, 75
Denver and Rio Grande Western Railway, 48, 51
Detroit Electric Illuminating Company, 27
Dett, Nathaniel, 223
Dillard, Dr. James H., 146, 236
Dix, Governor, 158
Doane, Bishop, 120
Dodge, D. C., 48, 50, 157

Eastman, George, 215, 216
Edison Electric Illuminating Company of Brooklyn, 53, 76, 77
Edison Electric Illuminating Company of New York, 25, 26
Edison Electric Light Company, 24
Edison General Electric Company, 26, 53
Edison, Thomas A., 24
Education, conditions in the South, 96
Education funds, 96
Educational tours, 100
Egan, John J., 188
Electrical industry developments, 25, 26, 27
Eliot, Charles W., 108, 117
Embree, Edwin R., 240

Esch-Cummins Act, 187

Fairbanks, Charles W., 122
Farnham, Gilbert and Company, 12
Federal Reserve Act, 170
Federal Reserve Bank, 171, 181, 196, 200, 201
Federal Reserve System, 170, 188
Federal Trade Commission, 172
Finley, John H., 220
Fisher, Irving, 67
Foote, Allen R., 127
Fort Valley Normal and Industrial Institute, 116, 145, 215
French, Daniel Chester, 220
Frissell, Hollis B., 115, 128, 129, 145, 146

Garrison, L. M., 177
Gates, the Reverend F. T., 101, 102, 105, 142, 159, 160
General Education Board, 103-106, 114, 126, 133, 142, 143, 145, 159, 217
General Electric Company, 27, 53, 55
General Theological Seminary, 139
"Gentlemen's Agreement," 28
George Foster Peabody School of Forestry, University of Georgia, 113
George, Henry, 58, 67, 127
Georgia, secession of, 6
Gillett, F. H., 173
Gilman, Daniel Coit, 103
Glass, Carter, 187
Godfrey, Frank. N., 157
Godkin, Laurence, 175
Goetchius, Henry, 5
Gold Democrats, 62, 63, 123
Good Government Clubs, 57, 92
"Good Neighbor League," 244

Haertl, Dr. Paul, 212
Hale, William Bayard, 164
Hampton Agricultural and Mechanical Institute (Hampton Institute) 13, 33, 34, 35, 36, 69, 96, 99, 110, 114, 115, 117, 133, 136, 144, 145, 148, 159, 215, 223, 224, 246
Hanna, Hugh H., 64, 65, 126, 127, 148

INDEX

Harding, W. G., 194, 195
Harriman, E. H., 21, 75
Harvard University, 108, 117
Havemeyer, Henry O., 80
Hearst, W. R., 122
Hewitt, Abram S., 30, 31
High, Stanley, 244
Hill, David B., 58, 122
Hill, James J., 21
Hill, Walter B., 91, 108, 109, 110, 111, 113, 140
Hitchcock, Gilbert M., 185
Hodgson, Edward R., 107, 108
Hodgson, Mrs. E. R., 107
Hodgson, Harry, 107, 108, 110, 114
Hodgson, Roberta, 210
Holy Trinity Church, Brooklyn, 16, 118, 138, 139, 158, 209, 249
Hoover, Herbert, 227, 231
House, Colonel E. M., 169, 170, 175, 184, 188
House, Grace B., 115, 137, 140, 183
Houston, David F., 161
Howe, Louis McHenry, 233
Howell, Clark, 110, 239
Huntington, Collis P., 21

Ickes, Harold L., 236, 244
Illinois Central Railroad, 24, 75
In the Vanguard, 174, 199
Indianapolis Monetary Convention, 65, 126, 127, 148, 164, 171

James, Arthur Curtiss, 115, 137
Jay, Pierre, 170, 171
Jeanes, Anna T., Fund, 142, 145, 146, 147
Jesup, Morris K., 103
Johnson, Dr. Charles S., 240
Johnson, Tom L., 68
Jones, Senator, 125

Kansas-Nebraska Act. 4
Katrina Trask Alliance, 204, 218-219
Kiefer, Daniel, 180
Kings County Electric Light and Power Company, 76
Kirkland, Chancellor, 161
Knickerbocker Trust Company of New York, 147
Koop, Eugene, 234
Kuhn, Loeb and Company, 70, 75, 80, 134

LaFollette, Governor, 111, 210
Laughlin, J. Laurence, 67
League of Nations, 195
League to Enforce Peace, 178
Leavitt, Charles W., Company, 111
Lehman, Herbert H., Governor, 246
Lexow Investigation, 57, 92
Lippman, W., 226
The Little Town of Bethlehem, 152, 205
Lloyd, H. D., 134
Lodge, Senator, 185
Long Island College Hospital, 135, 139
Low, Seth, 92, 93, 95
Lunn, George U., 150, 225, 226

Maxwell, Henry W., 139
Mayoralty Campaign of 1901, New York, 91-95
Mazet Inquiry, 92
McAdoo, W. G., 161, 162, 163, 168, 169, 170, 187, 194, 195, 209
McCarren, Senator, 122
McCombs, William F., 162, 163
McIver, Dr. Charles D., 100, 129
McMurry, Dr. Charles, 214
Melish, the Reverend J. Howard, 118, 119, 150
Men's League for Woman Suffrage, 191
Mexican Coal and Coke Company, 83
Mexican Lead Company, 47, 82
Mexican National Railway, 22, 24, 31
Mexican Northern Railway Company, 48
Mexican railroads and mining, 133, 141
Mexico, 22, 82, 165, 169, 172, 192, 230, 231, 244
Mexico City, 227
Miller, Adolph C., 201
Mitchell, the Reverend Edwin Knox, 197, 198
Montezuma Lead Company, 47, 83
Moody, John, 127, 149
Moore, Henry T., 190
Morgan, J. P., 21, 26, 27, 28, 70, 78, 133
Morgan, Dr. Arthur, 242

Morgenthau, Henry, 161, 178
Morrow, Dwight W., 192
Morton Trust Company, 83
Moton, Robert R., 117, 146, 188
Murphy, C. F., 122
Murphy, the Reverend Edgar Gardner, 100

Nash, J. Sylvester, 120
National Arts Club, 152, 154
National Banking Act of 1862, 66
National Democratic Campaign Committee, 123
National Democratic Party, 123, 149, 168
National Industrial Recovery Act, 235
National Monetary Commission, 148
National Single Tax League, 180
National Sound Money League, 65
Negro, educational needs of, 214
Negro Rural School Fund (Anna T. Jeanes), 146
Nevins, Allan, 134
New Deal, 230-244
The New Freedom, 164, 166
New York Edison, 75
New York Edison Electric Illuminating Company, 55, 77-79
New York Gas and Electric Light, Heat and Power Company, 77-79
New York Reform Club, 65
New York Tax Reform Association, 127
New York Times, reorganization, 56
Nichols, Acosta, 20, 153, 220
Nichols, Kate (see Katrina Trask and Mrs. G. F. Peabody), 14
Noland, L. W., 156

Ochs, Adolph S., 56
Ogden Party, 108
Ogden, Robert C., 97-103, 150, 161, 246
Oliver, Senator, 126
Osborn, Fred, 240
Osborne, T. M., 127, 150, 220
Owen-Glass Bill, 170
Oxnard, Henry T., 81

Page, Walter H., 98, 101, 146, 159, 161

Palmer, General William Jackson, 22, 23, 48, 49, 50, 71, 74, 82, 136, 149, 150, 157, 159, 227, 246
Panic of 1873, 12
Panic of 1893, 55, 76
Panic of 1907, 147
Pardee, Allena Gilbert, 38, 198, 201-203, 218, 219, 221
Park, Robert Emory, 110
Parker, Alton B., 122, 123, 126
Parrott, the Reverend Edward M., 120
Party politics, 57
Peabody, Charles Jones, birth, 3; married to Helen A. Hoyt, 15; partner, Spencer Trask and Company, 20, 86, 90, 138, 209
Peabody, Charles Samuel, 15, 86, 128, 150, 246
Peabody, Elvira Canfield, 1, 2, 4, 5, 10, 11, 13, 35, 44, 86-88
Peabody, Eva Louise, 3
Peabody family, 7, 8, 11, 15
Peabody genealogy, 1, 2
Peabody, George, 96
Peabody, George Foster, birth, 1, 3; childhood training, 4, 5; goes to work, 12; studies at Y.M.C.A., 13; meets Kate Nichols, 14; member of Holy Trinity Church, 16; becomes partner in Spencer Trask and Company, 16; banker, 17; railroad interests, 21-24; as railroad director, 24; director in electric industries, 25, 26, 54, 75; attitude toward business practices, 28, 29; early political interests, 30, 31, 59-61; advocate of Single Tax, 33; Free trade advocate, 33; Hampton Institute Trustee, 33, 34, 35, 36; business affairs in 1890's, 47-56; Gold Democrat, 62; member Executive Committee, Indianapolis Monetary Convention, 64-67; economic philosophy, 67-68; friendship with Newton D. Baker, 68; member of Board of Trustees, Colorado College, 69; activities in sale of Rio Grande Western, 74-75; activities in sale of New York Edison Electric Company, 77-79; activities in sugar beet industry, 79-82; friendship with Palmer, 82; director of Mexican Coal and Coke Com-

INDEX 277

pany, 83; director of Morton Trust Company, 83; methods of work, 83-85; home life in early 1900's, 86-89; support of Shepard for mayor of New York, 91, 92-95; educational interests, 96-106; leader in Southern Education Conference and Board, 97-103; treasurer of General Education Board, 104-106, 142; acquaintance with John D. Rockefeller, Jr., 105-6; University of Georgia trustee, benefactions to the University, 107-120; friendship with Harry Hodgson, 110; honorary degrees, 114, 117, 118; Chairman of Board, Penn School, 115; member of Board of Tuskegee, 116; church activities, 118-119, 129-131; Treasurer of National Democratic Party, 121-126; testimony regarding campaign funds, 125-126; member of Board, American Church Institute for Negroes, 130-131, 215-216; his wealth, 133-134; retirement from business, 132-135; attitude toward wealth, 134; his benefactions, 135-141; Jeanes Fund trustee, 142-147; activities at time of Panic of 1907, 147-148; views on currency, 148; political views, 149; resigns from General Education Board, 160; deputy chairman of New York Federal Reserve Bank, 170-171, 188, 201-203, 206; Saratoga Springs Commissioner, 155; resigns as Chairman of Saratoga Springs Commission, 171; relationship with Wilson and Wilson Administration, 161-173, 177; peace advocate, 174-175, 178, 179, 182; friendship with Carnegie, 179; supports country's war efforts, 182; advocate of League of Nations, 183-4, 195; member New York State Reconstruction Commission, 186; views on railroads, after World War I, 187; friendship with Will W. Alexander, 189-190; member of Board of Trustees, Skidmore College, 190; President, Men's League for Women Suffrage, 191; Mexican enterprises in 1919, 192; marriage to Kate Trask, 197, 201; Kate's death, 202; friendship with Franklin D. Roosevelt, 207, 208, 232-3; views in campaign of 1924, 210, 211; activities in Saratoga Springs conservation program, 212; on Southern conditions and educational needs, 214-215; adopts daughter, 218-219; home life in 1920's and 1930's, 219; love of music, 223; compiles book on Palmer, 227; at eighty, 230; and New Deal, 233, 234-5, 240-243, 244; at Warm Springs, 245, 246; George Foster Peabody Memorial Highway, 247; death, 248

Peabody, Mrs. G. F. (see also Katrina Trask), 199, 201, 202
Peabody, George Henry, 1, 4, 6, 7, 8, 10, 11, 13; death, 15
Peabody, Pocahontas, 45
Peabody, Royal Canfield, 3, 15, 86, 87; gift to Columbus, Georgia, Y.M.C.A., 90; 128, 208
Peabody, Mrs. Royal C., 116, 128
Peace Cause, 139
Penn Normal Industrial and Agricultural Institute (Penn School), 115, 137, 183, 191, 216, 223, 224
Philadelphia and Reading Railroad, 55
Plumb, Glenn E., 187
Politics, New York City, 91-95
Post, Louis, 67, 127, 149, 150
Purdy, Lawson, 127

Reed, Robert R., 184
Reform Club, 92
Reformed Church, Brooklyn, 13, 87
Rio Grande Western Railroad, reorganization, 23, 24; 47-48, 52; sale of railroad in 1901, 68; 70, 71, 72, 73, 74-5, 79-80, 87, 134
Rise, Mighty Anglo-Saxons, 140
Rockefeller benefactions, 101-105
Rockefeller, John D., 102-106, 142-144
Rockefeller, John D., Jr., 98, 102-106; 142, 159, 206-207, 214, 215, 224-225
Rockefeller, Mrs. John D., Jr., 106, 142
Roosevelt, Franklin D., 176, 194;

interest in Warm Springs, 207; 210, 228; President, 232; agricultural program, 237, 241
Roosevelt, Theodore, 122, 163
Roper, Daniel, 211, 233
Rouillard, the Reverend Irving G., 202
Ryan, Thomas Fortune, 83, 124, 126, 127

Sanitary Commission, 102
Saratoga Springs, 37, 39, 167, 171, 196, 202, 205, 207, 219, 224, 228-229, 247
Saratoga Springs Commission, 152, 153, 212, 228
Shackelford, Thomas J., 110
Shaw, Albert, 98, 101, 159
Sheehan, W. F., 122, 123, 124
Shepard, Edward Morse, friend of George Foster Peabody, 30, 31; corporation lawyer, 31; political views, 33; 56, 57, 58, 59; independent candidate for mayor of Brooklyn, 1895, 61; 88; candidate for mayor of New York, 92-95; 100, 103, 121, 122, 123, 128, 130, 149, 150, 155, 157; last illness and death, 158, 159; 246
Shepperson, Frances Mildred, 150
Shepperson, Mary Clement, 150
Sherman Silver Purchase Act, 54, 61
Single Tax, 127, 128
Skidmore College, 136, 190, 191
Skinner, E. M., 138
Smith, Alfred E., 186, 211, 212, 225, 226, 227
Southern Education Board, 98-103, 114, 126, 142, 143, 150
Southern Education Conference, 69, 97-99, 102, 108
Spaulding, Swift and Company, 12
Spencer, Samuel, 111
Spencer Trask and Company, 16, 19-20, 21, 24, 26, 27, 29, 47, 49, 55, 56, 67, 70, 75, 76, 78, 82, 86, 133, 148
Spreckels, Claus, 80
St. Augustine's School, 215
St. Louis, Alton and Terre Haute Railway, 24, 47, 52, 53, 68, 75
St. Paul's School, 130-131, 215
Starbuck, Kathryn R., 136, 191-192
Stewart's A. T., store, 12

Stiles, Dr. Charles W., 101
Stires, the Right Reverend Ernest M., 249
Straus, Nathan, 5
Straus, Oscar, 5
Sturges, Mrs. Mia Potter, 220
Sugar beet industry, 70, 79-82
Syracuse Convention, 59

Taft, William H., 126, 145, 163, 195
Taggart, Thomas, 123, 125-126
Tammany Hall, 92, 93, 122
Tannenbaum, Frank, 231, 238
Tarbell, Ida, 134
Tennessee Valley Authority, 242
Terrell, Governor, 111
Thomas, Norman, 210
Towne, Charles H., 24
Towne, Laura M., 115
Trask, Alanson, 15
Trask, Christina Nichols, 15, 38, 39, 40, 196
Trask, Kate (Katrina Trask), 15, 16, 38; writer, 41, 42; 57, 106; heart ailment, 128; 129, 139, 151, 153, 155, 174; peace advocate, 174-175, 181; supports war causes, 182; 193, 194, 196; marriage to George Foster Peabody, 197-198; 201; death, 202, 203; 205, 213, 219, 220, 222
Trask and Francis, 19; Trask and Stone, 19
Trask, Spencer, friend of George Foster Peabody, 14; marriage to Kate Nichols, 14; background, 19; 24, 26, 27; at Yaddo, 40; 42, 44, 46, 57, 75; railroad accident, death, 152-154; 156, 159, 220, 222
Trask, Spencer, Jr., 38, 40
Tumulty, Joseph P., 177
Tuskegee Institute, 96, 116, 117, 133, 144, 145, 215

Underwood Tariff, 169
University of Georgia, 107-121, 142, 160, 191, 214, 224; centennial banquet, 108; Peabody's gifts to the University, 135, 136, 213
University of Washington and Lee, 118
University of Wisconsin, 111-113

INDEX

VanDyke, the Reverend Henry, 120, 197, 220
Villard, Oswald G., 161, 233
Virgin Islands Council, 244
Voorhees School, 116
Waite, Marjorie Peabody, 204, 205; adopted daughter of George Foster Peabody, 218, 219; at Yaddo, 221-222, 224; at Warm Springs, 245, 247

Wallace, Henry A., 237
Warm Springs, 207, 208, 245
Washington, Booker T., 116, 117, 137, 145, 146
Westinghouse Electric Manufacturing Company, 147
White, Browne and Company, 12
White, Payson and Company, 12
Williams, John Skelton, 200
Willis, H. Parker, 65, 67, 170
"Willoughby Street," 60

Wilson, Woodrow, 161, 209, 226, 246
Wise, Rabbi Stephen S., 179
Without the Walls, 198
World War I, 171

Yaddo, 37, 38, 39, 40, 45, 88, 106, 128, 132, 151, 152, 155, 165, 190, 193, 196, 199; artists' retreat, 203, 205, 218-219, 220-222
Young Men's Christian Association, Peabody's gifts to, 135, 137
Young Men's Christian Association of Brooklyn, 13
Young Men's Christian Association of Columbus, Georgia, 89-91, 137
Young Men's Democratic Club, 31-32
Young Men's Democratic Club of Brooklyn, 57, 91
Young Men's Democratic Club of Brooklyn, 57, 91

www.ingramcontent.com/pod-product-compliance
Lightning Source LLC
Chambersburg PA
CBHW030131240426
43672CB00005B/99